2

The
Longest Race

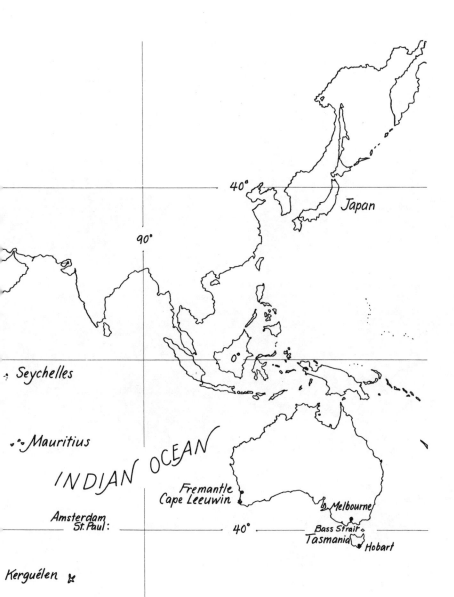

40°

90°

Japan

Seychelles

Mauritius

INDIAN OCEAN

Fremantle
Cape Leeuwin

Melbourne

Amsterdam
St. Paul:

40°

Bass Strait
Tasmania

Hobart

Kerguélen

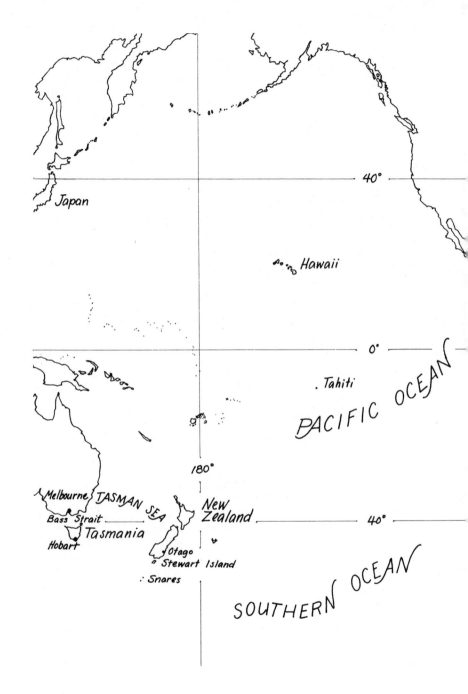

England
Ireland

Plymouth

Lisbon

Azores

Madeira

Canaries

ATLANTIC OCEAN

Sargasso Sea

Cape Verde

Galápagos

St. Peter and
St. Paul Rocks

Recife

Ascension

St. Helena

Rio de
Janeiro

Trindade

0°

90°

Buenos
Aires

Rio Salado

Tristan
da Cunha

Cape Town

Falklands

Cape Horn

DRAWINGS BY HEATHER O'CONNOR

The
Longest Race

BY **Hal Roth**

W · W · NORTON & COMPANY

NEW YORK · LONDON

First Edition

The text of this book is composed in photocomposition Baskerville, with
display type set in Baker Argentina and Helvetica. Composition and
manufacturing by the Maple-Vail Book Manufacturing Group. Book
design by Marjorie J. Flock.

Grateful acknowledgment is made to the following: John Farquharson
Ltd. for permission to reprint excerpts from *A World of My Own* by Robin
Knox-Johnston (published by William Morrow & Co., 1970); Nautical
Publishing Company for permission to reprint excerpts from *Capsize* by
Commander W. D. King (1969) and from *Trimaran Solo* by Nigel Tetley
(1970).

Excerpts from *The Strange Last Voyage of Donald Crowhurst* by Nicolas
Tomalin and Ron Hall are reprinted with permission of Stein and Day
Publishers. Copyright © 1970 by Times Newspapers Ltd.; and excerpts
from *Journey to Ardmore* by John Ridgway are reprinted by permission of
A. D. Peters & Co. Ltd. (published by Hodder & Stoughton Ltd., 1971);
and excerpts from *The Long Way* by Bernard Moitessier are reprinted by
permission of Granada Publishing Ltd.

Library of Congress Cataloging in Publication Data

ISBN 0-393-03278-7

W. W. Norton & Company, Inc., 500 Fifth Avenue, New York, N.Y. 10110
W. W. Norton & Company Ltd. 37 Great Russell Street, London WC1B 3NU

1 2 3 4 5 6 7 8 9 0

Contents

Illustrations

The Nine Contestants

John Ridgway • 29, married, one child, English, former paratroop officer and transatlantic rower, in *English Rose IV,* a thirty-foot Westerly fiberglass sloop. Started on June 1st 1968. Withdrew July 21st. (51 days)

Chay Blyth • 28, married, one child, English, former soldier and transatlantic rower, in *Dytiscus III,* a thirty-foot Kingfisher fiberglass sloop. Started June 8th. Officially disqualified September 14th (98 days). Really disqualified himself on August 15th. (68 days)

Robin Knox-Johnston • 29, divorced, one child, English, merchant marine captain, in *Suhaili,* a thirty-two-foot double-ended wooden ketch. Started June 14th. Finished April 22nd. (313 days)

Bernard Moitessier • 43, married, four children, French, veteran small-boat sailor, in *Joshua,* a thirty-nine-foot steel ketch. Started August 21st. Withdrew for personal reasons March 18th. (209 days)

Loïck Fougeron • 42, married, French, in *Captain Browne,* a thirty-foot steel cutter. Started August 21st. Withdrew on November 27th because of storm damage. (98 days)

Bill King • 58, married, two children, English, retired submarine commander, in *Galway Blazer II,* a forty-two-foot wooden schooner. Started August 24th. Withdrew on November 19th because of storm damage. (87 days)

Nigel Tetley • 44, married, two children, English, navy lieutenant-commander, in *Victress,* a forty-foot Victress trimaran. Started September 16th. Sank on May 21st. (246 days)

Donald Crowhurst • 36, married, four children, English, electronics engineer, in *Teignmouth Electron,* a forty-foot Victress trimaran. Started October 31st. Empty yacht found July 10th. (253 days)

Alex Carozzo • 36, bachelor, Italian, merchant marine officer, in *Gancia Americano,* a sixty-eight-foot plywood ketch. Started October 31st. Withdrew November 25th because of illness. (26 days)

Beaufort Wind Scale
For an effective height of 10 metres above sea level

BEAUFORT NUMBER	DESCRIPTIVE TERM	MEAN WIND SPEED EQUIVALENT IN KNOTS	DEEP SEA CRITERION	PROBABLE MEAN WAVE HEIGHT IN METRES
0	Calm	<1	Sea like a mirror	—
1	Light air	1–3	Ripples with the appearance of scales are formed, but without foam crests	0–1
2	Light breeze	4–6	Small wavelets, still short but more pronounced; crests have a glassy appearance and do not break	0–2
3	Gentle breeze	7–10	Large wavelets; crests begin to break; foam of glassy appearance; perhaps scattered white horses	0–6
4	Moderate breeze	11–16	Small waves, becoming longer; fairly frequent white horses	1
5	Fresh breeze	17–21	Moderate waves, taking a more pronounced long form; many white horses are formed (chance of some spray)	2
6	Strong breeze	22–27	Large waves begin to form; the white foam crests are more extensive everywhere (probably some spray)	3
7	Near gale	28–33	Sea heaps up and white foam from breaking waves begins to be blown in streaks along the direction of the wind	4
8	Gale	34–40	Moderately high waves of greater length; edges of crests begin to break into spindrift; foam is blown in well-marked streaks along the direction of the wind	5–5

(please continue on next page)

BEAUFORT NUMBER	DESCRIPTIVE TERM	MEAN WIND SPEED EQUIVALENT IN KNOTS	DEEP SEA CRITERION	PROBABLE MEAN WAVE HEIGHT IN METRES
9	Strong gale	41–47	High waves; dense streaks of foam along the direction of the wind; crests of waves begin to topple, tumble and roll over; spray may affect visibility	7
10	Storm	48–55	Very high waves with long overhanging crests; the resulting foam, in great patches, is blown in dense white streaks along the direction of the wind; on the whole, the surface of the sea takes a white appearance; the tumbling of the sea becomes heavy and shock-like; visibility affected	9
11	Violent storm	56–63	Exceptionally high waves (small and medium-sized ships might be for a time lost to view behind the waves); the sea is completely covered with long white patches of foam lying along the direction of the wind; everywhere the edges of the wave crests are blown into froth; visibility affected	11–5
12	Hurricane	64 and over	The air is filled with foam and spray; sea completely white with driving spray; visibility very seriously affected	14

This is a true story. It is not fiction. To the best of my knowledge all the facts are correct. My purpose has been to tell a story of high adventure that changed the lives of nine men. If there are any errors or mistakes in interpretation, the faults are mine.

1. *Without Stopping*

IN 1966–67, AN ENGLISH SAILOR named Francis Chichester sailed around the world in a fifty-three-foot ketch named *Gipsy Moth IV*. The voyage took nine months and included a seven-week stopover in Australia. Chichester had wanted to retrace the routes of the clipper ships and hopefully to beat their sailing times. The sixty-five-year-old sailor failed to beat the goal he had set for himself by a small margin, but he completed a first-rate voyage.

Chichester was a master at publicity and personal ballyhoo and financed his various sailing efforts with partial sponsorship from newspapers, magazines, commercial firms, and trade associations. He wrote books, endorsed equipment, cooperated with film ventures, and even made radio broadcasts while underway. Unlike many solo sailors, who tend to be quiet and withdrawn individuals, Chichester appeared to enjoy the x-ray of publicity and acclaim, and his battling-the-sea routine sold lots of books. His writing is filled with overblown passages about fighting the elements, troubles with bad designs, inferior equipment, slipshod boatbuilding, fickle weather, and uncooperative waves and winds. If you read parallel accounts written by other sailors in the same races you wonder if Chichester and the others were in the same race or even on the same ocean. Nevertheless, this crotchety mariner was the stuff that heroes are made of, and sure enough, it wasn't long before he was knighted by Queen Elizabeth herself. His vessel *Gipsy Moth IV* was put on permanent display on a concrete pedestal in Greenwich and became a kind of national shrine for English schoolchildren.

All this success and publicity rankled other sailors who wondered if Chichester's voyage could be bettered, perhaps with less notoriety. After all, reasoned some, people go to sea to get away from the noise of publicity. Yacht club purists said that Chichester was crass and money-crude. "Baloney," retorted Chichester, "I needed the lolly. How else do you think I paid the bills?"

"Chichester had returned safely to England that summer and I wondered what adventure remained untried," wrote Bill King, a former commander of English submarines and also an expert small-boat sailor. "It struck me that I could set out to sail alone around the world *without* stopping to refit in Australia. . . . It would be one step further in human effort and endurance. An absolutely new experience."

King ordered a new vessel to be built in a hurry, supposedly in secret, to be paid for by himself. It wasn't long, however, until he heard rumors that the great French sailor, Bernard Moitessier, who owned the yacht *Joshua*, was also thinking about a world-circling trip without stopping. An English merchant marine officer named Robin Knox-Johnston was trying to raise funds to build a fifty-three-foot steel two-master. Captain John Ridgway was said to be interested. Finally, in March 1968, *The Sunday Times* of London pulled all these separate efforts together by announcing a nonstop, round-the-world race for singlehanded yachts. The prizes were to be a Golden Globe for the first man to finish and £5,000 for the fastest time. The rules forbade outside physical assistance, and no food, water, fuel, or equipment could be taken on board after starting.

The challenge was to sail the thirty-thousand-mile course without stopping. If the goal was met and the record established, then the contest could never be repeated in the same form. It was the old story: the leader, the groundbreaker, the first to climb the mountain, the first to push aside the impossible. This sailing race was truly the contest of contests.

It must be emphasized that *The Sunday Times* has no desire to encourage suicide attempts [warned the newspaper]. To have a hope of success, yachtsmen must have seamanship of the highest order and a yacht and equipment of high quality. The judges will be ready to comment on the advisability of making an attempt.

The psychological problems raised by seven or eight months alone at sea are largely unknown. Sir Francis Chichester was troubled by hallucinations after only four months. The necessary combination of sea experience and physical stamina would appear to favour men in their forties . . . but younger or older contestants might well have other factors in their favour.

"There was no need to be officially entered, and the rules were simple," noted the Frenchman Moitessier. "All you had to do was to leave from any English port between June 1 and October 31, 1968, then return to it after rounding the three capes of Good Hope, Leeuwin, and the Horn.

"The idea came to *The Sunday Times* after they heard that Bill King and *Joshua* were preparing for the long way," said Moitessier. "My old pal Loïck Fougeron was also readying for the trip. . . . After *The Sunday Times* announcement we decided to sail our boats to Plymouth, hoping to be able to carry off one or even both of the prizes, the good Lord willing."

Already there were five entrants: Bill King, who lived on a farm in Ireland; Robin Knox-Johnston from England; John Ridgway from Scotland; and Bernard Moitessier and Loïck Fougeron from France. Soon there would be four more. Donald Crowhurst and Nigel Tetley from England; Chay Blyth from Scotland; and Alex Carozzo, an Italian from Venice.

The nine challengers were about to attempt something never before tried by man. Each not only hoped to sail a small yacht completely around the world without putting into port, but the entrants planned to *race* one another during their nonstop solo efforts. In the Southern Ocean the men would have to battle icebergs, freezing cold, and awesome storms. In the tropics the nine contestants would fight calms and the scorching sun. There would be no stops in port, no splendid dinners, no luxurious rests in comfortable hotels while boasting to newspaper reporters. This race was tough, the ultimate, the Everest of sailing. The contest meant thirty thousand miles of risky navigation across the most fearsome oceans known to man. The trip would take nine months of continuous sailing, a gritty test of endurance and determination.

There would be moments of splendid tranquility and moments of despair: hours when a man might rejoice in aloneness, and hours when he might cry out for companionship and help. Of course if the going got too difficult, he could always put into port somewhere. But then he would lose his entry in the great race and have to admit defeat. The humiliation of failure was not pleasant once you made the commitment to go—especially if all or part of your entry was paid for with other people's money.

Each of the nine would be responsible for keeping a good course, watching out for big ships, intricate celestial navigation, storm management—everything. If one of the solo sailors got sick he would have to dose himself or die; if he sailed into trouble he would have to sail out or perish. If he fell overboard his life was gone for there would be no shipmate to return to pick him up. If he broke a leg or got his head bashed in from a swinging boom there would be no one to bind up his wounds or take him to a hospital. If he ran short of equipment or a piece of gear failed or wore out he would have to improvise something. If he got bored he would have to devise amusements.

Each captain would have to cook himself wholesome and nourishing meals or else risk weakness and scurvy. Each man would have to pace himself so he wouldn't burn up his energy faster than it could be replaced by food and sleep. He would have to deal with problems as they came up and laugh at himself once in a while and try to keep a sense of balance and good cheer. Otherwise he might go mad. . . .

He would be without the companionship and tenderness of women; there would be no loving embrace; no gentle hand to wipe his brow or to pass him a warm drink on a stormy night; no sympathetic listener to defer to his leadership; no one to admire and encourage him.

To enter the race at all was a daunting prospect.

To finance the race raised another whole set of problems. A good example was Bill King's new yacht *Galway Blazer II*. King hired an English naval architect named Angus Primrose to design a sleek, superlight vessel forty-two feet long that displaced only 4½ tons. She had no engine and was driven by a Chinese lugsail rig set on two masts arranged without stays or shrouds. *Galway Blazer II* was beautifully built of laminated wood by Souter's, a famous shipyard in Cowes in the south of England. Wilfred Souter and his men constructed the hull and deck of four layers of mahogany. The first layer of thin strips was laid over a form or pattern of the hull. Each succeeding layer of wood was crisscrossed and glued to the preceding layer so that a laminated hull of great strength and lightness resulted.

Initially the vessel was to have cost £7,000. But during the six months of her construction the costs jumped to £10,000. Fortunately the increase was met by *The Daily Express* newspaper, which offered King £3,000 if he would "speak to no other paper" during the race. After the launching and during trials and outfitting the costs escalated further. King had to find another £7,000, which obliged him to throw in "the final savings for my old age," to collect £200 for television and film rights, and to get an advance for a book "which might never be written." In addition King leased the grazing rights on his farm, sold all his cattle and sheep, and put his car on the market. All this effort was just to get to the starting line. Was any competition worth so many pledges and sacrifices?

2. *The Early Starters*

THE FIRST MAN TO SAIL was John Ridgway, who already had the incredible adventure of rowing across the Atlantic Ocean with Chay Blyth during the summer of 1966. Army Captain Ridgway and Sergeant Blyth had spent ninety-two days in an open boat while they rowed from Cape Cod to Ireland. Now on June 1st, 1968, the day the round-the-world competition began, Ridgway sailed away from the Aran islands in Galway bay in western Ireland in a thirty-foot sloop named *English Rose IV*.

The twin-bilge keel Westerly 30 fiberglass yacht had been specially prepared by the builders. Ridgway wanted simplicity, so the engine and all through-hull openings had been eliminated. The ship carpenters had installed heavy teak drop boards in place of the usual weak door to the cabin. Instead of vulnerable windows, the men at the yard bolted small circular metal portlights in place. Ridgway elected a hand-cranked Clifford and Snell Lifeline radio, and at a stroke got rid of charging engines, fuel stowage, storage batteries, and a bulky and expensive long-distance radio. The Horlicks company packed eleven hundred pounds of special rations—enough for 400 days—in 400 separate packages. A pilot friend brought eighty charts and eight books of pilotage instructions. Sixteen sails were loaded on board.

The £4,250 cost of Ridgway's basic vessel was met by trading endorsements and advertising rights (in case the voyage was successful) for pledges of fiberglass material, resin, spars, winches, rigging wire, paint, and so forth that had gone into his vessel. Ridgway raised a further £4,000 for fittings and additional equipment by signing newspaper and book contracts and finding one additional sponsor. "I was not willing to embark on a voyage, untried by anyone before, with the added mental strain of financial worry," said the twenty-nine-year-old Ridgway. "If the worst came to the worst, then there must be no question of . . . [my wife] having to face creditors."

JOHN RIDGWAY

Ridgway considered himself a hardboiled adventurer and thought of the race as an experiment in physical survival and human toughness. To him the voyage was a military project. One made a program, delegated authority for the preparations, and then carried out the program like an exercise in an army field manual. According to Ridgway the sailing was a secondary problem. In spite of his military approach, however, he was apprehensive about crossing the Indian Ocean in winter, which he regarded as a greater hazard than Cape Horn itself. He also believed in occasional prayer.

Ridgway decided to leave from the Aran islands because it was there where his Atlantic rowing trip had ended, where he had made many friends, and where he could be sure of a quiet start. Unfortunately, on the morning of June 1st, there were two rival television launches that were filled with competing reporters, photographers, and soundmen. As *English Rose IV* got underway, one launch nudged the yacht on her stern pulpit and narrowly missed the self-steering gear. "I was furious," said Ridgway. "All my pent-up self control evaporated, and I screamed abuse at them. At the press conference I had taken great pains to point out the need for care while we were at sea. I knew this to be one of the most hazardous phases of the entire voyage."

Ridgway's outburst was in vain because a little later the other television launch slammed into his yacht, midships on the starboard side. The heavy, green trawler rolled her twenty-five-ton hull against the stressed monocoque hull of the yacht. "There was a horrible crunch. Everything and everybody shuddered . . . I looked down at the splintered strip of wood that masked the bolts joining the deck to the hull. I felt that awful sickness; defeat filled my mind. The bloody despair of trying to do anything with anyone—all that mattered to them were their blasted pictures."

With thirty thousand miles to go, Ridgway sailed out into the Atlantic and then headed south, praying that the collision damage was only superficial. If things got worse he could always put into the south coast of England for repairs and start out again. For two days the wind was light and fitful. Finally a west wind blew up and *Rosie,* as Ridgway called his vessel, hurried southward, apparently in good order. Soon Ridgway was south of the approaches to the English channel.

One evening with a blood-red sunset, 240 miles west of the French coast at the northern end of the Bay of Biscay, I was lying back on my bunk [wrote Ridgway]. . . . The clock on the bulkhead over the chart table said 2200 hours. I rolled out to check the log and the main steering compass. Far out on the port side, a catamaran seemed to be coming our way. A quarter of an hour passed and there was no mistaking his intentions. The number 12 on her side meant she was in the Atlantic race, which had started from Plymouth on the day I left Aran. My competitors' sheet told me number 12 was the *San Giorgio,* a giant fifty-three foot catamaran, sailed by Alex Carozzo, "the Italian master navigator" as the Observer newspaper had called him. Our meeting was quite a coincidence.

As he closed with *Rosie,* a black-bearded figure at the wheel raised a megaphone to his lips.

"Hello there, can you give me a position?" I smiled to myself. It was the supreme accolade for one who passed O level Navigation at the fourth attempt.

"I'll try. I'm not in your race, you know. I'm sailing south—round the world."

"What is your name?"

"Captain Ridgway."

"Oh, I have read about you. I hope to be joining the race when I return from America." He wheeled the big multi-hull around *Rosie* with typical Italian verve and élan. I dreaded a collision.

From the position at three-thirty that afternoon, I quickly calculated our present position and called it out to him over my own powerful Tannoy hailer. He wrote busily on a scrap of paper.

"Thank you, goodbye, and good luck." He swung away to starboard, and headed for the crimson sunset. I returned to my bunk. . . .

"Hello there." Ten minutes had passed; he was back again, sweeping his acrobatic circles around us.

"I lost the paper! Can you give me another position check?"

It was like some kind of pantomime, two madmen screaming at each other in the gathering dusk, way out on the ocean. We could have been the only two men left alive in the world, for we both spoke with sufficient gallantry, savouring the moment.

I gave him the position again, and this time I stayed in the cockpit and watched him go over the horizon, feeling a strong bond with this man I had never met.

On June 8th, Chay Blyth, the second contestant in the race, sailed from England in a small red yacht. Blyth, Ridgway's partner in the Atlantic rowing effort, left from the Hamble river near Southampton in a borrowed thirty-foot sloop named *Dytiscus III.* The vessel was a shoal-draft Kingfisher with twin bilge keels, a class of family cruising yachts that was barely suitable for the English channel and was certainly a poor choice for the Southern Ocean and Cape Horn.

Not only was Blyth's vessel marginal, but Blyth had practically no sailing experience. Of the nine men who competed in the race, Blyth was near the bottom of the list in sea miles. Yet the twenty-eight-year-old paratrooper, the youngest man in the race, had proved himself a tough nut in the Atlantic rowing marathon. Prior to leaving on the round-the-world race, Blyth surrounded himself with expert advisors who gave him crash courses in celestial navigation and in handling a small vessel. On the morning when Blyth sailed, however, he had so little confidence in his sailing ability that he enlisted friends to help him

CHAY BLYTH

raise and set his sails. His friends then got on board their own vessels and—like bodyguards—escorted *Dytiscus III,* one in front and one behind. Blyth was to watch the sailor on the yacht ahead of him and copy every more his friend made. The yacht in back was to head off boats that came close because Blyth had no idea how to avoid them. Once through the busy waters of the Solent area and out to sea, there would be less traffic, and presumably Blyth would be able to deal with the sailing. At least the eyes of the press would be off him. In retrospect this little ruse seems incredible, yet it was carried out and Blyth did get away on June 8th.

Prior to leaving in the £5,000 vessel, twin metal tracks were riveted to the mast for poles to boom out twin headsails. Both the fore and aft deck hatches were sealed. The chain locker was filled with foam to make a watertight bulkhead and to add buoyancy. The engine was replaced with a thirty-gallon water tank. Experts installed a large radio and Blyth learned how to operate and repair a small Honda gasoline generator. Meanwhile hundreds of food packets, charts, sails, foul weather gear, books, music tapes, and a motion picture camera were loaded on board.

On June 13th, Blyth entered the Bay of Biscay off the west coast of France. By now the captain had learned that his vessel's directional stability was poor—her bow often yawed from side to side. Yet Blyth pushed on.

"Sunday, June 16, brought me my swordfish—a splendid fellow who came quite close, leaping out of the water," wrote the Scots exparatrooper. "I dashed for my camera but I was not quick enough. It was also the day when I worked out a sight which indicated that I had sailed out of my first set of books and charts; and the day for my weekly shave and all-over wash . . . It is really marvelous, the feeling of sluicing the salt from your beard and then of banishing the beard itself. Suddenly, you are clean again. You feel you can take whatever the next seven days have in mind for you."

Right from the beginning, Blyth's advisors had had doubts about the running ability of the chunky, shoal-draft yacht and during a mild gale on July 1st, Blyth began to agree with his friends. "The waves curled around it, lifting the stern, and *Dytiscus* simply turned sideways on. . . . These were conditions with which the self-steering gear had never been intended to cope. So I lowered the sails again, and once I had lowered them there was nothing more I could do except pray. So I prayed. And between times I turned to one of my sailing manuals to see what advice it contained for me. It was like being in hell with instructions. I was lonely and frightened. And I realized that this was but a foretaste of what was going to come once I reached the Roaring Forties in my strong but totally unsuitable boat."

In spite of doubts about himself and his yacht, by July 18th, his 42nd day at sea, Blyth was south of the equator. He had grown increasingly familiar with his vessel. And he continued to improve his sailing skills.

Robin Knox-Johnston, the third man to depart, was a professional merchant marine officer who was especially keen for an Englishman to be the first person to sail around the world nonstop. He was terribly worried that a Frnechman might achieve this distinction. After an earlier Atlantic Ocean race, which a Frenchman had won, a French magazine had boasted: "Frenchman supreme on the Anglo-Saxon ocean," the inference being that English seamen were inferior to French sailors. "This had made my blood boil at the time," said Knox-Johnston.

He was born in Putney—a part of London—in 1939, one of five children of northern Irish stock. In addition to his schooling, when he was eight he took up boxing, which he continued until he was seventeen. In training he generally did poorly, but in matches he nearly always won. He was good at individual sports—boxing, running, and swimming—but poor at team games.

Knox-Johnston joined the merchant navy as an apprentice when he was eighteen. After three years of sailing between London and East Africa and achieving a reputation for being both hardworking and stubborn, he passed his second mate's examination (in 1960) and joined a ship running between India and the Persian gulf. He eventually got his first mate's certificate and by twenty-five he had his master's papers. Later he commanded a coasting vessel in South Africa. Married for a short time and then divorced, Knox-Johnston had a young daughter named Sara.

The twenty-nine-year-old seaman hoped to compete in the round-the-world race in a new fifty-three-foot steel vessel designed by Colin Mudie. Like the other contestants, however, Knox-Johnston was stuck for money. He wrote to fifty business firms and asked for help and sponsorship. No one offered any funds so he decided to enter the race in *Suhaili,* a sturdy, somewhat rotund ketch that he already owned. (The word *Suhaili* is the name given to the southeast wind in the Persian gulf by Arab seamen.)

Knox-Johnston had had *Suhaili* built in Bombay in 1963–64. He and a crew of two had sailed her to South Africa, and then to England in a nonstop seventy-four-day passage from Cape Town. The ketch was built of teak and measured a little over thirty-two feet long (plus bowsprit) with a beam just one inch over eleven feet. Though she was serviceable and a good sea boat, she wasn't fancy at all. Rough or not, however, the captain needed money, so he enlisted the help of a literary agent. Prior to sailing, Knox-Johnston got partial sponsorship from English and American book publishers, the *Sunday Mirror* newspaper, and *True* magazine in the United States.

When *Suhaili* left the port of Falmouth on June 14th, she lay suspiciously low in the water, so low that a stranger might have thought her to be sinking. The reason, of course, was that a few days earlier Knox-Johnston and his friends had loaded an entire truckful of food into the small white ketch, enough food for one man for 330 days. Into *Suhaili* went some 2500 cans and jars and packages, each averaging near a pound in weight. For example, Knox-Johnston took 216 cans of corned beef, 72 cans of runner beans, and 24 tins of apricots. He put on 72 cans of orange juice, 28 pounds of nuts, 350 pounds of potatoes, and 250 pounds of onions. Somewhere in the boat were 24 dozen eggs, 56 pounds of rice, 112 pounds of sugar, 216 cans of condensed milk, and 14 pounds of hot curry powder. The captain included 1,000 vitamin tablets, 24 tubes of toothpaste, 3,000 cigarettes, and a case each of Grant's scotch and Martell brandy.

Like the other contestants, Knox-Johnston filled up the forepeak of his yacht with a mass of spare sails, extra line, rigging wire, and tools. He had nine five-gallon drums of kerosene and diesel oil, eighty-six gallons of fresh water, an emergency life raft, a battery charger and spare gasoline, an armload of nautical charts, and seventy-five big books for navigation and recreational reading. He had clothes, bedding, oilskins, a large radio set, a spare tiller, a rifle and ammunition, twenty sailmaker's needles, two cameras, fishing equipment, twenty-four tea towels, and a massive first aid kit. The list of gear went on and on and resolved itself into two problems: where to put everything and how to find anything.

It is astonishing how much food a man consumes in a year and how many things he must have in order to keep a sailing vessel going across an ocean.

Three of the nine contestants had now left England. Ridgway was two weeks ahead of Knox-Johnston with Chay Blyth somewhere in between. When *The Sunday Times* had made the rules for the race it had set the starting dates between June 1st and October 31st because it was thought prudent not to arrive in the Southern Ocean until the southern winter was over. Indeed some people thought that Ridgway, Blyth, and Knox-Johnston had left too early and would get into unnecessarily heavy weather in the south. Yet little by little the first three men were gnawing at the thirty-thousand-mile carrot at the rate of roughly 75 to 100 miles a day.

In the meantime, *Galway Blazer II*, Bill King's new yacht, was rapidly nearing completion. Moitessier and Fougeron, the two French entrants, were in Plymouth putting on supplies.

Another contestant was Donald Crowhurst, a thirty-six-year-old electronics engineer, an ex-flying officer in the Royal Air Force, a former army lieutenant, and a onetime village politician. Crowhurst was extremely bright, but his character was streaked with behavior that was uneven, moody, and at times cheeky and overpowering. He had a wife and four small children and operated a struggling electronics business in a small village located in a rural part of southeast England. After a vigorous but unsuccessful attempt to borrow Chichester's *Gipsy Moth IV* for the race, Crowhurst decided to build a forty-foot Victress trimaran designed by an American named Arthur Piver, who was at that time the leading proponent of multihulled craft. Unfortunately Piver had recently been lost off the coast of California in one of his small trimarans, which may have capsized, come apart, or have been run down by a large ship.

A trimaran is an unballasted vessel with three slim hulls linked together by crossarms. The great beam gives the multihull considerable stability, and without ballast the total weight or displacement is minimal. On its pencil-like hulls the vessel can skim across smooth water at great speed and needs only small sails to drive the yacht. Unfortunately, in disturbed water and gusty winds it is possible for a trimaran to flip over. A capsize is an unusual occurrence, but when a trimaran is upside down, the vessel is more stable than when upright because of the weight and drag of the mast and sails hanging down in the water. Though various schemes have been suggested, there still is no way for a man on board a capsized trimaran to right his vessel.

The performance of a trimaran against the wind in rough seas is not much better than a normal monohull. Yet with a following or beam wind a trimaran is capable of speeds of at least twice that of a conventional ballasted monohull. The choice becomes a trade-off between the thrill and achievement of high speed and the risk and danger of capsize.

Crowhurst had elected a trimaran. Like the other contestants he had no money and had to go around pleading for funds, trying to convince reluctant people to pledge assistance in return for publicity.

"My estimates indicate that the boat would only cost about £6,000 so that with yacht mortgage facilities the outlay is very modest in comparison with the returns, which do not merely accrue to this company but include film rights, communication and story rights, and advertising revenue," said Crowhurst.

Not only did Crowhurst envision fame and riches from the publicity, but he claimed to have invented a whole series of electronic devices to make the trimaran safer. One gadget monitored the yacht's performance while the captain was asleep; anything unusual would be signaled to the crew by warning lights and alarms. Another electrical invention eased the sails automatically by letting out the sheets* if the vessel was overpressed

---

*A sheet is a line attached to the corner of a sail to control its trim. To ease the sheets means to let out on the lines controlling the sails—often the mainsail and a jib.

by increasing wind. Crowhurst worked out a scheme with an automatically inflating rubber buoyancy bag at the top of the mast to right the trimaran in case of capsize.

Like con artists who have been operating since the time of the Egyptian pharaohs, Crowhurst brazenly claimed to have all this equipment in operation and tested "after long development." He said he was applying for patents. In truth, these inventions existed only in Crowhurst's mind and had not been built or tried out at all.

In spite of statements that he had "been to sea in small boats over a period spanning almost thirty years," Crowhurst actually had little sailing experience and had never made an ocean passage in a small sailing vessel. He was like many small-boat fanciers who allow themselves to be carried away by the romance of the idea and attempt to let whim and fancy replace experience and actual sea miles. Reading an exciting sea story transforms these sea dreamers into intrepid captains and born-again Walter Mittys. This fancifulness is well known to naval architects and yacht builders. Nevertheless, Crowhurst was extremely convincing in his arguments and created quite a plausible case for his entry. Even the usually conservative yachting magazines accepted his statements and said that his inventions were sensible.

The man who had invested in Crowhurst's electronic business finally agreed to sponsor a new trimaran. But the race was about to start and Crowhurst's new trimaran wasn't even begun. Armed with financing, however, Crowhurst arranged with two boatyards to build the yacht in a hurry. One firm was to construct the hulls. A second company was to assemble the trimaran and complete the interior and rig.

"I must say that at this point I was most impressed," said John Eastwood, one of the owners of the second boatbuilding firm. "Donald seemed to know precisely what he wanted. He had a good technical background and an imaginative mind."

The hulls were built and delivered to Eastwoods on time and two dozen workmen rushed to complete the vessel. Crowhurst's continuing inventions and changes, however, interfered with the work and caused one delay after another. For example, the normal mast and rigging and sails could not be used because of the masthead buoyancy bag arrangement, so a special rig had to be designed, ordered, and custom made. Crowhurst wanted an oversize rudder and different interior shelving. There was a dispute about the fiberglass sheathing that the builder wanted to eliminate in favor of paint. Besides the design changes, there were problems because of material shortages, all of which were aggravated because of the rush job. Soon the yard men were put on a seventy-hour work week; later a night shift was arranged with workmen coming from nearby boatyards. Bothersome shortages plagued the hurried building. For example, one item was soft rubber on which to bed down the tops of the watertight hatches in the two floats of the trimaran. Only hard rubber seemed to be available and it was unsatisfactory because it was too stiff and unyielding. The hard rubber problem was only one item on a long list.

Building a yacht in a hurry was tantamount to teaching manners to a child overnight; it just wasn't possible without terrible penalties and unending difficulties.

3. *Sharks and Giant Yachts*

WHILE DONALD CROWHURST WAS IMMERSED IN the hellish business of trying to build a complicated new yacht in a few months, the first three competitors hurried southward, getting further and further from England. By July 1st, John Ridgway and Chay Blyth, the first two starters, had crossed the equator and passed into the South Atlantic. Robin Knox-Johnston, the third man to leave, had sailed only twelve hundred miles in sixteen days, but he was largely across the horse latitudes or variables, the light-weather area between the trade wind and the westerlies, and he looked forward to better daily runs.

I had settled in by this time [wrote Knox-Johnston], and was working to a daily routine which I had developed on my previous voyage but which, obviously, had had to be adapted to lone sailing. I tried to get to sleep at 10 p.m. if the sailing conditions allowed, and apart from a check at 2 a.m. (more frequently in the shipping lanes or bad weather) I slept through until 6 a.m. when I got up and made my rounds of the deck, setting what adjustments seemed necessary to the rudder, Admiral [the self-steering] and sails. Breakfast followed, usually fried eggs and something else, followed by a mug of coffee and the first cigarette of the day. If it was fine enough I always sat on deck for this. Nothing can compare with the freshness of the early morning at sea.

During good weather in warm waters, Knox-Johnston often went for a swim. Around noon he would pay out one of the sheets for a trailing safety line and jump overboard. He dived ahead of the boat from the bowsprit and swam as hard as he could until the stern came up to him. Then he would grab the safety line and haul himself on board. Next he scrubbed himself with saltwater soap before jumping in for a rinse. This routine kept him clean and fit. He was careful not to miss the safety line. . . .

During his third week at sea, Knox-Johnston was alarmed by a persistent leak. Even in easy going he had had to pump twice a day—more if the sea was rough. If the yacht leaked in settled waters of the tropical Atlantic, what would she do in the stormy waters of the Southern Ocean?

ROBIN KNOX-JOHNSTON

Two days past the Cape Verde Islands [he wrote] we ran into a calm patch and I reduced sail. Donning a mask and snorkel, I dived overside and went straight to the spot level with the mainmast about a foot above the keel where we had had trouble on the previous voyage. The trouble was there all right and a large gap was showing along the seam for about eight feet. I swam under the keel and checked the other side. It was the same, and as *Suhaili* pitched and rolled easily in the water I could see the gap opening and closing slightly. I swam to the surface, hauled myself on board, lit a cigarette and started to think the problem over. What really worried me was the thought that maybe all the floors, the brackets that join the frames to the keel, were working loose and that this was just the beginning of real trouble. It would be suicidal to carry on with the voyage if this were the case but at the same time it was very difficult to see if the danger was serious, as the floors were for the most part hidden by the water tanks which were built into the boat. Those I could see I checked and they seemed firm enough, so I convinced myself that they were all basically strong and the trouble was just a continuation of the old problem and could be put right by caulking. If I was wrong in this, I just had to hope that not all the floors would go at once and I would be able to manage to make a port before *Suhaili* broke up. . . .

Having decided that caulking was the answer, I had to think of some way of doing it five feet below water. Normally dry twisted raw cotton is hammered into the seam, stopped with filling compound and painted over, but I could not do that. I decided to try and do the job with cotton anyway and hope that the fact that it would be wet would not make too much difference. We had had to do the same thing when in the middle of the Arabian Sea. It had not been easy, but at least I had had two other people helping me and keeping a lookout for sharks. This time I would have to do the job on my own and hope that I would notice any sharks whilst they were still circling.

I got out the cotton and twisted up some pieces in 18-inch lengths, a convenient length to handle although ideally I should have done the whole job with one piece. Next I put a long length of line on a hammer and lowered it overside near where I had to work. Finally I dressed myself in a blue shirt and jeans to hide the whiteness of my body, something that sharks, great scavengers, always associate with refuse, and strapped my knife to my leg. I put the cotton on deck where I could reach it from the water and taking my largest screwdriver as the most convenient caulking instrument, I went overside.

The job was impossible from the start. In the first place I would run out of breath before I had hammered enough cotton in place to hold it whilst I surfaced, and each time I came up for air I lost all the work done. Secondly the cotton was just not going in properly, and even when I changed the screwdriver for a proper caulking iron I made no progress. After half an hour of fruitless effort I climbed back on board and tried to think of some other way of doing the job.

A while later I was busily engaged in sewing the cotton on to a strip of canvas 1-½ inches wide. When the whole strip, about seven feet of it, was completed I gave it a coating of Stockholm Tar and then forced copper tacks through the canvas about six inches apart. I went into the water again and placed the cotton in the seam so that the canvas was on the outside; I then started knocking the tacks into the hull to hold the whole thing in place. The finished job did not look too bad but it was a bit ragged at the edges and I thought that it might be ripped off when *Suhaili* got moving again so I decided to tack a copper strip over the canvas to tidy it up. . . .

So far, although I had kept glancing nervously about me whilst I was in the water, I had seen no fish at all. But whilst I was having coffee break, having prepared the copper strip and made holes for the tacks so that I would have an easier job under water, I suddenly noticed a lean grey shape moving sinuously past the boat. The sharks had found us at last. I watched this one for ten minutes hoping it would go away as I did not want to have to kill it. I was not being kind to the shark; if I killed it, there would be quite a bit of blood in the water and the death convulsions would be picked up by any other sharks near at hand who would immediately rush in, and I would not be able to get the job finished. After ten minutes, though, during which the shark kept circling the boat and showing no signs of leaving, I got out my rifle and, throwing some sheets of lavatory paper into the water, waited for the shark to come and investigate. On its first run round, the shark passed about three feet below the paper, but then he turned and, rising slowly, came in again. I aimed the rifle at the shape and with finger on the trigger, followed it as it came in. Three feet short of the paper the top of the head broke surface and I squeezed the trigger. There was an explosion in the water as the shark's body threshed around but within half a minute the threshing ceased and the lifeless body began slowly to plane down until it disappeared into the blue. For the next half hour I watched carefully to see if any other sharks would appear, but apart from two pilot fish, which, having followed their previous protector down until they realized he would never feed them again, now decided to join a larger and apparently stronger master, *Suhaili* and I had the sea to ourselves. I went overside and in an hour and a half had the copper tacked over the canvas on the port side. A light wind getting up forced me to leave the starboard side until we were next becalmed. But in any case I was quite chilled from four hours immersion, and also a little tense from constantly glancing around expecting to see a shark coming in behind me, and I was quite glad to give the job a rest for a while.

Two days later, when becalmed again, I went overside and repeated the job on the starboard side without incident. The leaking into the boat stopped completely.

This modest account of an ingenious repair while at sea and all alone demonstrates the toughness and resourcefulness of the singlehanded sailor at his best. Knox-Johnston's caulking repair would properly have been a shipyard job when the vessel was out of the water. Yet he kept at it until he had the problem solved, stopping to kill a shark in the middle of the job: a remarkable incident of courage and fortitude.

Not only was Donald Crowhurst trying to complete a new trimaran for the race, but the Italian entrant, Alex Carozzo, was hard at work building an enormous sixty-six-foot ketch (as yet unnamed). This vessel was almost twice as long as the average length of the other eight entries and no one knew whether one

ALEX CAROZZO

man could handle such a giant craft. The thirty-six-year old Italian captain had no doubts at all, however, and appeared to have unlimited confidence in himself.

Carozzo was a slim, bearded Italian from Venice who was known as the Chichester of Italy. He was a bit pushy, but a likable chap, and when you saw him from a distance you immediately thought him a character out of Shakespeare. A bachelor, he was a merchant marine officer who during a trip to the Far East had built a thirty-three-foot hard-chine sloop in the hold of his cargo ship. He had then sailed his new *Golden Lion,* as he called her, from Japan to San Francisco by himself in eighty-two days during the winter.

When the round-the-world race had started, Carozzo was sailing an enormous catamaran named *San Giorgio* in another race across the Atlantic and actually met John Ridgway sailing in the Bay of Biscay (as we saw in the last chapter). Carozzo did not complete the Atlantic race but returned to England where he commenced the construction of a single-hulled vessel for the round-the-world competition. The new project wasn't even begun until August 20th, but the Medina Yacht Company claimed that its expert workmen could build the new yacht in a hurry and launch her well before the deadline. Fifteen men were soon toiling around-the-clock on three shifts to complete the new Italian yacht in record time. The local yacht watchers were dubious, but the black-bearded Carozzo, chain-smoking throughout, radiated confidence.

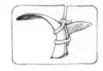

4. *The Middle Starters*

BACK IN SOUTHWEST ENGLAND, a fair wind blew from the north. Light patchy fog lay over Plymouth Sound. The date was August 22nd, and the two French entrants headed out to sea. Both men were slim, fit, and in good humor. The first was Bernard Moitessier, a long-time sailor who was forty-three years old when the race began. He had vast sailing experience, having built (and wrecked) two yachts, one on Diego-Garcia atoll in the Indian Ocean, and a second on St. Vincent in the Caribbean. In the years surrounding those two mishaps however, Moitessier had sailed thousands of miles across the Indian and Atlantic Oceans. He named his third yacht *Joshua*, after the pioneer American singlehander Joshua Slocum. The vessel—designed by Jean Knocker of Rue, France—was a thirty-nine-foot steel double-ender with a lofty two-masted ketch rig. *Joshua* could be steered from inside the cabin where the captain could keep watch from beneath a closed bubble hatch reinforced with steel. The ingenious Moitessier had built his three yachts largely with his own hands, generally scrounging materials and doing things on the cheap because he had little money. For years he lived as a sea gypsy, eking out a minimal material existence but reaping a richly satisfying life in spiritual terms.

In 1965 Moitessier and his wife had sailed from Tahiti to the Mediterranean via Cape Horn, a phenomenal nonstop voyage of 14,216 miles that took 126 days at sea. At that time the voyage was by far the longest nonstop passage ever completed by a small vessel, and it earned Moitessier publicity, awards, and a growing reputation: along with the proceeds from a book he had written about the trip.

Now at the start of the 1968 round-the-world race, the wiry Moitessier slipped away from Plymouth in his beloved, red-hulled *Joshua* and moved smoothly and steadily toward the open Atlantic. He was rested and confident and hoped that he could gradually overtake the leaders. During his previous Cape Horn trip Moitessier had averaged 113 miles a day; since then he had made various improvements in *Joshua* and had added and subtracted equipment. He felt that his skills were sharper.

Moitessier steadfastly claimed that he was not making the trip for money. "Money is all right as long as you have enough for a cup of tea," he told a reporter. "I don't care for it any more than that. The people who are thinking about money and being the fastest around the world will not win. It is the people who care about their skins. I shall bring back my skin, apart from a few bumps on the head."

The second French entrant, Loïck Fougeron, sailed a thirty-foot cutter named *Captain Browne,* which had been designed by a Belgian named Louis Van de Wiele. Originally called *Hierro,* Fougeron had renamed his vessel *Captain Browne* in honor of an old bearded English sailor who once roamed the Casablanca waterfront and whose pictures now graced the yacht's cabin. Fougeron had bought the four-year-old yacht in Belgium in January and had sailed her to England via Casablanca and Toulon. He had arrived in Plymouth in the early summer and commenced work at once to prepare her for the race.

Captain Browne was a gaff cutter with a sturdy steel hull, a long low coachroof with five small circular portlights along each side, a tiny cockpit, fairly high freeboard, and a stout transom-hung rudder. She sported a short, thick pole mast with ratlines across the shrouds so a man could climb aloft to check ahead.

Fougeron, who was forty-two years old, was a handsome, quiet Breton, born by the sea, who had lived in Casablanca for twenty years where he managed a motorcycle engineering company. On an earlier voyage he had crossed the Atlantic in a converted lifeboat. He had no singlehanded experience but he was confident that he would be able to look after himself and *Captain Browne*. The French captain had been meticulous in his preparations and even put aboard spare valves for his pressure cooker. He planned a basic diet of rice and carried forty gallons of fresh water in his tank plus another forty gallons of Evian mineral water in cans. During the months of the voyage Fougeron's wife stayed in Morocco. She did not like the sea but gently tolerated her husband's passion for a sailor's life. Before he left Plymouth, Fougeron cut down his dinner service to one plate and one cup and—apologizing profusely—offered visitors a gulp of gin straight from the bottle. He was very superstitious and went to great lengths to placate the old gods and traditions. For example he *never* mentioned rabbits at sea, a sure sign of bad luck.

In order to have a little company during his long voyage Fougeron decided to take along *Roulis,* a spirited kitten from Morocco.

On August 24th, two days after Moitessier and Fougeron had left Plymouth, Commander Bill King, the sixth entrant and, at fifty-eight, the oldest man in the race, sailed into the Atlantic on *Galway Blazer II.* Though Moitessier and King were both well-seasoned sailors, their backgrounds could not have been more different. King had begun his sea career at the Royal Naval College when he was fourteen. Three years later—in 1927—he went to sea in a British battleship. At twenty-one he was posted to a submarine in Hong Kong and traveled all over the Far East. Back in England he became second-in-command of *HMS Nar-whal.* At the beginning of World War II, King served as a submarine commander and led an incredibly active life for the next six years. He patrolled the Dutch coast, torpedoed eight ships off Norway, blew up a tanker by shellfire, duelled with German submarines, fought in the Mediterranean, and traveled to Singapore and Malta. In between times he played polo, skied, delighted in tennis and fox hunting, and hobnobbed with the titled and famous.

After the war, King got married, had two children, and became an expert at ocean racing aboard fast yachts. When *Galway Blazer II* was finally launched on May 24th, it was King's lovely sixteen-year-old daughter—holding a bouquet in one hand and a champagne bottle in the other—who did the christening while an audience of dignitaries clapped its approval. The fitting out of the new yacht, the sea trials, the various changes and improvements, and supplying took nine weeks more. It wasn't until August 24th that King finally sailed from Plymouth into the Atlantic.

Now six yachts were away on the race: Ridgway, Blyth, Knox-Johnston, Fougeron, Moitessier, and King. The trimaran of Donald Crowhurst and the giant ketch of Alex Carozzo were still in the building yards. Nigel Tetley was preparing to depart. But just about the time that Fougeron, Moitessier, and King were leaving England, news came from Captain John Ridgway, the first starter.

Ridgway, in *English Rose IV*—his *Rosie*—had crossed the Bay of Biscay, slipped past the Spanish and Portuguese coasts, and headed for Madeira, a small island 475 miles west of Casablanca on the northwest coast of Africa. *Rosie* found mostly northeast winds, so Ridgway dropped his mainsail and hoisted twin running sails, one to port and one to starboard forward of the mast, each held out with a pole. The self-steering vane guided the yacht nicely and she made 100 miles a day with scarcely any effort. It was all too easy.

At night Ridgway put up a kerosene lamp to warn shipping. Every few hours the captain rolled out to check the compass and log reading. As he sped along under twin headsails, with all the mast loading on the backstays, Ridgway wondered what would happen when the wind came from ahead, and the sailing pressure was changed to the side rigging. Then, much of the sailing load would be concentrated on the shrouds, their turnbuckles, the shroud plates that were bolted to the side decks, and the side decks themselves. It had been midships on the starboard side where the trawler had rolled against *Rosie* on the day she had left Ireland; now when the wind blew hard and his vessel touched seven knots, ominous creaks came from this area. When Ridgway reduced sail the noise stopped. During an inspection of the mast and shroud plates the captain discovered hairline cracks in the gelcoat around the lower shroud plate on the *port* side of *Rosie,* on the *opposite* side of the yacht from the collision. What did *these* cracks mean? Also the foot of the mast, stepped on deck, appeared to have shifted in its mounting shoe.

Ridgway, who was a big worrier, grew increasingly morose. "The collision had upset me more seriously than I cared to admit," he said. "The loneliness tied my stomach in knots. I found myself far too tense after a day in the cabin." He began to send radio signals, but his set refused to work. Something had gone wrong inside. He would have to get along without radio transmissions.

Each day got a little warmer, the sea turned a deep blue, and Ridgway ate the last of the avocado pears from England. He generally had lunch—sardines, crackers, and cheese—in the cockpit. Dinner was often a favorite curry. At Madeira he met a reporter from his sponsoring newspaper who came out in a local fishing boat. Ridgway passed across his diaries, films, and tapes, had a brief talk, and pushed on southward. *Rosie* continued running before the northeast trade wind that sometimes freshened and necessitated smaller sails. The little sloop had had fabulous luck with fair winds and at times covered 140 miles in twenty-four hours. Every day Ridgway oiled the self-steering gear and rubbed candlewax on the lines and sails at the points of wear.

On the morning when he passed the Cape Verde islands the wind picked up, the yacht rolled to one side and broached, and the twin headsails were backwinded, stopping the thirty-foot vessel. The rising wind ripped one sail right off the headstay and all the bronze hanks were torn open. Ridgway fought the sails to the deck. "I crept below and burst into tears," he wrote. "For some reason I could not shake off the emotional strain of loneliness. I noticed that I had cried at some point on each of twenty-seven consecutive days. Something must surely be wrong—I was just unable to relax."

A few days later *Rosie* slatted on the quiet waters of the doldrums, the region of oily calms between the northeast and southeast trade winds, and doddered along at fifty or sixty miles a day. Sometimes Ridgway sniffed the cod-liver smell of plankton that often signaled whales. "Soon we were up with them,

English Rose IV

shiny jet black with vertical foreheads dropping straight down to their mouths. . . . Like small submarines they would surface and dive; passing right under the yacht they assumed a beautiful brown color, but they would never surface closer than twenty-five yards."

Early on the morning of July 8th—Ridgway's thirtieth birthday—he tacked to the west. *Rosie* was through the doldrums and close-hauled on the port tack, heading a little west of south, into a twenty-knot southeast trade wind. The next destination was Tristran da Cunha, 2,250 miles to the south. Now the lazy days and easy living were over. *Rosie* slammed into head seas and bucked and pitched. From time to time the wind freshened and Ridgway reduced his sails accordingly. "As a wave moved along the hull, we would be left floating on air, and then the bows would fall like a lead balloon, plunging into the trough with a bow-shaking crack," he wrote. Ridgway hoped that *Rosie*'s designer had made the yacht strong enough.

Sometimes squalls brought more wind and rain. If there was not too much spray flying about, Ridgway caught rainwater by hanging a bucket at the forward end of the main boom and lifting up the after end of the boom with the topping lift to form a belly in the mainsail down which the rain poured. At first the water was a little salty but it soon washed everything clean and could then be bucketed into the tank and containers.

Ridgway kept inspecting the shrouds and fittings on *Rosie*'s port side because these were the parts that supported the mast as the yacht bounced along on the port tack. "We were about 600 miles south of the equator and some 600 miles east of Brazil," wrote Ridgway. "This was no time to lose the mast, for we had no engine. With a small no. 2 jib and heavily reefed mainsail we were making nearly four knots. The seas were long and high, the white crests sparkling in the sun. Every so often *Rosie* would stumble, taking a sea awkwardly, then she would shudder to a halt, decks streaming. [Suddenly] I was horrified to see the deck bulging around the damaged shroud plate while the cracks opened and closed, bubbling spray."

The army captain from Scotland quickly dropped both sails and lashed the single lower shroud to a strong point on deck.

He then undid the two bolts holding the shroud plate to the deck and replaced it with a new plate, adding a six-by-fifteen inch piece of ¾-inch plywood for a backing piece underneath the deck before he tightened the bolts. Then he reconnected the lower shroud and sailed on. Everything seemed to be okay.

"Next morning I noticed that the plywood had taken on a curve and was creaking ominously," wrote Ridgway. "I checked the situation from every angle. There were at least 700 miles of trade winds ahead and it was the southern hemisphere's equivalent of January. I thought for several hours on the predicament. One thing was sure, if the deck plate went, then the mast would definitely go with it. The only way to avoid the strain on the plate was to turn and run downwind to some South American port. The strain would then be transferred to the twin backstays. If I did this it would mean the end of the voyage, the end of the chance of a lifetime. To go on meant the Roaring Forties in winter; no one in his right mind would go there in a damaged boat."

The captain tried to puzzle out what had happened. He concluded that when the trawler had struck *Rosie* on the starboard side, the impact had caused the mast to whip and to strain the deck around the lower shroud plate on the port side.* Ridgway turned downwind and sailed to Recife, Brazil, which he reached on July 21st, fifty-one days after he departed from England. "It would be easy to say I would have won the race but for the damage . . . but I don't think I would have made it anyway," he wrote later in an honest admission.

The first man to leave the race was out. Eight were left.

* This type of flimsy construction and load concentration is totally unsuitable for an ocean-going yacht. The normal arrangement is for a long, substantial metal chainplate to be bolted to the side of the hull with six or eight ten- or twelve-millimeter bolts, or for a large transverse plywood knee to be massively glassed to the hull and deck underneath and then to bolt a chainplate to the knee. A single lower shroud fastened to a U-bolt pulling on a small area of thin deck is exactly what *Rosie* was designed for: Sunday afternoon sailing around a town harbor. A more versatile sailor (Moitessier, Knox-Johnston, or Tetley) might have beefed up the deck with a large strongback: or have fashioned a pair of chainplates out of something on board, bolted them to the hull, and pressed on. Ridgway had no background for this sort of repair.

On July 23rd, Chay Blyth was 480 miles south of the equator and far out in the South Atlantic, almost midway between Africa and Brazil. *Dytiscus III* was banging along close-hauled in the southeast trade wind. She headed a little west of south, about sixty or seventy degrees off the wind, which generally blew between twenty and twenty-five knots. Blyth logged 95 to 120 miles a day while his Kingfisher, heeled to twenty or thirty degrees, zipped along in big seas. "Jiggling like a tambourine on overtime," wrote the captain.

Blyth ran his life on positive, up-tempo lines and spent a lot of time thinking about his wife and infant daughter. Four days earlier he had celebrated his daughter's first birthday with an on-board party: a special breakfast of grapefruit juice, scrambled eggs, coffee, and biscuits. A birthday clean-up and shave. During the day he opened a parcel that had been packed by his wife and found a little cake (with one candle) and a few special treats of candy and paté, a pocket solitaire game, and a book of crossword puzzles. Blyth listened to a tape that his wife had made before he left. The tape had music, the sound of his daughter squealing, the doorbell ringing, and the dog barking. It was just like home.

So far in the race Blyth's major concern was that his thirty-foot twin bilge keel sloop was entirely wrong for ocean sailing. On the rough Atlantic the light shallow-draft Kingfisher tended to yaw and bob around instead of tracking straight and true like a heavier, deep-draft vessel. Nevertheless *Dytiscus III* was going along quite well. Blyth's immediate curse was a series of small, never-ending leaks typical of production yachts. The ventilators leaked, a forward pump leaked, the coachroof leaked, the shroud plates leaked, and there was a puzzling mystery leak in the forward anchor compartment. Blyth rushed around with a tube of synthetic rubber compound trying to squeeze in caulking here and there. The yacht had no proper bilge drainage so the captain had to mop up the water with a cloth.

All this was small stuff. When *Dytiscus III* was about 750 miles west of Ascension island, however, Blyth discovered that salt water had gotten into his thirty-gallon gasoline supply through the air pipe to the starboard bilge keel tank. He considered the

Dytiscus III

discovery a disaster. "The petrol was a sickly white," said Blyth. The Honda electrical generator would not run on the contaminated fuel, which meant no power for the navigation lights or the radio.*

"Try as I might, I could not bring myself to fancy the prospect of crashing through the night with no lights," said Blyth. "But it was the radio business that really bothered me. My wife would neither know where I was nor how I was, and if I decided to stick it out it would be another eight months at least before she would know that I was alive."

Blyth went through a lot of self-doubts and arguments with himself as he sailed south. "Morally, had I the right to let my wife wait eight months, with people constantly asking if she had heard anything, just to satisfy my ego?" Blyth considered putting into South Africa to replenish his gasoline and then to continue. He would be disqualified, but what did he care? He added up his problems: broken doors, leaks, torn sails, no mileage log, and salt water in the petrol. He finally decided to sail to Tristan da Cunha, an obscure Atlantic island at thirty-seven degrees south latitude, about 1,460 miles west of Cape Town, where he hoped to send a letter to his wife.

Dytiscus III ran out of the southeast wind on August 1st. The weather was cooler so Blyth put on warm clothing. On some days he made only sixty miles in light southwest breezes. When fresher winds finally came they were too strong and the thirty-footer broached before a gale. Then came fog and calms, followed by another gale with rain and lightning. ("At sea and at night, it terrifies me," wrote Blyth.) The weather got steadily colder and the captain added a pullover and thick stockings to his outfit.

Blyth arrived at Tristan da Cunha on August 15th. His vessel was in reasonable order. He was not short of food and he was rested and alert. Yet his actions were enough to make a seaman wince. "Sent up first flare," he wrote. "It's a big decision to make, because a flare means a ship in distress. I am not in distress, but I have got to make somebody see me somehow."

A ship from South Africa, the *Gillian Gaggins,* was anchored

---

* It never occured to Blyth to filter out the water by straining the gasoline.

near the island pumping gasoline ashore. After asking the ship's engineer to repair his generator, Blyth moved bodily aboard the large vessel. He accepted food and lodging and a load of new gasoline. These actions disqualified Blyth, of course, and though he eventually sailed to East London in South Africa, he is no longer part of our story.

Now two men were out of the race. Seven were left.

Nigel Tetley was the next man to sail in the round-the-world competition and the only entrant we haven't met. Lieutenant-Commander Tetley, like King, was a career officer in the Royal Navy. He was born in Pretoria, South Africa, and had been close to the sea ever since he was a boy, when he learned to row on a Scottish loch. Tetley had joined the navy in 1942 directly from Marlborough college and had served all over the world, finally working up to the command of a frigate in 1957. Forty-four years old and happily married to a geography teacher in Plymouth, Tetley had two teenage sons from an earlier marriage.

This handsome, pleasant man had owned and sailed a whole series of dinghies and yachts. During the winter of 1962–63 he had had his *Victress* trimaran built and had gradually modified and strengthened the big three-hulled craft as he tried her out on trips to Holland, Denmark, and Sweden. The multihull was the same design that Crowhurst was building except that Tetley's vessel had been properly completed and was nicely outfitted. In addition Tetley had added a center keel to improve steering and windward performance. The yacht had a total beam of twenty-two feet and carried 900 square feet of sails on two masts rigged as a ketch. *Victress* sported a large, high coachroof surmounted at the rear by a boxy cabin that allowed inside steering.

In 1966 Tetley and a friend sailed *Victress* in the gruelling two-thousand-mile round-Britain race. Tetley and his blond wife, Eve, lived aboard *Victress* year round, keeping warm in cold weather with a stove fueled by anthracite coal. Like Knox-Johnston, Tetley had tried hard to find a sponsor. He sent off letters to dozens of tea, tobacco, and drink firms.

Dear Sir [wrote Tetley]
     You may have seen a leader in *The Sunday Times* some weeks ago

announcing a Round The World Sailing Race for yachts leaving the
United Kingdom by October 31st, 1968.

Being very keen to compete and a serving Naval Officer also, I have
taken the initial step of applying to the Admiralty for unpaid leave from
early September to cover the period up to my normal retirement date,
age 45 in February, in order to take part.

Although my present yacht, a 40-foot trimaran, would be capable of
making the voyage, a yacht built specially for singlehanded sailing would
be much better, and I am writing in the hope that your firm may be
prepared to sponsor all or part of the building cost in return for advertising rights.

The yacht I have in mind is a 50-foot trimaran, to a design by Derek
Kelsall and myself, which could be built in his boatyard at Sandwich for
an estimated £10,000 fully fitted. This is a realistic figure for a light
weight, yet extra strong, trimaran of sound design and first-class materials.

My sailing experience covers thirty years, and includes the Round
Britain Race in which I achieved fifth place in my family trimaran *Victress.*

In view of the short times now remaining to build and equip a new
boat, I would greatly appreciate an early answer. . . .

As Knox-Johnston had discovered, a sponsor was a hard fish
to find. "The replies . . . all wished me luck, but regretted that
no special funds could be allocated for the project," wrote Tetley.
"What they really meant, was that the whole thing was much too
risky a proposition."

Tetley realized that if he wanted to enter the race he would
have to sail the family yacht, just as Knox-Johnston had done.
"But how would she stand up to the wild Southern Ocean?" wondered Tetley. No multihull had ever been through the fourteen
thousand miles of the roaring forties before. Could the *Victress*
do it? He would find out.

The days of speculation and indecision were over [wrote Tetley]. I
notified *The Sunday Times* of my entry. Some financial help would still
be needed if *Victress* was to get all the equipment she needed. How I
disliked the thought of publicity. If only one could complete the voyage
without anyone knowing until it was all over: to be remembered as a
seaman, not a conquering hero. As every sailor knows, the sea can never
be conquered, merely held at bay. But sponsorship would only come

through accepting publicity. If one took money, one should give a fair return. . . .

During the week, Michael Moynihan came down to interview me for *The Sunday Times.* He was racking his brains for a likely sponsor and when I demonstrated *Victress's* stereo system, he immediately hit on the idea of a record company. I was delighted at the prospect. That weekend *The Sunday Times* printed an article under the title "Around the World in 80 Symphonies." It showed a picture of Eve and me seated in the cabin, drinking beer and laughing our heads off. Bob Salmon, the photographer, was very good at making us laugh.

Unknown to us at the time, Richard Baldwyn, a director of Music for Pleasure, was returning by air from the south of France and, as the aeroplane was about to land, had just read the piece in the paper. Suddenly the captain announced there was some doubt whether the wheels would go down. While their fate hung in the balance, he made a silent vow that if the plane landed safely, he would help with the venture. The next morning, Terry Bartram of Music for Pleasure telephoned me at Naval Headquarters at Plymouth. Could he come down? Tomorrow? Certainly! This sounded like real efficiency. In the afternoon a telegram arrived from a rival company. Publicity was showing results: the sponsors were biting.

Tetley had worked out an arrangement for downwind self-steering using twin headsails held out on long poles led from the foredeck. He immediately hired an expert machinist to build a mechanical self-steering unit as well. Tetley strengthened the masthead fitting on the mainmast and installed additional rigging. Meanwhile Eve studied books on diet and food and began to load stores aboard *Victress.* In addition to helping pay some of the bills, the Music for Pleasure people made sure that Tetley had plenty of music for the yacht's sound system. No matter what happened, there would be music for every mood: stirring marches for the morning, chamber music at noon, string quartets in the afternoon, symphonies for the evening, plus a variety of singers, Scots balladeers, flute concertos—a little of everything.

Just before Tetley's departure on September 16th, a report came in from *Suhaili,* the leader in the race. No longer did Robin Knox-Johnston have time to play chess by radio or while away the hours singing songs from Gilbert and Sullivan. He had been in a frightful storm off the Cape of Good Hope and there had been some damage. The merchant navy captain had made repairs, however, and was continuing eastward into the Indian Ocean.

"Robin's radioed report appeared in the *The Sunday Mirror*. He said that throughout his service in the Merchant Navy he had never seen such seas," quoted Tetley. "Even allowing for press embellishment, the experience sounded hair raising and I wondered what madness I had let myself in for."

Nigel Tetley's departure was a little more emotional than he had planned.

As *Victress* headed for Plymouth Sound the knot of small craft fell back on either side. I was in luck, a fair wind blew from the north, wafting the trimaran down harbour like some stately queen attended by her courtiers. It felt strange to find her the centre of attention, though in the splendour of her new paint I knew she deserved it. I had one of Music for Pleasure's brass band records playing over the wheelhouse speaker, and I must have been unconsciously beating out the time, for I could see Eve, in a small boat near by, copying me. Just then, the music changed to a slow, soulful passage, my eyes blurred and the sobs came; I could not look at the club launch for several minutes. What had I to feel sorry about? It was Eve whom I had condemned to long months of loneliness and waiting. And there she was, standing up bravely in the bows of the open boat. "Come back soon!" she called as the launch, unable to keep up, turned away. Mustering all the confidence I could, I cried, "I will!"

As Tetley cleared England he began to hurry south in the Atlantic in hot pursuit of the four men ahead of him. According to his studies of the pilot charts, the winds during the months he had selected for his voyage were more favorable for running and reaching, which would mean high speeds for the spidery, three-hulled trimaran. Tetley was far behind the leaders; he was confident, however, that he would win the race.

5. *Different Captains*

WHILE DONALD CROWHURST AND ALEX CAROZZO struggled to get out of the boatyards and ready prior to the October 31st deadline—only six weeks away—the five men at sea sailed as hard as they could.

Of the five, Bernard Moitessier was the great romantic in the race. In temperament, he was a violinist who drew his bow hard against a tuneful ocean. Moitessier knew the flute calls of the wind, the bassoon notes of the waves, and the rhythmic snare-drumming of water along the hull. To him it was all a wonderful symphony filled with dreams and delight.

All *Joshua* and I wanted was to be left alone with ourselves [wrote Moitessier]. Any other thing did not exist, had never existed. You do not ask a tame seagull why it needs to disappear from time to time toward the open sea. It goes, that's all, and it is as simple as a ray of sunshine, as normal as the blue of the sky. . . .

The wake stretches on and on, white and dense with life by day, luminous by night, like long tresses of dreams and stars. Water runs along the hull and rumbles or sings or rustles, depending on the wind, depending on the sky, depending on whether the sun was setting red or grey. For many days it has been red, and the wind hums in the rigging, makes a halyard tap against the mast at times, passes over the sails like a caress and goes on its way to the west, toward Madeira, as *Joshua* rushes to the south in the trade wind at 7 knots.

Wind, sea, boat and sails, a compact, diffuse whole, without beginning or end, a part and all of the universe . . . my own universe, truly mine.

I watch the sun set and inhale the breath of the open sea. I feel my being blossoming and my joy soars so high that nothing can disturb it.

The other questions, the ones that used to bother me at times, do not weigh anything before the immensity of a wake so close to the sky and filled with the wind of the sea.

All the contestants except Moitessier and Fougeron, the two Frenchmen, carried radios to keep in touch with the rest of the world. Most people in a ten-month race would want news from home once in a while. In addition the contestants might wish to send messages to their families or sponsors. Certainly the men in the race would want to know how they were doing in relation to one another. This would mean occasional transmissions. Moitessier and Fougeron, aboard *Joshua* and *Captain Browne*, respectively, refused to take radios.

"The big cumbersome contraptions were not welcome," said Moitessier. "Our peace of mind, and thereby our safety, was more important, so we preferred not to accept them." Moitessier was a virtuoso with a slingshot, however, and did agree to shoot an occasional message and a few rolls of exposed film on board passing ships. "A good slingshot is worth all the transmitters in the world!" he said. "And it is so much better to shift for yourself, with the two hands God gave you and a pair of elastic bands."

In spite of his fierce independence, however, Moitessier sometimes relented when he thought of his wife.

September 1. We meet a ship early in the morning. I get out my mirror, and she answers with an Aldis lamp. She has understood and will radio my position to Lloyds. Françoise will know that all's well; I'm happy—right off, my day is made.

Feeling great, I go below to finish my mug of coffee; glancing out the hatch, what do I see . . . the ship coming back! She has made a big circle (I can see her wake on the calm water) and is bearing down on me from astern. Wow! I get pretty rattled . . . She comes by about fifteen yards off, towering like a wall far above my masts. The ship is enormous; she must be well over 300 feet long. When the bridge draws abreast, an officer shouts through a megaphone, "We will report you to Lloyds. Do you need anything?"

I wave "No" with my hand, my throat is so tight. The monster takes forever to go by; I pull the helm all the way over to get clear, afraid she would wobble in her course and sweep both my masts away. But the captain of the *Selma Dan* has a good eye and knows what he is doing. I have cold sweats just the same, and my legs feel like rubber. At this range I could pelt the bridge with my slingshot, but there was no time to prepare a message. And I dare not try to get them to understand by signalling: they are so nice they would turn around and come back. I have had enough thrills for one day, and I know someone who is not about to take on any more ships with his mirror for a while.

Little by little the Frenchman—with the advantage of his long experience—gained on those ahead.

The average speed climbs day after day, on a sea full of sun [wrote Moitessier]. I am glad to see that *Joshua* sails definitely faster than before. This improvement is largely due to the fact that she is much lighter. Also, the longitudinal weight distribution is far better; she is less loaded down with useless gear, and I was able to completely clear out the forward and aft compartments. In the old days, we had two dismantled dinghies in the forepeak, one dead and the other useless, not to mention an incredible pile of junk collected over the years. When in Plymouth, I unloaded engine, anchor winch, dinghy, all unnecessary charts, a suitcase full of books and *Sailing Directions* that did not cover my route, four anchors, 55 pounds of spare zinc anodes, 900 pounds of chain, most of the ¾″ diameter line, and all the paint (275 pounds!) after splashing a last coat on deck and topsides. . . . Naturally, I did not completely disinherit myself, in spite of cutting to the bone. Though I kept a strict minimum of charts, they covered all possible landfalls around Good Hope, Australia, Tasmania, the northern and southern islands of New Zealand, the Horn waters with parts of the Patagonia channels, and even a few atolls in the Pacific. . . .

Continued fair weather, but very little wind. The speed is still impressive, as *Joshua* can carry more than 1560 sq. ft. of canvas. I rigged a 54 sq. ft. storm jib as a bonnet under the main boom, in addition to the genoa bonnet, and a lightweight 75 sq. ft. storm jib as a second staysail. The sea is calm, my rig picks up the slightest breeze. I watch the boat slipping along at nearly 7 knots on a smooth sea in the setting sun. What peace! Two weeks already, and a daily average of 143 miles since Plymouth. . . .

The wake stretches on and on. The Canaries are now astern, the Cape Verde islands on the right, Africa to the left. Flying fish hunted by the dorados glide in big schools in front of the boat. At times, a beautiful rainbow plays with the foam of the bow wave. I film it, securely wedged on the bowsprit pulpit.

The doldrums are fairly close now. It is a zone of calms and light variable winds, with rain and squalls, caused by the meeting of the two trade wind belts near the equator. At the latitude of the Cape Verde Islands, the doldrums stretch approximately between the 15th and the 5th parallel north, or about 600 miles.

For the big square-rigged vessels of old, the doldrums meant long, exhausting days handling the heavy yards in the damp heat under a leaden sky, taking advantage of the least shift in the wind, continually coming about. For our small yachts, the doldrums are annoying but nothing more, since coming about is easy; the zone should normally be crossed fairly quickly. Just the same, a sailor will always take on the doldrums with an uneasy conscience. I wonder where my friends will cross? I have not quite settled on a course to the left or right of the Cape Verde Islands.

Joshua has been dragging along for days that feel like weeks. When the breeze drops completely, I have to sheet everything flat and drop the 650 sq. ft. genoa-bonnet combination, which would chafe too much, slatting against the staysail stay as the boat rolls. Every time the inconsistent breeze picks up, the genoa has to be raised again and the sheets trimmed to the inch to catch the faintest puff, to sail south at all cost. . . .

On a trip this long, every drop of fresh water is a gift from the heavens. I left Plymouth with enough water to reach New Zealand, though, and will have a dozen opportunities to top up my tank between here and Tasmania. Just the same, I collected 15 gallons yesterday and today, with a bucket rigged under the mainmast gooseneck.

While Bernard Moitessier patiently sailed through the fitful winds of the doldrums on *Joshua,* another yacht was close behind. It was Bill King aboard *Galway Blazer II.* Both men were expert sailors, both had distinctive yachts, and both were in the same race. Both had left Plymouth within twenty-four hours of each other. Both were thin, intense men full of nervous energy. . . . Yet the two sailors were galaxies apart in temperament, habits, background, and even equipment.

The vessel of each man reflected his personality: Moitessier's yacht was strong, well-equipped, powerful, and entirely adequate. Fully stored for the trip she displaced about twelve tons. Yet she was rough, without electricity, crude in fittings and finish, with a studied emphasis on practicality rather than fanciness. Like an earlier famous voyaging yacht named *Tzu Hang,* *Joshua*'s hull was painted bright red. She had the feel of distant

Galway Blazer II

oceans about her and looked comfortable on the water, as if she belonged there, a true workboat of the sea.

King's vessel·was strong, well-equipped, and a little more graceful than powerful in appearance. Her four-and-a-half ton displacement was less than half the weight of *Joshua. Galway Blazer II* had the latest electronic instruments, a life raft, a long distance radio, and the finest self-steering gear. Her interior furniture was nicely designed and built. There was a large comfortable chair with a seatbelt, and King's bed was a swinging cot that pivoted along its fore-and-aft axis and could be locked to any angle of heel. *Galway Blazer II* had a glass-smooth finish and impeccable paint and varnish that befitted a proper yacht. Yet somehow the grey and white vessel had an aura of daintiness, more a perfection of detail than of a solid, unified small ship.

Even the rigs of the two yachts were different. Moitessier had a well-tried lofty ketch rig with conventional solid wooden masts that were massively stayed in place with a forest of wires. Each of the heavy wire shrouds and stays was oversize and strongly fastened to the steel deck. The rig was thoroughly conventional, and every aspect of its handling had been practiced and perfected by seamen for generations. With its multiplicity of halyards, sheets, pendants, outhauls, shrouds, stays, preventers, guys, stropped blocks, and other rigging, *Joshua* looked a little like a tea clipper coming from China in an old nautical painting.

King, meanwhile, was sailing southward with an entirely different rig. *Galway Blazer II* had two large diameter hollow spruce masts on each of which was fitted a fan-shaped Chinese lugsail— a roughly rectangular sail supported by six full-length horizontal battens whose after ends held the controlling sheets that were led to the cockpit area. The forward part of each sail lay along its mast which was free-standing and without support wires of any kind. Without stays and shrouds the sails could be eased right ahead for downwind sailing.

The performance of the lugsail rig was outstanding across the wind and with the wind. Against the wind the performance was mediocre; also in light airs the sailing ability was poor because of the limited sail area. Yet the sail arrangement had the great advantage that it could be easily shortened from the safety of an inside position and there was no sail changing at all. *Galway Blazer II* had two circular control hatches protected by spray hoods. All King had to do to adjust the sails was to poke his head out and to haul on or ease a few lines. The arrangement must have reminded King of his days as a submarine commander because controlling the yacht from the deck hatch was a little like running a submarine from a conning tower.

While *Galway Blazer II*'s rig had great handling abilities for ordinary sailing, such unstayed mast arrangements had never been tested in the severe weather of the Southern Ocean. King had prepared for the worst by fitting an emergency bipod mast arrangement that was kept on deck.

Once at sea, King showed that he was no idler and was soon averaging 150 miles a day. On August 26th, near the coast of Spain, *Galway Blazer II* logged 188 miles in twenty-four hours with a fair northeast wind. Unfortunately King had problems with the Chinese rig whose fourteen-foot fiberglass battens began to break. He was obliged to sail under the foresail alone while he handed the mainsail, extracted the broken battens, and put in spare stiffeners made of hickory. Little by little King made adjustments to the Chinese rig, which he found both exasperating and marvelous in turn. The unconventional sail plan wasn't nearly as close-winded as her competitors, but King's yacht moved well at an angle of sixty-five degrees off the wind.

As befitted an old salt, King gradually succumbed to the spell of the sea. "I fell into the wonderful basic routine of living as a sea creature with nothing between me and the sky and the depths, with only the sun and stars to guide me," he said in a glowing moment.

King was a slender, spare man with a deeply tanned face and a halo of silver hair. He looked more like a college professor or a clergyman than a world-circling sailor. He was a vegetarian who ate sparingly. No cases of whisky went with him. Years before he had made a sailing trip across the Atlantic and had lived on soaked raisins, almond nut paste for protein, whole-wheat biscuits, and cress grown in jars for vitamin C. "Never had I felt better than after twenty-three days of this carefully balanced diet," he said, "and I was sure it would suffice me for a year if necessary. Flying fish always add themselves to the menu in tropical waters. I would take no medicines and only one large tin of instant coffee to use as a stimulant when I must not sleep."

Throughout the northeast trades King often logged 160 miles a day. But when he left the splendid northeast wind and entered the doldrums, his speed plummeted to only 40 miles a day.

BILL KING

Gradually King slatted his way south toward the wind belt of the southeast trade wind, which began 300 miles north of the equator at his longitude. *Galway Blazer II*'s Chinese rig was slow and underpowered in the poky winds of the doldrums. One of the disadvantages was that there was no way of hoisting a light-weight ghosting sail for very light breezes. It wasn't until September 27th that King again found a good sailing wind. "Today as the sun got up we came into the true trade winds," he wrote. "Their chief herald was the lovely sky; long French-bread, roly-poly, flocular clouds, replacing solemn menacing piled-up black-ness, and a nice steady wind enabling me to set course for the next point."

Sometimes King wondered about himself:

After the morning chores I tried to rationalize my various anxieties [he wrote]. Up to now they have been entirely connected with the feeling that I could never get my boat ready this summer. Now, of course, I am beset by other bogies. Why have I undertaken this venture? To teach myself a lesson? I do not experience either a fear of death or dejection at the prospect of spending eight or nine months alone; but I do have a choking fear of failing to be able to cope with the possible situations which may arise. Things will be going wrong from now on, things I did not think of in time, and which now must be put right by myself.

King said that he undertook his long voyage to purge himself of a portion of his past: to be healed of the terrible mental scars inflicted by the war during the six years that he had spent as a submarine commander—an experience that most of his fellow submariners did not survive. During World War II he had lived half his life submerged. The worst months were the patrols up and down the Norwegian coast during the summer of 1940, when the long days and short nights meant that King's submarine had to keep submerged eighteen hours out of twenty-four. "At the end of those eighteen-hour dives the air became so deficient in oxygen that our breath came in heavy gasps," he wrote.

Fortunately life on board *Galway Blazer II* wasn't all grimness and introspection. Often King looked out of the yacht and away from his black memories and was thrilled by the beauty around him.

Last night the fresh trade wind slackened and, instead of spurting and scooting off the wave crests, we sailed serenely on under a star-spread sky [wrote King]. I sat riveted by the beauty of it for hours; the mast wheeling against the veil of the Milky Way, the apex of our universe. How tiny we seem when one becomes aware of the immensity of the firmament. How much more aware one is in a little boat on a wide sea under a jewelled darkness . . .

King had the bad luck to accidentally burn his hands with acid while servicing the yacht's batteries. Later he fell and bruised his ribs on the cockpit coaming. These mishaps reminded King how slight the margin of error in personal accidents was for a lone adventurer. An injured man would not be able to sail his ship across an ocean.

This evening I learnt that Bernard Moitessier has worked out a big lead [wrote King]. This, of course, must be a great disappointment to me and destroy my peace of mind. I built this boat specifically to pioneer this trip, not for ocean racing. When it transpired that a race was on, there was nothing else to do but to join it, but now I have to realize I have little chance of winning it. Already I face the same sort of emotional situation that must have faced Scott when Amundsen reached the South Pole first, or the earlier Everest Expedition which did not quite make it, after superhuman efforts. This sort of thing is a test and discipline of one's character which must be faced, but I did not set out to test my character. I just wanted to achieve a terrific new experience and forget six ugly years spent fighting *under* the sea.

I cannot *drive Galway Blazer* against faster boats. I will plod on around the world, revelling in my boat's special poetic beauty, in her strength and power. I will put disappointments from me—but I wish now I had no radio contact. Much as I like Mike [King's newspaper radio correspondent], family, and value news, I would rather be alone and immersed in the job.

6. *The Late Starters*

ON SEPTEMBER 21ST, the first day of spring in the Southern Hemisphere, five of the nine entrants in the race were sailing southward in the Atlantic. The leader, Robin Knox-Johnston, had already turned east and was south of the Cape of Good Hope at the southern tip of Africa. Moitessier was nearing Ilha Trinidade at 20 degrees south latitude, some 600 miles east of the Brazilian coast. Loïck Fougeron and Bill King were both still slatting their way through the frustrating dead air region between the northeast and southeast trade wind zones near the equator. Nigel Tetley had just left England in his blue trimaran *Victress*.

John Ridgway and Chay Blyth were both out of the race, one because of damage, and the second because of disqualification.

The last two men—numbers eight and nine—had not left England. The Italian Alex Carozzo was madly working on his enormous sixty-six-foot ketch. In just two days, on September 23rd, Donald Crowhurst was to launch his Victress trimaran which had been named *Teignmouth Electron*.

The name Teignmouth (pronounced TIN-muth) had come from Rodney Hallworth, Crowhurst's publicity agent, who was also the public relations man for the town of Teignmouth, a summer resort of thirteen thousand people located in Devonshire on the southwest coast of England. Crowhurst's home was nearby, and Hallworth proposed that if the yacht were named Teignmouth, and Crowhurst started his voyage from there and agreed to mention the place as often as he could, Hallworth would start a £1,500 fund-raising campaign. Crowhurst's company was Electron Utilisation so the name *Teignmouth Electron* was coined.

In truth the naming of Crowhurst's new vessel was not very important just then because it was doubtful whether she would get away before the October 31st deadline. The original launching date of August 31st had come and gone as had the "final" date of September 12th. In spite of Eastwoods's efforts of a seventy-hour work week plus a night shift, the yacht simply wasn't ready. Crowhurst wrote Eastwoods a stern letter. "The entire project is now in jeopardy;" he said in part, and set September 23rd as the absolute last date for getting into the water.

Eastwoods countered with a bill for £900 for Crowhurst's continuing alterations and demanded that all other arrears be settled as well. Another volcano erupted over the fiberglass deck sheathing called for in the design. Eastwoods said there was no time. Crowhurst fumed. He argued that the figerglass was necessary and part of the contract. Eastwoods rejoined that painting was good enough because the deck thickness had been doubled at Crowhurst's insistence. The yard had tried to telephone Crowhurst about the matter but he was away. The painting had already begun, and if he wanted to launch on September 23rd . . . .

According to Nicolas Tomalin and Ron Hall, Crowhurst's biographers, it was a time of crisis.

That night, with Donald Crowhurst in an angry, unhappy mood, was the only time during the entire venture when Clare [his wife] pleaded with him to refuse delivery of the boat and give up the project. Somewhat to her surprise, he seriously considered her arguments. "I suppose you're right," he said, "but the whole thing has become too important for me. I've got to go through with it, even if I have to build the boat myself on the way round." Clare afterwards felt she had put her case too strongly because after this Donald became more secretive about the further difficulties that arose. And there were many more of those.

When *Teignmouth Electron* was finally launched on September 23rd, it was Clare Crowhurst who made the christening remarks and swung the traditional bottle of champagne against the bow.

Unfortunately the bottle didn't break. The builder had to step in behind her and help finish the christening and try to laugh off the bad luck omen.

The builder's yard was in Norfolk in the east of England facing the North Sea. Crowhurst and the crew were to sail the sleek new Victress trimaran to Teignmouth on England's southwest coast facing the English channel, a distance of about 325 miles. By the time the yacht was rigged and various squabbles with the yard were settled, however, it was already September 30th. Crowhurst and his two crewmen hurried into the North Sea and shaped a course south for the Strait of Dover. Crowhurst became violently seasick in the ocean swell but gamely steered as *Teignmouth Electron* streaked south with a fair wind. The three men on board calculated that they would be in Teignmouth in three days. Unfortunately the wind changed, the contrary tidal streams were strong, and the Victress trimaran—an absymal performer to windward—scarcely made any progress at all. Crowhurst began tacking back and forth across the English channel and even used the trimaran's outboard motor at times. But after seventy-two hours of steady sailing and a great deal of back and forth work, the vessel had only made a little progress toward Teignmouth. Indeed she was just a little west of Boulogne, France, scarcely 40 percent of the distance to Teignmouth.

Crowhurst was puzzled and angry and began experimenting with small and large sails trying to find more effective combinations. Peter Beard, one of the two crewmen, asked Crowhurst whether this sort of sailing performance was really adequate for ocean passages—especially the difficult work of coping with big seas and strong winds. In an astonishing reply Crowhurst told Beard that the question was academic because the winds during the round-the-world race would always be behind him and fair. Beard asked what would happen when the winds were against *Teignmouth Electron*. What would the captain do?

"Well, one could always shuttle around in the south Atlantic for a few months," said Crowhurst. "There are places out of the shipping lanes where no one would ever spot a boat like this." Then he took Beard's logbook to show him how it could be done. He drew Africa, and South America. He placed two small triangles between them to represent the Falkland Islands and Tristan da Cunha. With his pencil he lightly traced a lozenge-shaped course, round and round, between the two. It would be simple, he said, no one would ever find out. Crowhurst laughed: it was obviously a joke. The diagram is still in Peter Beard's logbook.

It had taken four days to reach Newhaven on the Essex coast halfway to Teignmouth. Crowhurst's crew had planned only three days for the entire trip and had to leave for other commitments. Crowhurst telephoned the builder for crew and waited for replacements. Meanwhile a southwest gale thundered up the English Channel and the wind howled in Newhaven. Crowhurst fumed and paced the floor of a waterfront bar. Already he was into the first week of October. The race deadline was only three weeks away. He should have been in Teignmouth long before and have attended to half a hundred small and large modifications. By this time all his stores and tools and radios and electronic gear should have been on board. Crowhurst should have been in hot pursuit of Knox-Johnston who was already in the Indian Ocean; he should have been chasing Moitessier and Fougeron and King and Tetley who were far south in the Atlantic.

Finally the new crewmen arrived, but the foul weather raged on for another two days. It then took an additional forty-eight hours to sail fifty miles to the Isle of Wight where the new crewmen promptly quit. It was here that Crowhurst met Alex Carozzo, the Italian who was in the race. Both men had the parallel problems of feverish, almost hopeless preparation difficulties. They commiserated with one another and inspected each other's yachts. The meeting was a bit like Alain Gerbault and Harry Pigeon, two early world-circling sailors, who in 1925 met each other in Panama. There, in steaming Balboa, on the shore of the Pacific, each man looked at the other's vessel with interest and curiosity, but returned to his own yacht, which he preferred above all others.

Crowhurst managed to recruit an expert local sailor and began bashing into the westerly winds again. After thirty-six hours the wind direction finally changed and the trimaran soon finished the remaining eighty miles to Teignmouth, sometimes reaching twelve knots. The three-day delivery had taken thirteen days. It was now October 15th.

Crowhurst hoped that his problems would be over once he got to Teignmouth and back to the resources of his family, friends, home, and business. Hallworth's fund-raising had lagged (only £250 so far toward the goal of £1,500), but his publicity was good and had attracted some encouraging support among the leaders of the community. However there was an element of skepticism and mocking doubt among the waterfront locals who can always be relied upon to heap scorn on any idea or program whether it has merit or not.

The boatyard pulled *Teignmouth Electron* out of the water, and carpenters started to work on a number of projects which had either not been completed or needed changes. The hatch on the floor of the cockpit had leaked badly. Unlike Tetley's Victress trimaran whose cockpit was covered by an enclosed wheelhouse, Crowhurst's cockpit was open. During normal ocean sailing a good deal of water flew around, and the cockpit got spray from time to time plus an occasional wave top. A leak in Crowhurst's cockpit was particularly bad because the precious electric generator was underneath; if the generator failed there would be no power for lights, radios, and the electronic devices.

Crowhurst had hoped to use radios that he had built himself, but there was no time for proper certification; so he had to purchase commercial radio equipment. The installation of the antennas and ground plates was complicated and required specialists. Lists of food stores for 300 days plus emergency rations for another 120 days had to be drawn up and bought. Many of the food items were difficult to find in the half-closed summer resort area. Crowhurst's requirements included tools and parts for the electronic equipment which hadn't been constructed yet. With time so short he intended to take along all the components and to build what he needed while underway. Every morning there were long shopping lists; people rushed off in all directions to stores and supply houses.

Crowhurst needed drill bits, solder, shackles, spare line, sail needles, rubber sheeting, gasoline cans, water jugs, oilskin patching kits, bedding compound, and signaling flags. He needed charts, navigation tables, nautical almanacs, light lists, logbooks, tidal tables, pilot books, and pencils. He needed underwear, woolen clothing, sea boots, watch caps, and warm gloves. The lists included copper tubing, plumbing fittings, hacksaw blades, black tape, bottles of aspirin, and toothbrushes. It seemed that for every item bought and crossed off the shopping lists, however, two more things were added.

Workmen bolted a brace to the self-steering gear to strengthen its mounting, which was plagued by vibration troubles at high speed. The special masthead buoyancy bag (deflated) was lashed aloft.

Crowhurst's efforts were newsworthy so reporters scurried around town interviewing people and asking a lot of nosy questions. Television cameramen filmed the beamy, white-hulled *Teignmouth Electron* while workmen and technicians sawed, filed, welded, pounded, and painted. The cameras whirred and BBC interviewers asked Crowhurst leading questions. At first Crowhurst cooperated and even delighted in giving cocky, exaggerated responses.

Talking to yourself is very important [he said]. When one has been awake for a couple of days, soaking wet and perhaps hasn't had enough to eat . . . you can restore a sense of urgency by telling yourself what the consequences of your lack of attention to detail are. . . . this is a tremendous help because the very process of speaking, forming the words, helps to crystallise one's thoughts in a way that no mere process of thought can ever do.

Donald Kerr, the BBC announcer, asked Crowhurst whether he had ever been in a situation in which he thought he was going to drown.

There was an occasion on the South Coast [said Crowhurst]. I was sailing with a following wind . . . blowing about force seven.* The boat was set up for self-steering and I must have been about twenty miles from shore. There were no guard rails, I didn't have a safety harness, and I fell overboard. I thought, as the boat sailed on, that I was either

---

*A Force seven wind is a moderate gale with winds of twenty-eight to thirty-three knots. See the Beaufort wind scale chart at the front of the book.

going to drown or else I was in for a very long swim. I realised of course that it was entirely my own fault and I didn't waste any time blaming myself. I just made a mental note that this sort of practice had to be avoided in the future and got on with the thinking about what one had to do about it. I was very lucky on that occasion because my boat, in point of fact came up into the wind. My self-steering arrangements had relied on a little manual assistance from myself from time to time. . . . But she did sail on something like a quarter of a mile before coming up into the wind and it was quite long enough to give me a fright.

This incident was, of course, pure fantasy. Fortunately there was little time for such grandiose interviews. Crowhurst's time was short and there was a lot to do. Expert small boat sailors know that before a race or a sailing deadline the captain has to be at the yard and to take full charge of everything. He must constantly test and check the work, and enlist the cooperation of everyone. When the men work *with* such a person and are on his side, good progress is possible. Otherwise the situation is a disaster.

All hell broke out during those two weeks he was here [said one of the shipyard workers]. Everyone was trying to help, but nobody rightly knew what to do. As for Crowhurst, he didn't look the man to go at all. He hadn't an inkling where anything was, or what was happening. He didn't test nothing. He didn't stay with his boat, as a skipper ought to. He'd suddenly clear off for something, and we'd be wandering around trying to find him. If it wasn't some mysterious drive up to London it was a wine-and-cheese publicity party up the Royal. That's no way to start off round the world.

You couldn't tell what was going on inside of him. He just wasn't integrated with us, if you know what that means. He was in a daze. We'd have admired him much more if he'd simply said "I've lost me nerve. Let's drop the whole business." Obviously he was in a blind panic and didn't have the guts to call it off. So what if it made him bankrupt and penniless? Life is very sweet, brother, even without money, and even looking a fool.

And that boat of his! It was just bloody ridiculous. A right load of plywood it was. The attitude here was he couldn't get further than Brixham.

To his friends, Crowhurst was a kaleidoscope of shifting impressions. One man thought him determined, confident, and

eager, but a bit disorganized. Another said that he was cheery
and raring to go.

"Crowhurst was strange, not all there," recalled a third friend.
"He had gone peculiarly quiet. It worried me. It was a mood I
had never seen before. I knew Donald's explosive fits of temper,
and I would have welcomed a familiar outburst or two; that would
have meant he was trying to get things done. But in those last
few days he seemed absolutely subdued, as if his mind was par-
alyzed."

A fourth man told him not to go. "You won't be ready in
time," he said. Crowhurst replied: "It's too late. I can't turn back
now."

During the sixteen days that Crowhurst was at Teignmouth
he grew increasingly tense, confused, and forgetful. He wasted
time on trifles and neglected important jobs. He continued to
write letters, for example, soliciting money when there was no
chance of replies in time. One day his wife noticed that water
was running out of one of the trimaran's floats when it was out
of the water. This might have indicated a dangerous leak. The
captain shrugged off the warning.

Crowhurst took *Teignmouth Electron* out for a few hours to try
all the new sails and to work out his downwind running arrangements. A BBC photographer and interviewer went along. Crowhurst seemed slow and clumsy and was exasperated when various
pieces of hardware and hatch bedding proved unsatisfactory.
The afternoon was a disappointment for everyone. Two days
later when the BBC people looked over the yacht again, things
were no better. The vessel still needed a great deal of fitting out.
Stores and equipment were piled haphazardly on the decks. Mrs.
Crowhurst—who had gotten a cracked rib when Donald had
accidentally fallen against her—was varnishing eggs in a nearby
shed. The BBC man no longer saw a news story about an interesting sporting event. The newsman detected signs of trouble
and quietly changed his story line.

A water-filled float in a trimaran is particularly dangerous
because it can lead to a loss of stability and perhaps cause a capsize. With three hulls, however, the bilge pumping arrange-

ments are complicated. Generally a series of separate watertight compartments is built, with a suction hose from each compartment leading to a selector valve, which is then connected to a pump. By changing the selector valve setting, each compartment can be pumped out in turn. Often in a trimaran the pumping system is split into two halves, each served by a separate pump. *Teignmouth Electron* had two powerful Henderson hand bilge pumps, but lacked a vital connecting hose. After urgent calls, the manufacturer flew a piece of special noncollapsible hose to an airport near Teignmouth. In the confusion, somehow, the hose never got to the yacht, although Crowhurst thought it had been put on board.

In addition, a great pile of important parts either got offloaded from the trimaran or was left behind on the slipway by mistake. Or the parts may have been thrown out as rubbish. Mrs. Crowhurst put a bag of personal gifts for Donald on his bunk. The empty bag was later found on the slipway.

Finally with only twenty-four hours to the race deadline, the BBC crew took pity on Crowhurst, stopped filming and recording, and began to help him directly. The newsmen hurried out to buy flares and lifejackets. In the late afternoon the BBC men dragged an exhausted and trembling Crowhurst to a restaurant for something to eat. "It's no good. It's no good," he kept mumbling.

Why didn't someone object to this nightmare scene and cry stop! Why didn't Crowhurst's sponsor tell Donald to give up? Why didn't a group of Crowhurst's friends take him aside? Why didn't Mrs. Crowhurst refuse to let her husband go? And finally, what about the race officials at *The Sunday Times*? Where were they? Or was their intention only to sell more newspapers? It's hard to believe that the executives of the newspaper could have been so cynical.

Crowhurst seemed to have been caught up in a great Ferris wheel of publicity. The wheel was turning and no one had enough sense to throw the brake lever. It was quite true that Crowhurst lacked proper sailing experience. His vessel was clearly untried and not ready. It was late in the year and bad weather might come at any time. The race was extremely hazardous and intended mainly for professional seamen, a class of men that certainly did not include Crowhurst.

Of the nine entrants in the race, five were professional sailors. Four were not and it's perhaps predictable that those four were not strong contenders. It was the old salts who kept plugging away to the bitter end. In the future, the rules for solo distance sailing races would be drastically changed to require long qualifying trips in the intended vessel far in advance of the starting date. The vessel itself would be inspected closely. But in 1968, when such singlehanded competitions were relatively unknown, the sponsors had a free and easy attitude. If an entrant was foolhardy he had only himself to blame. Besides, the competition was designed to sell newspapers by promoting an unusual race, a circulation scheme that was decades old. (Recall the wager of Phileas Fogg in *Around The World In Eighty Days*.) The zanier the race the better. Within gentlemen's limits of course. But what were the limits?

Crowhurst had accepted sponsorship and press exposure. At his elbow he had a professional journalist pounding the drums of publicity and telling the world that his man would win. Perhaps Crowhurst was too proud and too much of a showoff to admit that he was ill-advised to carry on. An Argentine once described a famous sailor from his country, a person with unbounded egotism, as "a man with a touch of vanity." This certainly applied to Crowhurst, who wasn't a bit shy when it came to claims for himself.

Publicity acting upon vanity translates to acid dripping on thin metal. It takes an uncommonly strong man to combine the two elements, to hold up the resistance of common sense, the barrier of silent reserves, the reassurance of laughing at oneself. Crowhurst had none of these defenses.

His biographers talked at length with Mrs. Crowhurst about the last night in the hotel. It had been a hell of a day and the Crowhursts didn't get to bed until 0200.

Donald lay silent beside Clare. After struggling for the right words, he finally said, in a very quiet voice: "Darling, I'm very disappointed in the boat. She's not right. I'm not prepared. If I leave with things in this hopeless state will you go out of your mind with worry?" Clare, in her turn, could only reply with another question. "If you give up now," she said, "will you be unhappy for the rest of your life?"

Donald did not answer, but started to cry. He wept until morning. During that last night he had less than five minutes' sleep. "I was such a fool!" says Clare Crowhurst now. "Such a stupid fool! With all the evidence in front of me, I still didn't realise Don was telling me he's failed, and wanted me to stop him."

Late the next afternoon—October 31st—after a false start because the masthead buoyancy bag had been lashed over the sail halyards which made it impossible to raise the sails—Donald Crowhurst waved goodbye to forty friends and the BBC on three motor vessels which accompanied the trimaran to the starting line. The gun was fired at 1652 and the captain of *Teignmouth Electron* steered out to sea, tacking into a wind from the south. He was soon out of sight with thirty thousand miles to go.

On the same day, Alex Carozzo also left England. The last two months had been a marathon for the cocky Italian, but he had accomplished wonders. The Medina Yacht Company had somehow built Carozzo's huge sixty-six-foot ketch in an incredible forty-nine days, and *Gancia Americano,* as she had been named, was launched on October 8th.

The giant two-master was flush-decked with a bold sheer and chine-built of marine plywood sheathed with fiberglass. Carozzo had transplanted the sails and rigging from his catamaran which he had put up for sale. The new yacht had two steel rudders, one for self-steering, and the second for minor course corrections. Her most startling feature was a thirty-six-inch centerboard in front of the vessel's eight-foot keel to help keep the ship on course while running before giant seas. A small cockpit served as the control center. The builder, Terry Compton, couldn't quite believe that his company had produced the enormous yacht in only seven weeks. Seven months would have been more usual time.

"It's a bloody miracle," said Compton. "I don't know how we managed to do it. She's built like a battleship and is certainly as strong as any other boat in the race. It's unlikely now that she'll catch up all the others, but she should take the prize for the fastest time."

Carozzo calculated that *Gancia Americano* could sail twice as fast as the other entries. However the exhausted Italian faced the thorny problem of outfitting his jumbo entry for a voyage of six months or more and checking that everything was installed properly and worked. He made remarkable progress but the October 31st deadline for leaving was at hand. Carozzo therefore asked the race committee for permission to sail a few days later. His request was rejected so the Italian captain put all his sailing supplies and foodstuffs on board *Gancia Americano*. On October 31st he officially departed on the race, but anchored a few hundred feet off Cowes where he had a long sleep before beginning to sort and stow and check everything prior to his real departure.

For better or worse, all the contestants had left England.

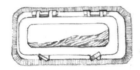

7. *What Do They Do All Day?*

A SAILING YACHT IS DESIGNED to be steered by a human hand, a hand that makes continuous small corrections as the wind shifts slightly and the vessel is pushed from side to side by wave action and water movements. If the helmsman lifts his hand from the tiller, and a reasonable balance of sails is set, a good yacht will always head into the wind and stop. This design measure—weather helm—is important to safety in case the helmsman lets go of the tiller for any reason. The man on watch might need to deal with the sails during a squall. Or he might fall over the side. Then the tendency of the yacht to head into the wind and stop would perhaps save the helmsman's life.

Usually a yacht can be made to sail herself to windward if the tiller is pulled a little toward the wind and tied off. Self-steering *across* the wind and *with* the wind are more complicated, especially if the wind is strong, and substantial seas are running in the ocean. While it is possible to set downwind twin running sails or to lead small control lines to the tiller from the sheets, these systems are cumbersome and require a good deal of trial and error and fine tuning. A yacht with two masts and a number of separate sails has more potential self-steering adjustments.

The owners of model yachts sailing on a pond in a park have long been able to control their vessels by linking an air rudder—a sort of pivoting weathervane—to the ship's rudder. By suitable adjustments to this wind blade, any course can be sailed. When this system is scaled up to an ocean sailing yacht, however, it is soon apparent that a very large wind blade is needed in order to have sufficient force to steer a full-size vessel. An obvious improvement was to design a device that would mechanically amplify the turning action on a small wind blade into a force with enough muscle to steer a full-size yacht. A number of sailors worked on this problem in the 1950s and 1960s, led by a clever inventor named Blondie Hasler. Four of the entrants in the round-the-world race used Hasler self-steering devices. The other five sailors also had mechanical self-steering, some made professionally and some cobbled together a few days before departure. Most of the units—then and now—relied to some extent on Hasler's brilliant invention, which has greatly expanded the sport of single-handed sailing.

This is not the place to describe the intricacies of self-steering devices, which involve shafts, wheels, paddles, linkages, pivots, bearings, blades, and so forth. What interests us is their *effect* on short-handed sailing. A good unit means that the captain generally doesn't have to sit and steer his vessel at all. Once the gear is working properly it will respond to every shift of wind. If the breeze is steady, the course will be steady too. The wind pilot functions on all points of sailing in both gales and zephyrs, in darkness and sunshine, in snow and clear weather. A good self-steering device seems almost human in its operation except that it doesn't require coffee and sandwiches, periodic rests in bed, and aspirins during a storm. Life at sea becomes a good deal more tolerable and pleasant.

Many of the owners of these mechanical helmsmen get so attached to their automatic friends that they give them pet names—Alfred, Columbus, George, Frankenstein, Picasso, and so on. Of course a lone sailor on board a yacht with a self-steering mechanism must be careful not to fall overboard because the vessel will continue to sail onward, with no one to bring her back to the man in the water.

A self-steering gear can guide a yacht all the way across the Pacific Ocean or the Bay of Biscay. Such a device can also steer a yacht directly into the shore, a sandbank, a reef, a lighthouse, or another vessel if the captain fails to keep a lookout and to adjust the mechanism from time to time. Around land and in shipping lanes the solo sailor must keep his eyes on the compass, other vessels, distant land forms, and lights and buoys every ten, fifteen minutes or so. Out at sea and far from land and shipping, a singlehander can relax somewhat—enough to sleep for a few hours. Even with a self-steering gear, however, a person by himself has plenty to do.

"What happens at night?" is a question often asked. Strangers to long-distance sailing can readily understand that a person can sail and cook and navigate and splice lines during the day. Somehow people who are unused to ocean sailing have trouble understanding what happens at night. Many people think that a yacht is stopped at sunset each evening, the sails are lowered, an anchor is dropped, and the crew has dinner and goes to bed. Not quite! If a vessel is to get anywhere in reasonable time, the yacht must be run on a twenty-four-hour basis. Sometimes one of these small ships is stopped in case of a severe storm, but this is unusual. Often during storms the wind is fair and *with* the vessel which enables the yacht to make excellent mileage toward its goal.

In reality, sailing vessels—including all the romantic ships of history—are very slow movers. A 200-mile daily run was quite respectable for a clipper ship in the old days, a distance that a modern passenger jet aircraft can do in less than thirty minutes. An average day for a thirty-five-foot yacht at sea in all sorts of weather is much slower—say 90 to 110 or 120 nautical miles in twenty-four hours. An exceptional run might be 150, but there are also 50-mile days.

KNOTS
(*rate of speed
per hour*)

2 knots equals	48 miles per day
3	72
4	96
5	120
6	144
7	168
8	192

A second question that people ask is: "What do those solitary seamen do out there all by themselves? How do they fight boredom? How do they pass the time?" To answer this question let's run through an imaginary twenty-four-hour period for a lone sailor far out at sea. Let's look at what such a person actually does.

Midnight: Up to check around the horizon to make sure that the vane is steering okay. The yacht is some fifteen degrees off course; so the captain changes the steering vane control line slightly and then watches the compass for ten minutes or so to verify the new setting. He then sits at the chart table for a few minutes and studies the course ruled on his chart, which suggests that he will pass about thirty-five miles to windward of an island to his south. The captain climbs up in the main hatchway and stands looking to the south, staring into the blackness of night, trying to see the island. He listens carefully for surf. He neither sees nor hears anything, so after a careful look in all directions he climbs down into the cabin and goes back to sleep.

0200: Up to look around again. The course is good and the wind is about the same—fifteen knots from the northeast. The barometer has dropped a little. The captain notes these things in the ship's logbook. He is hungry, so he primes the kerosene Primus stove with alcohol while he pumps a little water into the teakettle. This week the captain is on an herb tea kick so after the kettle boils he makes tea and has a few crackers with strawberry jam. He switches on the radio receiver and listens to a heavy-throated woman announcer on one of the English language broadcasts of Radio Moscow. The woman is lambasting the Australians on some obscure political issue. The captain concludes that government political broadcasts of all nations would be far more successful if they would play more music and lay off the hard political stuff. The weather is a little cooler and the captain is glad to climb into his bunk again where it is warm. Wait a minute! Back up again to turn on the 100-fathom depth sounder, which might show something in case the yacht is near one of the shallow banks around the island. Nothing shows on the depth sounder so back to the bunk and sleep.

0400: An easy night so far. The captain is about slept out, but it is pleasant in his warm berth. He bestirs himself and climbs up into the companionway. Hello, what's that? A light ahead and to the right, maybe four or five miles away. Probably a fishing boat from the island rising up and down on the ocean swells. He takes a compass bearing of the light (145 degrees) and writes it down. He should leave it well to starboard. Soon it will be dawn. A good time for a round of star sights, but there is about 50 percent cloud cover so the captain decides to skip the morning stars and rely on sun sights later in the day: especially since there is plenty of sea room ahead. Our solo sailor walks around the deck and checks the sails and running rigging for chafe, shining a flashlight up and down as he walks with one hand sliding along a lifeline. Hello, what's this? A lanyard from the cockpit bucket has fallen across one of the self-steering lines and has gotten drawn into a small block and has half sawed the vane line in two. The captain gets out a piece of spare small line to replace the chafed line. While he is busy with the line the yacht comes head to wind and the sails flap noisily. The sailor secures the new vane line, pulls the tiller hard over, and starts the vessel going again. It takes a few minutes to get back on course. The captain stuffs the bucket into a cockpit locker and resolves to keep odd lines away from the steering vane. Incredible how two lines can rub each other to destruction in a few hours.

0600: Daylight and pink clouds in the east ahead. The wind is a bit fresher (northeast, twenty-two knots) and the yacht is overpowered a bit and would probably go just as fast with less sail. Is it worth the effort to change down further (there is one reef in the mainsail already) or should he wait awhile? Maybe the wind will ease off. Might as well wait. The next sail change will be to the number three jib. Where is it? Under the saloon table or is it in the forepeak? Time for a good breakfast in any case. Bacon and eggs, toast, and fresh coffee. No, the bread is about shot with mold so he'll have hot cereal instead. The captain fires up a Primus stove, opens a can of Hungarian bacon and peels off five slices. "I wonder what a pig farmer outside of Budapest would think if he saw his bacon being cooked here?" says the captain. While the bacon is frying he looks out at the dawn and sees Venus low in the sky to the northeast. A good chance for a navigational fix if he combines it with a later sun shot. The captain changes the course to the south a little, away from the wind so there won't be so much spray across the decks. He gets out his sextant and works his way along the port side deck to a spot clear of the shrouds. To overcome the up and down motion of the yacht as she rides over the ocean swells he wedges himself in place between a lifeline stanchion and the coachroof so that he will be secure enough to use both hands for the sextant. The captain holds the sextant up to his eye and quickly adjusts the micrometer screw. When the shiny reflection of the planet just touches the horizon line on the lower mirror he glances at his watch, which is set to Greenwich time. As he goes below and puts the instrument in its box he smells bacon. His frying pan has upset and the bacon, grease, and eggs are all over the galley floor. What a mess! It never fails when he tries to do two jobs at the same time. At least he got a good shot of Venus. He writes the time and angle in the navigation workbook. Then he starts breakfast all over again.

0800: Overcast and a steely look at the sea. No sun observations this morning. A little more wind. Oilskins and boots on. Number three jib to the foredeck. Number two down, unhanked, into a bag and tossed below. Number three hanked on. One hank refuses to open; so back to the cockpit shelf for pliers and the oilcan. Finally the sail is up and drawing. A few storm petrels dancing around above the water. Marvelous to watch the soft gray birds flitting just over the wake of the yacht. What on earth can such delicate birds find to eat way out here? The yacht is going okay and the motion is a bit easier now so below and oilskins off.

1000: The captain is at the chart table working out the observation of Venus. He takes a few figures from the Nautical Almanac and the navigation tables and makes some calculations. Then working from the 39th parallel of south latitude he draws a position line on the chart that comes out seven miles from his dead reckoning position. Not too bad, but he needs a second position line so he can cross the first and get a definite position fix. Maybe the sun will break through the clouds later. Back to the current repair project: to overhaul the distance recording log. The problem is that both ball bearing assemblies on the revolving shaft are shot. There are some old spares, but they too are corroded and rough. Maybe he can use one of the old bearings that is not too bad and combine it with the better of the new ones still in place. Plus lots of grease rubbed in around the tiny balls. What a rotten bit of engineering to use plain steel instead of stainless steel. Too bad he didn't bring new bearings. Finally, the distance recording log is back together. The captain attaches it to its bracket outside the port cockpit coaming and eases its propeller over the side. Marvelous, it works. But for how long? The yacht is going at 5½ knots according to the instrument. Enough tinkering for a while. Back to his bunk and a book called *In Company of Eagles* by Ernest Gann. Fascinating stuff about World War I flying. Richtofen and all that. The captain wonders how the Red Baron would have made out in a singlehanded yacht at sea? Probably okay, but may be not enough glory and medals and combat for him. Plenty of open cockpit flying in a yacht at sea though.

1200: Today is the captain's thirty-fourth birthday. Out with a bottle of wine carefully saved and sheltered from breakage. The damned cork disintegrates when pulled and cork fragments shoot all over the galley. Cursed corks! The bottle was kept on its side so the cork was wet but it still pulled apart. The standards of everything are going down. Oh well, the wine is delicious. An ambitious spaghetti sauce simmers slowly and fills the yacht with an aroma worthy of Naples itself. The sauce is excellent over spaghetti cooked so it's just chewy. A second helping empties both pots and fills the captain's stomach to a delightful degree. Still no sun for a latitude shot; so the captain washes the dishes, pumping salt water into the galley sink and scrubbing the pots as the yacht bashes her way across the wrinkled surface of the sea. It's amazing how these small yachts can take such pounding day after day. No sense thinking about it because worrying won't help. The captain decides to have a good wash; so he heats a little water, strips down, and has a sponge bath, spilling only half the water as the boat rolls. Talcum powder and fresh clothes feel great and are good for morale. The oilskins go back on, however, in case a boarding sea slops across the decks when he is outside. He can't afford to get his clean clothes wet with salt water on the first day.

1400: A small crisis. All the sleeping and eating and washing should have been a tipoff that things were too easy. The captain notices water on the cabin sole and innocently pulls up a floorboard. The bilge is full of water! He immediately lays into one of the hand pumps and soon empties the bilges. Where is the water coming in? From forward somewhere. The captain lifts up all the floorboards as he works his way toward the bow. The water is trickling in from the chain locker. The sailor hurries out on deck and goes forward. Hooray! the leak is solved. The wooden plug that closes the access hole for the anchor cable has somehow come out and has vanished overboard. Every few minutes the foredeck is sprayed with water and some of this has found its way below into the chain locker. It takes the captain half an hour to whittle a new tapered plug from a scrap of soft pine. He greases the plug and tamps it in place with a hammer. What a relief! Now, however, the captain is all wet with sweat and spray.

1600: Oilskins off and into the bunk for a sleep. The hell with everything.

2000: Barometer up. The wind is lighter and now out of the southwest. Broken clouds and a bit of moonlight. The Southern Cross and Scorpius are just visible between the clouds, which periodically open and close. Gorgeous constellations. The compass course is terrible because the wind has changed and the vane has followed it around. The first thing is to decide the strength of the wind. Judging by the feel on the captain's face and the small whitecaps it is blowing about seventeen knots. With a fair wind, however, the apparent wind will be less, say twelve. The captain will have to change to the running rig. He takes over the helm, gets back on course, and adjusts the self steering vane to the new wind. He then shakes out the reef in the mainsail, eases the mainsheet, and ties the boom forward with a preventer line to the stem. Then he unhooks the spinnaker pole, adjusts its inboard end to shoulder height on the mast, and passes the jib sheet through the outer end of the pole. Back in the cockpit he eases the port jib sheet and hauls on the starboard sheet. Now both sails are drawing nicely and the course is good. The captain shines a flashlight on the sails and notices that the mainsail is rubbing on the port shrouds. He gets a small tackle out of the cockpit locker, walks forward on the port side, and hooks it between a deck fitting and the main boom. He pulls on the hauling part of the tackle, and the boom moves lower little by little, taking the sail away from the shrouds. A large bird is flying behind the yacht but it is too dark to identify the creature. The new southwest wind has a touch of the Southern Ocean and is definitely cooler. Where is the long underwear? Time for a few notes in the log.

2200: The compass course is still good to the east-southeast. The kerosene cabin lights are out and need filling. The captain gets a jug of kerosene from the bilge and at the same time he tops up the Primus cooking stove. . . . Isn't it marvelous how the yacht goes on day after day? The important things seem to be a goal, something to look forward to, food to eat (not fancy, but wholesome, hot, and sufficient), and sleep (naps are okay, but they must add up to six or eight hours). One can get used to the interruptions. Also something to occupy the mind. Best to read books about nonsailing. Greek history is interesting but those Greek names are impossible and the Greek heroes are always murdering one another. Was there a Greek mafia? James Bond is good but too fanciful and those books have all been read anyway. The captain goes to a wooden box in the forepeak and pulls out a silvery sphere. It is a large, thick-skinned orange wrapped in aluminum foil. The sailor strips off the foil, peels the orange, and slowly eats the thick sections while he stands in the hatchway and looks out at the sea and the stars. In spite of all the small problems of ocean voyaging the captain knows no greater satisfaction and pleasure than taking his own vessel across the seas of the world. He takes a deep breath. The tiny yacht knifes her way through the long night. Twenty-four hours have passed.

8. *Capsize*

WHILE ALEX CAROZZO AND DONALD CROWHURST were still in England and frantically working to get away before the October 31st deadline, the leader in the race was far south in the Atlantic. On Robin Knox-Johnston's eighty-fourth day at sea he was 700 miles southwest of the Cape of Good Hope, the southern tip of Africa. He had just crossed the 40th parallel of south latitude and had entered the Southern Ocean, that vast globe-circling expanse of cold water, strong west winds, and albatrosses north of the ice shelf of Antarctica. Knox-Johnston planned to sail eastward along the 40th parallel all the way to Australia, but his north–south position would vary somewhat depending on the wind. Since there was unlimited sea room, all Knox-Johnston had to do was to keep his vessel going roughly eastward. On day eighty-four *Suhaili* was at forty-two degrees south. She hurried along on an easterly heading under full sail with a fresh wind from the north.

Knox-Johnston had had good weather for the past few days. The barometer had begun to fall, however, and he knew that bad weather was coming: especially when he saw thin veiled clouds—mare's tails—high in the sky. Although he realized that it was crazy, Knox-Johnston half wished for the first storm to come. He wondered how he would get along in the enormity of the Southern Ocean, which reached right around the world south of Africa, Asia, Australia, and America. He reckoned he would be in the Southern Ocean for four months or longer.

On September 5th, a shower of cold hail rattled on *Suhaili*'s deck and announced the first storm. As the cold front overtook the yacht, the reading on the barometer suddenly rose two millibars. The wind shifted abruptly from the north to the west–southwest and increased to gale force. Knox–Johnston quickly made a drastic sail change. He put three reefs in *Suhaili's* mainsail, two reefs in the mizzen, and hoisted the storm jib in place of the working jib. After an adjustment for the new wind, the Admiral—Knox–Johnston's pet name for his self-steering gear—continued to keep the yacht on an eastward course.

When wind blows across a stretch of ocean for many hours, seas build up and continue for a long time even if the wind dies away. The stronger the wind and the longer it blows, the bigger the seas—up to a point. If the wind is steady and say Force five, seventeen to twenty-one knots, the seas grow reasonably even and not too big, two meters or less in height. When a new weather system appears, however, the wind often switches around and blows from a different direction. The new wind begins to build up its own wave pattern that interacts with the leftover wave train from the old wind. The new waves and old waves generally slide into one another with some spray and slop and a bit of curling white water. As the old wave train dies out and the new train takes over, a regular pattern of seas from one direction again becomes dominant.

With moderate winds the interaction of overlapping swells is not too severe. The problem occurs when a strong wind from one direction is replaced by a fast-moving gale force wind from a new direction. Then the old and new wave trains—both of which can be powerful—meet and intermingle over the course of many hours. This interaction occasionally results in large breaking waves from unexpected directions. Complicating this can be swells from a distant storm in a third direction, just enough to upset the first two. All old sailors know this game. You lie in your bunk listening to the big ones breaking out there and wondering if the next one has your name on it. You can go along for hours. Then suddenly a cross-sea or two or three can rise up and deal you cruel blows.

This is what happened to *Suhaili* on September 6th in the middle of the night. The wind switched from north to west–southwest and doubled in strength.

The next thing I remember is being jerked awake by a combination of a mass of heavy objects falling on me and the knowledge that my world had turned on its side [wrote Knox-Johnston]. I lay for a moment trying to gather my wits to see what was wrong, but as it was pitch black outside and the lantern I kept hanging in the cabin had gone out, I had to rely on my senses to tell me what had happened. I started to try to climb out of my bunk, but the canvas which I had pulled over me for warmth was so weighted down that this was far from easy.

As I got clear *Suhaili* lurched upright and I was thrown off balance and cannoned over to the other side of the cabin, accompanied by a mass of boxes, tools, tins, and clothing which seemed to think it was their duty to stay close to me. I got up again and climbed through the debris and out on to the deck, half expecting that the masts would be missing and that I should have to spend the rest of the night fighting to keep the boat afloat. So convinced was I that this would be the case that I had to look twice before I could believe that the masts were still in place. It was then that I came across the first serious damage. The Admiral's port vane had been forced right over, so far in fact that when I tried to move it I found that the stanchion was completely buckled and the ⅝ inch marine plywood of the vane had been split down about 10 inches on the mizzen cap shrouds. The whole thing was completely jammed. Fortunately I was using the starboard vane at the time, because I could not hope to try and effect repairs until I could see, and the time was 0250. It would not be light for another four hours. *Suhaili* was back on course and seemed to be comfortable and I could not make out anything else wrong; however, I worked my way carefully forward, feeling for each piece of rigging and checking it was still there and tight. I had almost gone completely round the boat when another wave came smashing in and I had to hang on for my life whilst the water boiled over me. This is what must have happened before. Although the whole surface of the sea was confused as a result of the cross-sea, now and again a larger than ordinary wave would break through and knock my poor little boat right over. I decided to alter course slightly so that the seas would be coming from each quarter and we would no longer have one coming in from the side, and went aft to adjust the Admiral accordingly.

Having checked round the deck and rigging, and set *Suhaili* steering more comfortably, I went below and lit the lantern again. The cabin was in an indescribable mess. Almost the entire contents of the two starboard bunks had been thrown across on to the port side and the deck was hidden by stores that had fallen back when the boat can upright.

Water seemed to be everywhere. I was sloshing around in it between the galley and the radio as I surveyed the mess and I could hear it crashing around in the engine room each time *Suhaili* rolled. That seemed to give me my first job and I rigged up the pump and pumped out the bilges. Over forty gallons had found its way into the engine room and about fifteen more were in the main bilge, although how it had all got in I did not know at the time. Doing a familiar and necessary job helped to settle me again. Ever since I had got up I had been in that nervous state when you never know if in the next minute you are going to be hit hard for a second time. I could not really believe that the boat was still in one piece and, as far as I could see, undamaged. It's rather similar to when you uncover an ant nest. The exposed ants immediately wash their faces and this familiar task reassures them and prevents them panicking. Pumping the bilges was a familiar task to me and when it was completed I felt that I had the situation under control and set about tidying up quite calmly. The only real decision I had to make was where to start. I couldn't shift everything out of the cabin as there was nowhere else to put things, so I had to search for some large object amongst the mess, stow it away and then use the space vacated as a base. It was two hours before my bunk was cleared. I found books, films, stationery, clothes, fruit and tools all expertly mixed with my medical stores, and for days afterwards odd items kept appearing in the most out of the way places.

While straightening up, Knox-Johnston saw water dripping on the chart table in the after part of the cabin. He traced the path of the water and found cracks along the edge of the cabin, cracks that extended around the entire coachroof. Every time that water fell on deck, some of it ran into the cabin. The captain also discovered that the cabin bulkheads had been slightly shifted by the capsize.

"The sight of this, and the realization that if we took many more waves over the boat the weakened cabin top might be washed away, gave me a sick feeling in the pit of my stomach," said Knox-Johnston. "If the cabin top went it would leave a gaping hole six feet by twelve in the deck; I was 700 miles southwest of Cape Town. The Southern ocean is no place for what would virtually be an open boat."

Some people would have sent out an SOS and headed for land. Knox-Johnston was made of sterner stuff; he decided to see what he could do. After organizing the cabin stowage a bit, he looked into the engine room and found that the ship's batteries had broken away from their mountings during the capsize. He lashed the batteries in place, took a tot of whisky, and turned in to sleep until daylight.

The next morning the gale was a little less strong and the seas were more even. After a bowl of hot porridge, a cup of steaming coffee, and a cigarette, Knox-Johnston felt better. He got out his box of nuts and screws and managed to put some fastenings between the sides of the coachroof and the deck to strengthen the cabin somewhat and to close the cracks that let in water.

Traditional wooden boats with a cabin above the deck are often weak where the coachroof structure meets the deck. This is because the continuous athwartship deck beams are cut away to give headroom in the cabin below. To deal with this problem, naval architects call for vertical reinforcing rods down through the cabin sides, and horizontal rods between the outer edge of the deck and the bottoms of cabin sides. These bronze or stainless steel fastenings lock the whole deck and cabin structure together. Unfortunately these rods are difficult and costly to install and are often omitted by builders ("we'll do it later") in spite of the designers' specifications. It was unfortunate that *Suhaili* lacked these reinforcements when she was capsized by a wave.

Sometimes the frustrations of the voyage were maddening.

I had just opened a new bottle of brandy for my evening drink, and having poured out a good measure I put the bottle on the spare bunk, jammed by the sextant box [wrote Knox-Johnston]. About an hour later a strong smell of brandy began to invade the cabin and I eventually traced it to the newly opened bottle. The bottle was sealed by one of those metal screw caps, and as the boat rolled in the sea, the movement had slowly loosened the top until the contents could escape. I was furious about this. As my allowance was half a bottle of spirits a week I had lost two weeks' supply, but I consoled myself with the thought that I had at least taken that day's ration from it!

The men in the race often exhibited remarkable cleverness. At one time Knox-Johnston needed to adjust the electric contact points on the magneto of his battery charger. He had no feeler gauge so he counted the pages of his diary. There were 200 to the inch so one page equaled $^5/_{1000}$ or .005. Three pages equaled .015, the required gap.

Two days later the storm eased enough so that Knox-Johnston could repair his self-steering apparatus. Unlike the other contestants, *Suhaili*'s gear was divided into two parts, each identical and each located outboard of the cockpit on a spindly metal frame, one unit to port and the other to starboard. Each half could steer the yacht independently, depending on the wind. During the capsize, the port blade had split and the supporting framework had buckled. The captain had a spare stanchion for the vane and managed to mount it and to get the port steering gear into operation again.

Suhaili was lashed by five gales in ten days. It would have been easy to have stopped the vessel and waited for the disturbances to pass but Knox-Johnston wanted to keep going. Besides, the wind was fair and kept blowing him toward Australia and New Zealand. The problem was a delicate balance between reducing sail too much and pressing on to the danger point. Going too fast risked a possible broach and capsize. Going too slow meant that he would never finish the race.

The motion in the thirty-two-foot yacht was incredibly rough during the gales. "I slept fully clothed, usually rolled up in the canvas on top of the polythene containers in the cabin," wrote the English captain. "As I would quickly get cramp in that position, I would then try sleeping sitting up. This would be all right for a bit, but sooner or later the boat would give a lurch and I would be picked up and thrown across the cabin. If I tried wedging myself in the bunk I could not get out so quickly in an emergency, and if the boat received a really big bang I would get thrown out of the bunk and across the cabin anyway."

Sometimes *Suhaili*'s master philosophized a bit and wondered what he had gotten himself into on this voyage.

The future does not look particularly bright, and sitting here being thrown about for the next 150 days, with constant soakings as I have to take in or let out sail, is not an exciting prospect [wrote Knox-Johnston].

After four gales my hands are worn and cut about badly and I am aware of my fingers on account of the pain from skin tears and broken fingernails. I have bruises all over from being thrown about. My skin itches from constant chafing with wet clothes, and I forgot when I last had a proper wash. I feel altogether mentally and physically exhausted and I've been in the Southern ocean only a week. It seems years since I gybed to turn east and yet it was only last Tuesday night, not six days, and I have another 150 days of it yet. I shall be a Zombie in that time. I feel that I have had enough of sailing for the time being; it's about time I made a port, had a long hot bath, a steak with eggs, peas and new potatoes, followed by lemon meringue pie, coffee, Drambuie, and a cigar and then a nice long uninterrupted sleep, although, come to think of it, to round it off properly. . . . .

Why couldn't I be satisfied with big ships? The life may be monotonous but at least one gets into port occasionally which provides some variety. A prisoner at Dartmoor doesn't get hard labour like this; the public wouldn't stand it and he has company, however uncongenial. In addition he gets dry clothing, and undisturbed sleeep. I wonder how the crime rate would be affected if people were sentenced to sail round the world alone, instead of going to prison. It's ten months solitary confinement with hard labour.

In spite of Knox-Johnston's grumbling he was making excellent time. In one two-day burst he logged 314 miles, but the rapid pace was hard on the captain and the banging about was beginning to wear down the ship's equipment, especially the self-steering gear, which needed a good deal of repairing. Would the ship hold together for the rest of the trip?

9. *Oysters and Pheasant*

FAR TO THE NORTH NEAR the Canary Islands off the northwest coast of Africa, Nigel Tetley adjusted the volume of a Schubert aria sung by Rita Streich on the yacht's music system. The big blue trimaran *Victress* sped southward before a fair wind from the northeast. Tetley had just finished a superb meal of roast goose, peas, and beans washed down with half a bottle of wine. He felt fit and rested although it was hellishly hot in the tropics. After two weeks at sea he finally had things under control.

Since his departure from England on September 16th, Tetley had had a succession of broken gear and small and large problems. During a sail change on the first day, one of the wooden spinnaker poles had splintered, and a second pole had somehow unhooked itself and been lost overboard. That night one of the rigging wires that supported the mast came loose. The mast bent alarmingly and when Tetley looked aloft the next morning his heart froze.

By noon the wind had eased to about ten knots so the captain climbed the mast to find out what happened. A diamond stay wire terminal fitting had cracked and the wire had pulled out. The movement of the yacht on the lumpy ocean made work up the mast difficult because the increased height aggravated the motion. Tetley felt seasick, but he managed to rope himself to the mast and to repair the rigging with wire clamps from his emergency kit. The mast was saved.

The speedometer and distance recording device had stopped on the first day. Either the cable to the instrument was broken or the tiny propeller under the hull was fouled. Tetley changed to a mechanical speedometer driven by a propeller towed behind the yacht at the end of a fifty-foot line. On the second day, however, when Tetley pulled in the propeller to clear it of weed, the propeller and line slipped from his wet fingers and fell into the sea and were lost. The captain had a twice-weekly radio schedule with England for the first part of the trip, but the transmissions from the yacht were bad. Tetley traced the fault to the aerial tapping against the metal rigging wires during high winds.

During a calm period one day, Tetley tied a line around his waist and dived into the sea to inspect the speedometer propeller under the hull. The little propeller was undamaged; so the fault had to be in the cable connection somewhere in the hull. Later Tetley climbed the mast to clear two fouled halyards. He fashioned a new spinnaker pole from a long oar. And so it went. Fix. Fix. Fix. Repair this. Change that. Modify this. No wind. Too much wind. Take down the small sails. Put up the big ones. Then change back. No wonder Tetley was so weary. Not only was there the work of keeping *Victress* going so he could try to win the bloody race, but he had to recover from the hard work and nervous strain of getting the yacht ready, the publicity, and the departure. It was not enough to be an expert sailor. The captain needed to be a business executive to deal with all the commercial details. Solo racing was exhausting!

Fortunately Eve, Tetley's wife, had done a thorough job of provisioning the vessel before the race. "I started a grand reading session, studying everything I could lay my hands on to do with diet, nutrition, and vitamin deficiencies, she wrote.

> The thought of Nigel having to eat only tinned or dried foods for up to ten months and still remain healthy kept me most evenings reading and re-reading until I had a grand list of "thou shalt haves". . . . We both agreed that as much variety as possible was to be aimed at, and to make all the food as attractive and tempting as we could. Anyone who has had to eat often alone, knows how miserable it can become, and how jaded one's appetite is, even if half an hour previously one felt starving. The newspapers swooped joyfully on to the "luxury" angle of the food. They didn't want to know about the bully beef and baked beans, but wrote up the pheasants, octopus, oysters, venison, etc. lyrically!

Tetley even had an electric mixer with which he was able to concoct milk shakes from full-cream dried milk provided by Nestles. Cutty Sark had given him two cases of whisky and Bass had chipped in with seventy-two bottles of beer and seventy-two half-bottles of wine. "It's cheaper to heat the body than the boat," Tetley had joked to a reporter before he left.

Eve's hard work was all worthwhile, as Nigel found out early on his voyage. "The long weeks of preparation had taken more out of me than I supposed," wrote Tetley. "The sea no doubt would toughen me in time, but what I needed most just then was food to give me energy. I waded into an enormous roast chicken which Eve had provided and, sitting back listening to Handel's 'Water Music', soon felt better."

By the end of the first eight days Tetley had logged 510 miles and was only 60 miles from the Atlantic coast of Spain. The captain joked to himself about stopping. "What about a run ashore in Corunna?" he mused. "Who would know?" But he satisfied his wandering spirit by opening a bottle of wine and selecting a roast duck for supper.

A continuing hazard for small-boat sailors is the chance of being run down by big ships. In theory all vessels have lookouts, but in practice the lookouts often relax at sea or scan the horizon only occasionally. During the last thirty years the number of trading ships has doubled, the average length has increased by 40 percent, and there has been a significant increase in speed. In spite of these changes the crews of big ships are proportionally smaller than in former years and more automatic devices are in use. It's not a bit unusual for small-boat sailors to see large ships hurrying along at sea on straight and undeviating courses with apparently no one on watch except the autopilot. Fishing vessels aggravate the problem because they also use autopilots and often make frequent course changes. There is much talk of radar, but a yacht's radar reflector is worthless if no one is watching the receiving scope on the larger vessel.

Fortunately the paths of cargo ships and oil tankers are well charted because big vessels generally take the shortest and most direct routes in order to save time and conserve fuel. It behooves small ship captains to cross shipping lanes quickly and at right angles if possible.

A professional mathematician and sailor named John Letcher has calculated that in the twenty-five hundred miles between California and Hawaii the chances of a small vessel being run down by a big ship are one in a thousand, assuming no lookouts on either vessel. If daylight hours are reckoned safe and if 90 percent of the large vessels are in charted shipping lanes, the collision risk drops to one in twenty thousand. Dr. Letcher's numbers are only statistical odds, however, and in the waters he analyzed he was run down twice, once by a cargo ship and once by a fishing vessel. Dr. Letcher was lucky to have escaped with his life. Certainly it is no false statement that in spite of mathematical odds and the vastness of the oceans, a collision is a nagging worry to the captains of small vessels who are completely helpless before the towering mass of a big ship that may be a thousand times (or ten thousand times) the tonnage of a yacht. Not only is a small sailing vessel dwarfed by a modern cargo ship or oil tanker, but these gigantic battering rams may be steaming along at fifteen knots or more.

On *Victress* Nigel Tetley tried to minimize his time near shipping lanes. He set his alarm clock to remind him to check around the horizon. Usually the skyline was empty, but a few times he saw the distant silhouette of a ship during the day or the white lights of a fishing boat at night. One morning Tetley looked out on a tunnyman, rolling heavily, that had run down to check on the sailing yacht. The fishing boat sheered off when her captain saw Tetley waving cheerfully. "A single-hander has to come to terms with the chance of being run down and learn to relax," wrote Tetley. Yet he was hard put to follow his own advice. He worried a good deal when near shipping lanes and fishing grounds. Fortunately most of the round-the-world course was well clear of shipping, especially the long route in the Southern Ocean.

By October 6th Tetley had entered the zone of the northeast trade wind, which meant that since he was traveling southwest he had a fair and steady wind behind him. On the second night, the trade wind increased to nineteen knots and *Victress* surfed for long stretches on he wave crests. "I had a long inward debate over the wisdom of leaving the mainsail set all night as well as the twins, a total of some 900 square feet of canvas," wrote Tetley. "It would have been a different matter with a crew and someone on watch all the time. The prudent course usually makes good seamanship, but in this case, banking on the constancy of the trade wind, I left everything up. All the same, sleep did not come easily with the yacht careering along."

The next day when Tetley calculated his position he found that he had logged 156 miles in the last twenty-four hours, his best run so far. He might win the race yet! Certainly the trimaran was sailing faster because each day Tetley was consuming about ten pounds of food and fuel.

Yet the trimaran had persistent leaks and the captain repeatedly found water in the forward compartments of the outer hulls. Fortunately, before he had left England Tetley had rigged up an inside bilge pumping position in the main cabin where he could pump out seawater from the bow sections of the outer hulls. The trimaran leaked because the vessel was still grossly overladen with food, supplies, and equipment. The overloading caused flexing and pounding as the thin plywood hulls sped across the rough waters of the ocean. Tetley thought that the water got in along the joints between the outer hulls and the crosswings of the trimaran. He had covered these joints with copper sheeting before he left, but the leaks continued.

Sometimes the whole sailing venture seemed too difficult and bizarre. Who in his right mind would try such a stunt? Sailing across a lake or an ocean might be explained away, but around the whole world nonstop? Alone and without human companionship? It was madness. Certainly the strangeness of the undertaking was felt by all nine men in the race. The longer one went the worse it got. Or would one finally adjust to a state of tranquility and balance? The sailing and the cooking and the navigation and the repairs were possible. But mental stability and ease were something else. Maybe a Buddhist monk would make the ideal single-handed sailor. After all, a spiritualist was a sort of mental hermit.

"Thoughts of packing it in came into my mind for the first time today, brought on I think by too much of my own company," wrote Tetley on his sixteenth day at sea.

It would be so easy to put into port and say that the boat was unsuitable or not strong enough for the voyage. What was really upsetting me was the psychological effect seven or possibly twelve months of this might have. Would I be the same person on return? This aspect I knew worried Eve too. I nearly put through a radio call to talk over the question in guarded terms; [I] then realized that although Eve would straightway accept the reason and agree to my stopping, say at Cape Town, we would feel that we had let ourselves down, both in our own eyes and those of our friends, backers, and well-wishers. It was just a touch of the blues, nothing more, due to the yacht's slow rate of progress.

Tetley began to find small flying fish on his deck rounds in the mornings. "I started reading for the first time on the voyage," he wrote. "An old *Sunday Times* colour supplement on motherhood—a husband with his wife at the moment of birth. Personally I think I would funk it."

Tetley frequently spoke with London on his radio although he was beginning to get out of range and would soon transfer to Cape Town. The news included a message from Eve that cheered Tetley greatly. Loïck Fougeron, the French entrant on *Captain Browne,* had been sighted off the Cape Verde islands. Bernard Moitessier in *Joshua* had not been seen since September 1st. Bill King aboard *Galway Blazer II* was out of radio contact, but was believed to be across the equator. Robin Knox-Johnston in *Suhaili* was making good time across the Indian ocean.

In order to get electrical power for his radio and lights, Tetley ran a small gasoline battery charger every few days. The ignition coil failed, however, which made the charger useless. Tetley was also able to charge his batteries by running the main engine, which had a generator. But one morning Tetley discovered water sloshing over the floorboards and salt water up above the level of the starter motor on the main engine. He quickly traced the trouble to a corroded through-hull fitting, pounded a cork into the leak, and pumped out the water. Tetley poured fresh water over the starter motor and dried it out, but the unit no longer worked. Without a starter the main engine was finished. Tetley began attempts to overhaul the starter. In the meantime he relied on a second small portable charging engine that he had brought along just in case. . . .

While passing the Cape Verde islands off the African coast on October 11th, the wind suddenly increased to thirty knots and the following seas grew big and nasty looking. Tetley steered by hand to help the vessel because he was afraid the yacht would turn sideways and get into big trouble. All at once the wheel went dead. *Victress* handled the situation perfectly on her own, however, and kept zipping along downwind. Hardly daring to breathe, Tetley hurried below to investigate the steering problem. The control wires had crumbled to powder inside their plastic sheaths. The captain quickly fitted new steering wires while the loud speakers purred with the sound of Nielsen's violin concerto.

In order to replenish drinking water, all the yachts in the race had water catchment systems which ranged from a flat spot on the deck drained by a hose led to a water tank to the simple expedient of a bucket hung under the forward corner of a sail. Sometimes a downpour lasted an hour or more. The first few minutes rinsed the sail and bucket. Afterward the captain could pour buckets of clean fresh water into the tanks and dump a few buckets over himself.

One afternoon when the wind was light and *Victress* ghosted along quietly, a shoal of porpoises surfaced around the yacht and splashed alongside for an hour. "When tired of playing at the bows they would fan out on either side and flush the flying fish like gundogs working a field of game," said Tetley. With good runs in the northeast trade wind his average mileage increased to 125 miles per day. Tetley was lucky to find a steady easterly wind instead of calms in the doldrums. He crossed effortlessly from one trade wind zone to the other while he baked bread and listened to the music of Saint-Saëns. On October 22nd he slipped southward across the equator.

By the third week in September, Loïck Fougeron neared the Cape Verde islands. The master of *Captain Browne* had only one big problem: his Moroccan cat Roulis. This wild, globetrotting cat was more trouble than the rest of the voyage combined. Fougeron had taken the cat for companionship, but at times it seemed the cat was in charge and Fougeron merely a servant who cleaned up after the animal.

Roulis had more energy than a box of exploding dynamite. She was a curse from morning till night and even got into mischief at midnight. First Roulis ate the aerial wire of the radio receiver. Fougeron thought the radio had broken down until he noticed the mutilated aerial. Then the cat began to chew the bags holding the powdered eggs and scattered dried egg all over the cabin. Roulis had fleas and Fougeron worried that the fleas might spread to his bedding and clothes. Finally, the cat was pregnant and growing fatter by the day.

"I envisaged making up a raft and putting Roulis out to sea, but I haven't the heart to do it," said Fougeron in a letter to *The Sunday Times*. "I'm afraid she will drown herself and, in spite of

The Sunday Times

The wild cat that was aboard the *Captain Browne*.

LOÏCK FOUGERON

all her tricks, I like her very much." The captain didn't want a litter of kittens aboard either, but he was unable to consider drowning the kittens. Obviously the cat had to be put ashore. So Fougeron made up a parcel with films and letters and when he saw a fishing boat he passed the cat and parcel to the men on the boat with the request that the animal and package be given to the British consul in the Cape Verde islands.

When Mr. Foulde, the consul, got the parcel and cat, he kept the cat and forwarded the parcel. A few days later, however, he cabled *The Sunday Times* and asked to be relieved of the cat because she was wrecking his house. The newspaper made arrangements to send Roulis to a friend of Fougeron who lived in Belgium. "Not to my home in Casablanca," said the captain. "Roulis might get eaten by the dogs out there."

Fougeron reported that the solitude of the voyage hadn't weighed him down—at least not yet. The French sailor had experienced no hallucinations; in fact he had not seen as much as a single siren swimming around his vessel. "It is hot, 28 degrees inside. I live like Adam and am brown as a Kanaka. Some tan and perhaps also some dirt. Water is rare and precious. I have only shaved once since I left Plymouth. I am going to do it again. I see a tramp staring out of the mirror at me.

"I use two litres of water daily," continued the French sailor. "The wine is getting bitter. I will have to drink it quickly." The master of *Captain Browne* reported an international menu.

Breakfast was porridge with powdered milk followed by Swedish bread with New Zealand butter, Dutch jam, and English tea. Lunch of mashed potatoes made from dried potatoes and powdered eggs diluted with a little milk. Dinner of English dried peas, Argentine corned beef, French cheese, and Moroccan wine.

"The automatic steering works perfectly," reported Fougeron. "I have had no trouble since leaving Plymouth. . . . Fishing last night, caught six fish. I will eat them tonight with the rest of the potatoes."

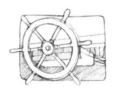

10. *Collision at Cape Agulhas*

THE SUN RISES, PEAKS, AND SETS, and one day gracefully makes way for the next," said Bernard Moitessier. "I have only been gone a month; my boat and I could have been sailing forever. Time stopped long ago. I have the feeling nothing will ever change; the sea will stay the same luminous blue, the wind will never die, *Joshua* will always carve her wake for the pleasure of giving life to sheafs of spray, for the simple joy of sailing the sea under the sun and the stars. . . .

Each morning the sun tinges the little clouds with pink and mauve as they drift along like snowflakes. Then the sun begins to climb, a clear light in the pale blue sky—the trade wind sky of the south Atlantic, where the weather is constant, without squalls or calms. The wind breathes into my sails the life of the open sea; it runs murmuring through the whole boat, to blend with the rustling of water parted by the bow . . . I listen to the sound of water along the side, and the wind in the rigging. By turns, I read *The Roots of Heaven* and *Wind, Sand and Stars*, in little sips. I spend long moments on deck, watching the flecks of foam rising in the wake. There are so many things in the flecks of foam and the water that runs along the side. I could not ask for more; I have it all.

Joshua had averaged 159 miles a day for a week since finding the southeast trade wind on September 17th. Such runs were phenomenal for a singlehander on a thirty-nine-foot ketch that measured only a little over thirty-four feet on the waterline.

Moitessier felt much better to be out of the calms and frustrating winds of the doldrums that had widened for him to a 900-mile zone of rain squalls, heat, and discouragement. He had figured on 600 miles. Sometimes the doldrums were a thousand miles from top to bottom; sometimes only one mile. To predict the width was like trying to forecast earthquakes or the mood of a woman on her birthday. He was glad that the doldrums were behind him.

Moitessier was a little concerned about his health. He had had problems with an ulcer and had to be careful. "I have to fill out a little," he said. "I did not have much fat to start, and there isn't any left. My inner barometer has been rising rapidly since last night, though. This morning I downed a huge mess of oatmeal and three mugs of Ovaltine with renewed appetite."

On September 29th, Moitessier called at Ilha da Trindade,* a remote three-mile-long Brazilian island 600 miles east of the mainland of South America and 1,230 miles south of the equator. There was a tiny settlement on the high and jagged volcanic island where Moitessier hoped to leave a package of films and a note to be forwarded to *The Sunday Times* in London. But when Moitessier stopped 300 yards from the beach and blew his horn and waved, the untutored villagers were mystified by the red-hulled ketch. The Brazilians had no boats, so no one was able to come out. Moitessier had no dinghy, and in any case he was not allowed to go ashore under the rules of the race. After jilling around for a while and uncertain what to do he reluctantly turned and sailed away.

A little south of Trindade, *Joshua* ran out of the steady southeast trade wind and into the poky breezes of the horse latitudes. The French captain had done well—some fifteen hundred miles in two weeks—since he had entered the trade wind 240 miles north of the equator. Now south of Trindade and away from

---

*Ilha da Trindade and Ilhas Martin Vaz are two small islands in the south Atlantic. The islands are owned by Brazil and have Portuguese names. Trindade is often confused with the island of Trinidad in the Caribbean. To further complicate the terminology, at one time Trindade was called Trinidade and is so indicated on old charts. In this book we will use modern names and spellings as far as possible.

Joshua

the headwind he changed direction abruptly from a south-southwest close-hauled course to east-southeast toward southern Africa. Moitessier wanted to get through the horse latitudes quickly and into the steady westerlies, but the winds he found were often feeble and false. One day, *Joshua* covered only twenty-three miles and was practically becalmed. Moitessier pulled on his wetsuit and went over the side to give the hull a scrub below the water and to pull off the gooseneck barnacles that had collected on a few places. The smoother the hull the better. Back on board he ghosted along slowly while he watched the sky for signs of changing weather that would signal wind.

Four main belts of wind circle the globe and affect sailing vessels. The boundaries of these wind zones are not precise and are influenced by seasonal changes, local disturbances, and unusual weather. As a general guide, however, these four wind zones are quite predictable and are well established.

In the high latitudes—both north and south—are the *westerlies* which prevail roughly from the 40th parallel of latitude toward the polar regions. The *trade winds* are the twin zones of constant, steady winds that sailors like and dream of and which run from near the equator to very roughly twenty-five degrees north or south. The trade wind north of the equator blows from the northeast; south of the equator the trade wind comes from the southeast. The *doldrums* are equatorial calms between the two trade winds. And finally the *horse latitudes* (or variables) are the zones of uncertain winds between the trades and westerlies. In the old days, sailing commerce was well organized to take advantage of the trade winds and the westerlies, and the ships made long east and west runs in these wind zones. Conversely, the square-rigged ships tried to slip through the doldrums and horse latitudes as quickly as possible. The contestants in the round-the-world race planned accordingly.

As Moitessier sailed further south and east and got closer to the tip of Africa and the Cape of Good Hope the wind began to come from the west. The weather grew colder. The captain put on sneakers and woolen trousers and began to pack away his light-weather sails. He changed the regular mainsail and mizzen for smaller and heavier sails with extra reinforcing over the areas of potential hard wear. Moitessier was a heavy smoker and he often puffed away on a Gauloise cigarette while he worked.

"There was a little gale yesterday, like a first brush with the high latitudes," he wrote on October 10th. "Mostly force seven or eight, always from the SW; the low was therefore far to the SE. Very manageable sea, and very beautiful; a little surfing, just to make sure everything is all right. The bow lifts like a feather." Two days later there was another moderate gale, but under severely reduced sail *Joshua* continued at seven knots and logged twenty-four-hour runs of 182 and 173 miles, with the help of some east-setting current.

"Food has picked up in the last two weeks, and I feel great," said Moitessier. "[I am] willing to take a reef, willing to shake one out, depending on the sky and the weather. Night and day, I sleep with one eye open, but I sleep well. . . . The temperature falls to 55° when the wind is SW and climbs to around 60° when it is from the NW. I don't usually like cold weather, but I feel brisk when the temperature drops, because I am well bundled up and the SW winds blow in a fair weather sky, even when they are strong."

In addition to the ton of excess weight removed before the race, Moitessier decided to jettison 375 pounds more. Over the side went a mass of extra food, twenty-five bottles of wine, kerosene, alcohol, a box of batteries, and a big coil of valuable ¾-inch diameter nylon anchor line. The captain reasoned that emptying *Joshua*'s forward and aft compartments would make her faster in light airs, require less sail in fresh winds, and help the yacht to be more stable and responsive. Discarding hundreds of dollars' worth of food and supplies was a drastic step, but it made the Frenchman feel better.

On October 19th, the fifty-ninth day of the trip, *Joshua* was forty miles southwest of Cape Agulhas, the extreme tip of South Africa. Moitessier had decided to try to pass his film and messages for *The Sunday Times* to a fisherman on the Agulhas bank. He photographed his log twice, page by page, and put the two films in separate watertight packages together with other films

of the trip so far. He was also anxious for news of the other eight
contestants in the round-the-world race.

I can see Françoise's joy as she realizes all's well aboard, that I have
not lost weight (she will not know that I have—none of her business),"
[wrote Moitessier]. "I can just see my children's excitement, shouting all
through the house, "*Joshua* is rounding Good Hope!"
   Yet it is a hard card to play, this need I feel to reassure family and
friends, to give them news, pictures, life—to bestow that infinitely precious thing, the little invisible plant called hope. Logic shouts at me to
play the game alone, without burdening myself with the others. Logic
would have me run SE, far from land, far from ships, back to the realm
of the westerlies where everything is simple if not easy, leaving well to
the north the dangerous area of . . . [converging currents and gales
near the land].
   But for many days another voice has been insisting "You are alone,
yet not alone," The others need you, and you need them. Without
them, you would not get anywhere, and nothing would be true.

Moitessier made his landfall near the lighthouse at Cape
Agulhas right on schedule and then sailed slowly west-northwest
along the coast. He hoped to find a fishing boat or a yacht, but
it was Sunday and the fishing boats would be in port. A gale was
forecast so the yachtsmen wouldn't be out either. All at once
Moitessier noticed a small black freighter coming up behind him.
He watched it carefully as it began to pass about twenty-five yards
to *Joshua*'s right. When the ship, a Greek vessel named *Orient
Transporter,* was even with him, Moitessier waved a package of
film. The man at the helm waved back and put his wheel over to
kick the freighter's stern toward *Joshua.* Moitessier tossed both
of his packages on the freighter's deck. Success! But look out!

Joshua begins to pull clear, but not fast enough [wrote Moitessier].
By a hair, the stern's overhang snags the mainmast. There is a horrible
noise, and a shower of black paint falls on the deck; the masthead shroud
is ripped loose, then the upper spreader shroud. My guts twist into
knots. The push on the mast makes *Joshua* heel, she luffs up toward the
freighter . . . and wham!—the bowsprit is twisted 20° or 25° to port. I
am stunned.
   It is all over. The black monster is past. I gybe quickly and heave-

to* on the port tack, drifting away from the coast. That is the main thing right now, so I can repair the shrouds without hurrying.

No doubt worried, the freighter has changed course. I wave them all's well, because in coming back to help, she would finish me off!

Poor Moitessier would have been far better to have accepted a battery and a low-powered radio from *The Sunday Times* for occasional short-range transmissions than to have tried to communicate directly with ships. Twice he had attempted to pass messages and twice he was threatened with destruction. Now he was aghast at what had happened near the Cape of Good Hope. "The beautiful trip is over," were words he tried not to say. "You can never continue non-stop with such damage . . . I have played and lost, that's all . . . later perhaps, it will hurt. But later is far away."

Nevertheless, Moitessier got out his tools to see what he could do. He repaired the two starboard shrouds whose cable clamps had only slipped. The spreaders were still OK thanks to their flexible mountings. "For the mast I feel nothing but admiration," he said. "At the moment of impact it looked like a fishing rod bent by a big tuna. It confirms the trust I had instinctively felt for the good old telephone pole. All in all, I have had a lot of luck in my misfortune."

The problem was that the bowsprit—almost seven feet long and made of a piece of reinforced three-inch diameter thick-walled steel pipe—was bent downward and twisted to port. To straighten it was a shipyard job.

Moitessier rested and pondered his next move. After a day of thinking, the captain decided to try to lever the bowsprit back into position with a boom and purchase arrangement. He took a spare mizzen boom and shackled one end of the ten-foot pole

---

*To *heave-to* is a maneuver designed to stop or slow forward way on a vessel. Generally a yacht is headed into the wind with a small headsail backed to force the bow to leeward (downwind). This action is balanced by putting the tiller to leeward which tends to head the vessel up into the wind. The drag of the rudder and the backed headsail roughly balance each other, and the vessel is almost stopped. Most modern yachts heave to from fifty degrees to seventy degrees off the wind and jog along at a knot or so while making a lot of leeway (losing ground downwind).

to a place on deck near the after end of the bowsprit. He then led the other end of the pole forward over the bow and held it up and a little to starboard of the bent bowsprit with a halyard coming down from the mast. Next Moitessier ran a four-part block and tackle from the forward end of the pole back along the starboard deck to *Joshua*'s cockpit. Finally he fitted a piece of chain between the end of the twisted bowsprit and the forward end of the pole.

Now came the big moment. The Frenchman led the hauling part of the tackle to a winch and started cranking in the line. As the powerful tackle began to contract, the forward end of the pole was forced upward and to starboard. Since the end of the pole was chained to the end of the bowsprit, the pole forced the bowsprit upward and to starboard too. Little by little the steel bowsprit began to point toward the horizon and to move to starboard. Marvelous! Moitessier was practically dancing with pleasure.

"I feel I am going to start crying. It's so beautiful . . . the bowsprit begins to straighten out, very, very slowly. I am wild with joy!"

By the end of the day *Joshua* was fully operational. The bowsprit rigging had stretched during the collision; so Moitessier clipped off a few links from the side and bottom chains and reshackled the stays. He straightened out the mangled pulpit and lifelines. "Worn out by fatigue and emotion I fall into bed after swallowing a can of soup for dinner." *Joshua* was able to go on. Wow! What a day!

"I am tremendously tired, yet I feel crammed with dynamite, ready to level the whole world and forgive it everything," said Moitessier. "Today I played and won. My beautiful boat is there, as beautiful as ever."

On October 24th, *Joshua* crossed the longitude off Cape Agulhas and headed into the Indian Ocean. Moitessier steered south-southeast to get away from the African coast and its turbulent waters where scores of yachts, freighters, naval ships, and tankers had been savaged over the years. The problem was that gales and storm force winds from southerly directions slammed into the Agulhas current running down the west coast of Africa from the north. The four-knot current and the opposing fast-moving gales created terrible breaking seas that were unpredictable maelstroms of fury and trouble. There were documented instances of large naval warships rising high on huge seas and then plunging deeply into the resultant "holes in the ocean" with disastrous results. Certainly tiny yachts were not meant for such places.

11. *A View of Death*

Six days after *Joshua* had sailed into the Indian Ocean, Loïck Fougeron, the second Frenchman in the race, saw the 7,700-foot volcanic cone of Tristan da Cunha rise above the horizon. Tristan da Cunha is an isolated group of four small islands in the mid-South Atlantic, a little over fifteen hundred miles from both South America and the southern tip of South Africa. The islands belong to England and are populated by 250 people whose families came in the nineteenth century and who today live chiefly on potato farming and fishing. When Fougeron passed this lonely outpost on October 30th, it meant that *Captain Browne*—his thirty-foot steel cutter—was three weeks (at 100 miles a day) behind Moitessier who had reached the Cape of Good Hope by a more northerly and direct route.

At thirty-eight degrees south latitude, Tristan da Cunha is midway between the horse latitudes and the westerlies. In such a zone you might expect the weather to be moderate; yet the islands are often ravaged by west-moving gales that dart up from the south.

For several days Fougeron had been running south toward the roaring forties with strong winds behind him. "A pale, dismal day breaks under a low sky, and the surface of the sea is streaked with zig-zagging white rays as the waves climb higher," he wrote. "They break against each other and chase us with their menacing crests. But *Captain Browne* spurts over each wave and pursues her route through the bubbling foam, safely guided by the self-steering device."

Fougeron had made good progress, but he was worried by the strong winds and hardly dared to rest. "No question of sleep here as in the trade winds," he said. "One has to snatch an hour or a moment to rest without removing boots or oilskins—just in case."

Sometimes the barometer shot up to surprising heights after an east-moving weather depression had passed *Captain Browne.* Then the wind would ease off or stop entirely. Fougeron would let out his reefs and put up bigger headsails. After a period of light weather, however, the heavy winds would again roar down on the yacht.

This is what happened on October 30th near Tristan da Cunha. At 1300 hours the barometer read 1051 millibars (1013 is normal) while the yacht rolled uneasily on a windless sea. At 1400 a light wind arrived and Fougeron soon had full sail up. By 1500 the wind had become so strong that the French captain had decided it was impossible to carry on and he was busy clawing down the sails. By 1600 the intensity of the storm had doubled. At 1700 the conditions were simply ghastly. The wind was so strong that it flailed the tops off the waves and drove the spume across the sea in horizontal streaks. From the shelter of *Captain Browne,* Fougeron looked out uneasily. Obviously this was no ordinary storm. "Never in my life have I seen the sea so high," wrote the captain. "Large albatrosses fly past at great speed, egged on by the wind."

Fougeron had unlocked the self-steering gear so the wind blade could feather into the wind. "I am scared it will be torn off," he said, "but left to turn freely it should withstand anything." As night fell on the raging ocean east of Tristan da Cunha, a fury of wind suddenly slammed down on the yacht and sheared off the wind blade as if its stainless steel shaft were made of Swiss cheese. In a second the blade disappeared downwind. What would go next?

A fierce wind rages in the rigging, and waves explode against the deck [said Fougeron]. . . . I am fearful that the revolving turret and hatches will be destroyed. . . . October 31st, 0200. The wind is at hurricane force. I . . . look at the sea, frightened and hypnotized at the same time. Clouds scudding across the bright moon make a Dantesque setting—as though the sea is a gigantic bubbling cauldron. I am not ashamed to admit my mounting fear.

I get the impression that a single wave would suffice to crush us, like a nut under an elephant's foot. I am tired, cold, and should like to eat and drink something hot. It's impossible to sleep. I curl up in the cramped bunk and wait for the sea to win its victory over me.

A few hours before dawn, while lying beam-on to the raging ocean, a huge wave roared out of the night, engulfed *Captain Browne,* and rolled the yacht partway over. Fougeron thought his life was finished.

The boat lunges sideways, driven by a frightful force. I am flattened violently against the side and then, in the middle of the bubbling waters, everything goes black. [There is] a cascade of kitchen materials, books, bottles, tins of jam, everything that isn't secured, and in the midst of this bewildering song-and-dance I am projected helter-skelter across the boat.

At this moment I believe it is the end, and that the sea will crush me and prevent me from ever coming to the surface again. I will join the legions of sailors who have perished along this ancient route. In a flash I think of my family, my wife, and all those I love and will never see again.

Captain Browne's heavy ballast keel quickly rolled the yacht back upright. The steel hull was undamaged, but Fougeron had to deal with rigging problems. Far worse than the damage to the mast and its supporting wires, however, was the damage to Fougeron's confidence. He was terrified, completely and thoroughly. In a twinkling he had lost interest in the round-the-world race. The fury of the storm, the noise, the capsize, the mess in the cabin, and the cold were too much for him. He wanted out. He wanted land. He wanted a quiet harbor and a peaceful sunset. He was through.

"Each wave unfurls in spouting foam, reaching higher than the mast," said Fougeron. ". . . My eyes burn, my teeth chatter . . . The sea is [a] moonlit landscape in a snowstorm. The waves rise up like cliffs. I am surrounded by buildings which collapse in order to stand up and fall down again.

"I loathe this sea, the sea that I love."

Captain Browne

Below in the cabin a hundred precious things were churned together and ruined. "I want to cry out at the sight of the shambles. Not a single book, utensil in its place. Books on the bunk, condensed milk, onions, dried fruit in the pages of paperbacks, broken glass on the floor, a packet of cigarettes, mustard, pencils, a small cask of wine . . . Miraculously my alarm clock still ticks."

Fougeron was cold, tired, and filled with despair. He looked around and saw only the menacing waves and the powerless hand of a man about to be swallowed and crushed. His optimism and his will to win the race had been destroyed by the storm. He felt wretched.

In spite of its violence, however, the great storm moved eastward and was gone in a day. Nevertheless, Fougeron had had enough. He headed for Cape Town, now fourteen hundred miles to the east. During the next two weeks the weather was generally poor, with calms, headwinds, and gales. The French captain remained sorely demoralized. The heart had gone out of him and he sailed his vessel badly.

The essence of small boat handling is to crack on sail in light airs and to reduce sail when it breezes up. But without proper food and rest, a sailor doesn't have the strength to handle sails or the wit to make reasonable decisions. Fougeron complained about losing weight. He wrote that he lived on cold coffee, sugar, alcohol, and vitamin C, hardly a reasonable diet. Without spirit and muscle he tended to leave up his small sails and to wait for the next storm. His daily mileage dwindled.

After fifteen days, Fougeron gave up trying to get to Cape Town. He changed his course for St. Helena, an island far to the north—only 960 miles from the equator. His new target meant that he was heading into the tropics again and would be able to run with the warm trade wind, the friendly following breeze. Now the going was easy.

On November 28th he arrived at St. Helena and anchored. "I am lulled to sleep by a soft surge, under a sky studded with stars," he wrote. "*Captain Browne* rocks gently at her anchor." For Fougeron the race was over. To withdraw from such a marathon was no mark of cowardice; perhaps it was a sign of common sense.

Fougeron had never gotten south of thirty-seven degrees south latitude, but he had peered into a window open to the view of death. He was the third man to withdraw from the round-the-world race. Six were left.

Not only was Loïck Fougeron rolled over in the terrible storm near Tristan da Cunha, but a second contestant was caught as well. Bill King on *Galway Blazer II* was about 380 miles east-southeast of Fougeron when the great storm came. Neither man realized that he was so near the other. Neither could have helped the other, because in a severe storm at sea a man can survive only by withdrawing snail-like into the protective shell of his ship. A sailor generally runs through a series of sail reductions and may drag a long line or two to slow his progress, but unless he is holed or damaged, the last thing he wants is to see another vessel, with its threat of collision and damage or worse. Nevertheless, all sailors sometimes wonder about the other fellows out there.

(At this very moment a sailor on some faroff sea is being buffeted and thrown by a storm. He is enduring the screeching of wind, the crash of a breaking wave, the terrible rolling, the difficulty of doing anything constructive, the half-sick lethargy, the interminable waiting, the wasted time. It all seems so stupid and futile and crazy. Again the question: Why would anyone go to sea in a small vessel?

Yet a storm does end. Then hope and confidence snap back like the first brightening rays of a morning sun that suddenly click above the horizon after a dismal night. The blue sky returns, the sun warms everything, a reasonable wind blows, and the yacht goes along easily over seas that now seem friendly. The terrible battering from the storm is forgotten, when by rights the captain should carry a grudge to his death and quit this sorry business. The shiny truth, however, is that an hour of pleasant ocean sailing toward a goal somewhere makes the whole enterprise worthwhile.

Sailing on the sea is a mixture of black and white, of love streaked with hate, a confusion of good and bad, of rhapsody versus misery. Ocean sailing teaches self-reliance together with awe and respect for the sea. It tells a man to value his sense of humor and balance, and to laugh at himself once in a while. The life is one of simplicity, without pretense, a direct line to nature. Nothing else is so free and easy and pleasant and satisfying. Nothing else is so tedious, demanding, humbling, and difficult.)

Commander Bill King had crossed the equator on September 30th and had run out of the southeast trade wind two weeks later. He was a bit demoralized by the radio reports of Moitessier's fast progress. Knox-Johnston was somewhere ahead also. King realized that he was behind in the race, but like a good contestant he hoped to make better progress. Perhaps he would run into some good slants of wind so that *Galway Blazer II*'s fine hull could make record runs and get up with the leaders. King was also wise enough to know that in any competition you can never tell when the leaders will stumble.

Now on his sixty-seventh day at sea—after more than nine weeks of sailing alone—King's thoughts of his place in the race were pushed from his head by an ominous development. He had become aware of a different feel to the sea; something big, something violent was coming. A few hours later King was deep into the worst storm he had experienced in half a lifetime spent at sea. He had watched storms from the tiny platforms of submarines and from sailing vessels all over the world. But nothing in his long background was like the wild ocean that now battered his graceful ocean cruiser.

On Wednesday, the 30th of October, the barometer started to plummet downward . . . and as the wind's howl rose, I reefed down through gale to storm force, [wrote King]. Finally I had just the peak of the foresail showing at about Force 10; but still the wind increased [with] huge slabs of foam down the backs of the waves and the tops flying away. Night fell and every now and then the sky would clear. . . . A brilliant moon illuminated the scene which increased in grandeur and horror; I was now down to bare poles. Finally, a new note of scream came in the wind and, during each squall, the sea started to come right away in spindrift. The boat behaved beautifully, running down wind, with the vane steering. But this new hurricane speed defeated the vane; it could not steer, nor could the control work.

King steered for twenty-four hours, standing in the enclosed cockpit. There was no opportunity to eat, but he wasn't hungry anyway, being spellbound by the storm raging around him.

I stood up with my head in a Perspex dome, feeling remote and detached from the storm [King wrote]. . . . I estimated the waves at forty feet but, when the hurricane arrived, all pattern seemed lost in a confusion of tumbling hills. At one patch of moonlight as we came down off the top of a monster, I distinctly saw a petrel flying across my path way below me. . . .

A sea top erupting into pointed mountain peaks would suddenly be pressed down into flatness, blown off by wind-scream, mercifully shutting out the grey-green light, so that only the immediate streaky shoulders of sea hills could be seen." The air might clear to reveal a quarter of a mile of racked, spume-laden ocean.

By 0500 the wind had eased a bit and King got the yacht to steer herself. But by 0930 the wind increased sharply again ("greater than before") and changed direction from the north to the west. King's barometer rose sharply. The center of the weather system to the south was moving southeastward of the yacht. Now came the worst problem of all. The old north wind had raised colossal seas that were running from the north. The new wind shrieking from the west began to send its gigantic seas slamming into the old seas from the north. "Everything the sea had done until then was eclipsed by the fury and confusion of the two huge seas running across one another," said the slim captain of *Galway Blazer II*.

King noticed that the top of his forward sail had started to come unfurled. He was afraid the foresail peak might be destroyed by the wind, so he stopped running with the storm and lay ahull, broadside to the west wind. The vessel seemed to ride as well sideways to the west wind as she had when she had run before the storm.

Toward evening—1700—on Halloween, the wind started to ease. King thought that the storm center had passed, so when the wind got down to forty-five knots he took down his two hurricane hatches and went on deck to see about a problem with the self-steering gear. He then returned to the enclosed cockpit to get a piece of line to secure the loose foresail. He was sitting under the open hatches coiling the line when the worst happened.

Galway Blazer II rolled over to ninety degrees and was hurled forward on her side by a huge breaking wave. "She was using her side as a surfer would his board, to speed and accelerate down the face of the wave," said King. "The masts must still have been in the air, their proper element, and I had time to think, 'she will come back again; that great lead keel will swing her upright.' "

At that instant a cross-sea erupted from the north. Instead of the yacht recovering, her masts were buried in the great cross-sea. The force of the water pushed on the masts which acted as levers and "started the mariner's most dreaded catastrophe: a complete roll over, upside down . . .

I was on my shoulders pressed against the deckhead, which was normally above me, [said King] my head pointing to the sea bottom, fifteen thousand feet below, looking at the green water pouring up through both hatches.

Curiously, I felt no fear at that moment. There was nothing I could do, except cling on to my wedged-in position. I knew she would quickly right herself by the down-swing of the two-ton lead keel. The boat had been specifically designed to withstand a disaster of this nature, without hull damage. I felt, perhaps, a pained surprise that I should have been defeated by the aftermath of the tempest, after riding out its fury. I stared, perhaps stupidly, at the inrushing columns of water, and . . . then, with a mighty flick up she came.

The cockpit was full of green water up to the top of the half door, perhaps three tons of it. My eyes flickered over the mess below deck and focused on the gymballed stove, hanging upside down.

King quickly closed the hatches and set to work to pump out the water. When he went on deck a little later, however, he was aghast. The foremast had snapped off about twelve feet up. The mainmast was still standing, but fractured and angled to starboard. The self-steering gear was a mass of twisted metal. King realized that it was the end of the race for him.

The delicate unstayed masts were sufficient for ordinary ocean sailing if watched over by an expert seaman, but in the roaring forties their use seemed a little risky. The trouble wasn't in the air but in the sea. Sooner or later, small vessels involved with really bad weather get into a severe roll, a broach, or a capsize situation, which means their masts get dipped into the water. If the vessel is going along at four or five knots, the ocean is very hard and yields only grudgingly. God knows it's risky enough with a time-proven rig whose masts are supported with a dozen strong wires. Without the familiar wires, the unstayed masts that get pushed into water can crumble like toothpicks in a prize-fighter's hands. Or as an engineer might say: "It's an unfair strain in an incompressible medium."

Galway Blazer II was at thirty-nine degrees south latitude, about one thousand miles southwest of Capt Town and 400 miles southeast of Tristan da Cunha. With one mast gone, the second mast damaged, and no engine, Bill King was in a tough spot. But he was as tough as the ocean that had stopped him.

Shortly after the capsize and rollover, and still lying broadside to the storm, the yacht was knocked down again, but only to ninety degrees and the mast was not put into the water. Meanwhile King cleared up the mess below and repaired the self-steering gear. On November 1st, he sawed off the remains of the foremast. Then he gingerly tried a reefed sail on the main-mast and hoped the spar would hold. It seemed to be okay. The following day there was a storm with sixty-knot winds. Again King lay broadside to the wind with no sail up and again was rolled to ninety degrees. On November 4th, he got underway and crept toward Cape Town at about fifty miles a day.

When *Galway Blazer II* was designed, King had specified an emergency mast for the vessel. The mast was made in the form of an A-frame and was stored flat on deck with its arms along the side decks and its apex at the bow. Each arm was 18½ feet long and made of four-inch diameter aluminum pipe hinged on deck to a slider that ran in a twelve-foot track, one on each side deck. The mast was erected by sliding the arms forward in the tracks and hauling on backstays. A short forestay completed the emergency mast from which King hoisted an eighty-five-square foot storm jib.

On November 13th, King was sailing before a gale under the storm jib alone. He had been in radio contact with Cape Town and learned that a large South African yacht with a crew of seven was coming out to tow him the last 200 miles. On the following day the two yachts made contact and *Galway Blazer II* was whisked into Cape Town.

Of the nine men who had started the round-the-world race, only five were left.

12. *The Impractical Sailor*

OCTOBER 31ST WAS THE LAST DAY that anyone could start in the round-the-world race. On that date Robin Knox-Johnston in *Suhaili* was far in the lead, halfway along the south coast of Australia, nearing Melbourne and the Bass Strait area north of Tasmania. Bernard Moitessier had recovered from his collision with the black freighter near the Cape of Good Hope, and *Joshua* was 900 miles eastward into the Indian Ocean. Nigel Tetley on the blue trimaran *Victress* was about to sight Ilha Trindade in the tropical regions of the South Atlantic.

The final two starters in the race had barely left England. The Italian, Alex Carozzo, had anchored *Gancia Americano* off a south coast port while he sorted out his gear. Donald Crowhurst aboard *Teignmouth Electron* had just disappeared over the horizon toward the Bay of Biscay.

As we have seen, John Ridgway and Chay Blyth had retired earlier, largely because of unsuitable vessels. Both Loïck Fougeron and Bill King had been knocked out of the race by a particularly violent, fast-moving storm near Tristan da Cunha.

Of the nine starters, four had withdrawn. Knox-Johnston was in the lead, but he was battling to keep *Suhaili* from being knocked apart by the seas of the Southern Ocean. Moitessier's *Joshua* was in far better condition and was making the fastest runs of any of the entrants; nevertheless the French captain was some 4,500 miles behind Knox-Johnston and had a lot of miles to make up. If Moitessier averaged 150 miles a day and Knox-

Johnston did 100 miles every twenty-four hours, Moitessier would need ninety days—*three months*—to catch up. To maintain such an average seemed impossible for a singlehander. Of course Knox/Johnston might fail to make 100 miles a day or he might even drop out.

The trimarans had been expected to make the fastest times of any of the yachts. The weight of their heavy stores, however, slowed them enormously. As the captains ate into their food and began to use up fuel and various supplies, the trimarans began to sail faster. In the fresher trade winds, Tetley averaged 140 miles a day, much more than earlier in the race. But he was more than seven thousand miles behind Knox-Johnston.

All the men in the race wanted very much to know about the others—where they were, how they were doing, their problems and solutions, record runs—*news of any kind, good or bad.* Though the entrants were sometimes thousands of miles apart, each felt drawn to the others by the bond of the race and by the trouble-some challenge of trying to sail a tiny vessel around the world nonstop. All the yachts had receivers and most had two-way radios. All listened, hoping for race information. But when the news came it was sparse, often rewritten by nonsailors, madden-ingly incomplete, and much of the time there was none at all. Football, tennis, cricket, horse racing, road racing, golf, political news, stock prices, wool quotations, the inane chatter of radio announcers—there was everything except what the sailors wanted to hear.

The entrants with sponsors generally had scheduled radio calls, but even these were often poor and incomplete. The race lacked a dependable communication scheme which tried the contestants' patience and sometimes kept them shadow-boxing with invisible competitors. Before the race was over, the lack of reliable news and the absence of reasonable monitoring by the race sponsor was to cause grievous problems.

At noon on November 3rd, Donald Crowhurst's sleek forty-foot trimaran *Teignmouth Electron* ran swiftly to the southwest before a fair wind. The yacht had left England three days earlier and now was well into the Atlantic off the northwest coast of

Teignmouth Electron

France. The pretty white and blue multihull was one of two Victress designs in the round-the-world race. The first was sailed by Nigel Tetley, the second by Crowhurst. Tetley's *Victress* had a high wheelhouse above a raised coachroof. This allowed a splendid accommodation arrangement below but rather spoiled the lines of the vessel when viewed from the side. In addition the raised coachroof and wheelhouse were structurally marginal and somewhat vulnerable to breaking waves.

On Crowhurst's Victress, he had eliminated the weight and windage of the raised coachroof and wheelhouse. For visibility ahead he had substituted a racy-looking blister with six small portlights facing forward. This modification saved a good deal of weight and made the yacht stronger, but reduced the living space and light below. *Teignmouth Electron*'s helmsman was somewhat exposed without a wheelhouse. The captain didn't plan to spend much time in the cockpit, however, because he had a self-steering gear.

Crowhurst was nervous about getting away to sea after the long business of building the trimaran, sailing around the east and south coasts of England, and collecting and loading the stores and provisions for the thirty thousand-mile trip. Fortunately it wasn't all drudgery, as he had noted in his log the previous day:

Earlier today porpoises came out to greet me. There were about thirty of them playing round the boat, accompanied by a mass of gulls. Sometimes as many as six pairs in a line (they seemed to prefer swimming in pairs) would jump on the starboard side and swim across the bows to port. All round the boat they were leaping around and inspecting me.

The first big problem on the voyage was the self-steering gear which persisted in shedding screws because the high speed of the trimaran made the steering gear vibrate and shake out the fastenings. Crowhurst should have had spare screws, but he had forgotten to bring any. He was able to keep the gear working by switching a few fastenings, but obviously this practice could not go on. And he was just beginning the trip! On the delivery passage in England, Crowhurst had been advised to weld the screws in place, but he had forgotten to in the rush to get away. He could have used lock washers, double nuts, a locking thread compound, cotter keys, safety wire, or have mashed the thread ends with a hammer. Eventually, he would have to do something.

Crowhurst had trouble with a boil on his forehead above his left eye. He decided to take vitamin pills. While fretting over his forehead he went to work on the Racal radio receiver, which had stopped working. Since he was a radio expert he took the set apart and checked each component. It was only after some hours that he was embarrassed to discover that the problem was a blown fuse.

While Crowhurst ate his meals, he studied a thick, blue book called *Ocean Passages For The World,* which outlined recommended sailing routes and discussed prevailing wind systems and currents. He felt a little like a clipper ship captain as he decided on his route southward in the Atlantic.

On Tuesday, November 5th, the second big problem appeared. Crowhurst saw bubbles coming out of the forward hatch on the port float of the trimaran. The port float was also low in the water. Could there be water inside? When the captain undid the twelve butterfly nuts and removed the circular hatch he found the compartment flooded up to deck level. No wonder the float was low in the water! Unfortunately just then the weather was nasty. According to Crowhurst the seas were running fifteen feet high and almost as much water ran into the open compartment as the captain was able to bail out with a bucket. It took three hours to get the water out and to screw down the hatch on a new gasket.

I cursed the people who'd been kind enough to help me stow ship, and I cursed myself for a fool [wrote Crowhurst]. I swore the boat was a toy fit only for the Broads or the pool at Earl's Court [the national boat show]. But when I'd got the job done, eaten some curry and rice with an apple and some tea, I experienced the great satisfaction that something I'd been fearing had happened and been dealt with. Now I must do all the other hatches. I looked into the port main hatch, and things seemed OK. I got out my vitamin pills. A whaler, French or Spanish, said hullo.

The next day was the sixth birthday of Rachel, Crowhurst's youngest child. Her father, who was extremely fond of his four children, made both a radio telephone call and sent a telegram to his daughter.

The wind had been blowing from the south, almost directly from the direction *Teignmouth Electron* had been trying to go. This had forced Crowhurst to tack. From November 2nd to the 6th, the yacht had logged 538 miles, but in those four days she had made good only 290 miles, or about 72 miles a day, toward her target. Finally on the 6th, the wind began to veer to the west and Crowhurst was able to head directly south at increased speed.

On the following day, sailing faster, the screws began to fall from the steering vane again. "That's four gone now—can't keep cannibalizing from other spots forever!" said Crowhurst. "The thing will fall to bits."

The boil on the captain's forehead was better, apparently helped by the vitamins and by penicillin pills that he had begun taking. Crowhurst complained of condensation and unpleasant smells in the small cabin; obviously the ventilation was bad and had never been properly thought out for a long sea passage. The captain wrote that he had great luck making toast for supper over a Primus stove while the yacht bashed along in winds up to 39 knots.

Crowhurst's biographers—Nicholas Tomalin and Ron Hall—have pointed out that there were really two Donald Crowhursts. One was real and believable; the second was contrived and posturing. On a BBC tape, Crowhurst said the following:

An involuntary gybe had hurtled my head against the cockpit side, and now I was conscious that my head hurt and my back hurt. I wondered if any serious damage had been done. Very tentatively I moved one foot and one leg, and then the others. I lay there for a minute, thinking how careless I'd been, and then, very slowly sat up. I sat very quietly for about three minutes, and then very gingerly got up. Everything seemed to be all right. I didn't know then that it was going to be three days before I was going to be able to move again. I gathered myself together, got to my feet, and finished making the attachment of the trisail to the boom, and continued my way eastwards.

This all sounded very heady and heroic. Unfortunately the words did not come from Crowhurst at all, but were stolen from Sir Francis Chichester's book *Gipsy Moth Circles The World* (pages 195–196) which was on board *Teignmouth Electron:*

I was flung in a heap to the bottom of the far side of the cockpit. I stayed motionless where I landed, wondering if my leg was broken. I relaxed everything while I wondered. For about a minute I made no movement at all, and then slowly uncurled myself. To my astonishment—and infinite relief—nothing seemed broken. . . . Picking myself up and collecting my wits, I carried on with my radio work . . . During the night I had some difficulty in moving my ribs and ankle, and feared a bad stiffening . . . I sailed out of the Forties that evening . . . I tried to celebrate the event with a bottle of Veuve Cliquot, but it was a flop drinking by myself.

Not only did Crowhurst copy the words of Sir Francis, but he preceded his message by drinking champagne from a bottle of Moet et Chandon. Clearly someone was in fantasyland.

By November 8th, the trimaran was west of Cape Finisterre, the northwest corner of Spain. Though he was in the shipping lanes, Crowhurst decided to take a long sleep and lowered the mainsail and mizzen. When he got up at 1100 and saw a big liner near him he began to hoist the sails. He found, however, that the mizzen halyard had gotten loose and had run partway up the mast. Before he climbed the mast to retrieve the halyard, Crowhurst carefully streamed a safety line astern in case he slipped and fell overboard. He went up the mast, captured the loose halyard, and soon had all the sails hoisted. While he was up the mast he noticed that the rubber buoyancy bag at the top of the mainmast was loose and that the inflation hose was not attached to the bag.

Teignmouth Electron's progress got slower and slower because Crowhurst began to lower the mainsail at dusk. This made it easy to stay on course but it spoiled any reasonable daily runs. Crowhurst became depressed and sluggish. His celestial navigation wasn't working properly. One day he lost his temper at the spar-maker back in England when he noticed that a screw had fallen from the mizzen mast. On November 12th he was too weary (or lazy?) to change course after a wind shift at 0200 and sailed north—in the wrong direction—for seven hours. He bestirred himself with a warning in the log: "If I did that every day it would take over a year to finish. *I must not allow myself to be lazy.*"

On the next day—the 13th—a new disaster materialized. First Crowhurst had had trouble with loose screws in the steering gear. Second had been water in the floats. Now he found that water was pouring into the yacht because of a faulty hatch in the cockpit floor.

Today has had a sinister significance all right [he said]. Plugging away to westward in a southerly gale the cockpit hatch has been leaking and has flooded the engine compartment, electrics and Onan [the generating plant]. Unless I can get the Onan to work I will have to think very seriously about the continuation of the project. With so much wrong with the boat in so many respects—it would perhaps be foolish . . . to continue. I will try to get the generator working, and think about the alternatives open to me.

Crowhurst was to write that seventy-five gallons of sea water had leaked through the floor of the cockpit in a single night. What could be done? Without electricity none of his beloved electrical devices could function. His radios wouldn't work. How could he talk to England? His children? His sponsor? His press agent?

The captain of the *Teignmouth Electron* began a long written analysis of his problems. Not only did he have serious leaks, loose screws on the steering vane, and doubtful electricity, but he had found that his mainsail and mizzen were cut far too full (too baggy) and chafed severely on the mast shrouds much of the time. Without electricity Crowhurst wouldn't have radios, which meant no way to send messages to his wife. It also meant no electric lights and no radio time signals for accurate longitude. He had found that the steering gear didn't work properly at high speeds and was liable to cause wild broaches that might be disastrous in the seas of the Southern Ocean. He had twin headsails for possible use when running before the wind; with this rig the yacht might steer herself, but the sails and gear had never been tried and there was no telling what problems would come up. The masthead buoyancy bag scheme for self-righting wasn't completed. Worst of all was his seasonal timing. Because of the various delays and problems, *Teignmouth Electron* was scheduled to arrive at Cape Horn in the middle of autumn which Crowhurst feared was too close to winter. He reckoned his chances of survival at 50–50. He didn't like the odds.

Crowhurst's logbook discussion of these problems covered nine pages of closely spaced print. These private notes to himself were quite logical and realistic. His analysis should have convinced him to steer for the nearest port. He didn't.

He was worried about humiliating himself by quitting. He was worried about the reaction of his family, his press agent, and the people of Teignmouth who had helped him. He was worried about losing face with his sponsor. He was worried that his sponsor, Mr. Best, might exercise the contract option that required Crowhurst to buy back the trimaran if the voyage was not completed.

The captain had vague plans about stopping in Cape Town or Australia. He had fanciful notions about starting the race again the following year. As fast as he thought up one scheme, however, he would discredit it and come up with an even more bizarre idea. Would the other contestants drop out and leave the Golden Globe and the £5,000 to Crowhurst? If the others dropped out he had plan A; if not he was ready with plan B, and so on. Maybe he could market his company's navigation instruments in Australia. Maybe he could sell the yacht. . . .

In listening to all this, one cries out for the earthiness, the practicality, and the common sense of a Knox-Johnston, a Moitessier, or a Joshua Slocum, people who simply *did* things without a lot of frenzied thinking and planning. You begin to wonder whether Crowhurst could have sharpened a pencil without a prepared outline. Yet in reading over his writings it's impossible not to be impressed by Crowhurst's intelligence. Though he was a fledgling sailor he had come a long way during the past year. He had started in the race only twenty weeks after handing the plans of his yacht to the builder. How many people could top that? His schemes to deal with *Teignmouth Electron*'s problems were reasonable. He would seal the leaky cockpit hatch and cut an access opening into the compartment from below. He would deal with the loose screws on the steering vane by tapping each screwhead and putting in a small locking screw. The general pumping arrangements were a mess but he would think of something. Maybe he could find the missing hose. . . .

But at the end of it all, Crowhurst was not really practical. He was unrealistic and stubborn. He tried to solve ordinary difficulties by overkill. His solutions were too complicated and fancy. He was simply a visionary engineer full of top-heavy ideas who repeatedly boxed himself into mental corners because of indecision and vanity.

It's no sin to admit failure born of ordinary human frailty. The sin is to be not strong enough to admit defeat. If the vessel was unsuitable and Crowhurst's resolve was faltering he should have quit. A simple act. In 1968, a singlehanded voyage from England to Madeira was impressive. A trip to Cape Town or Australia was extraordinary. Yet, after a tortured session of self analysis that clearly indicated he should give up, he couldn't bring himself to do it. Maybe later. He would try to get his sponsor, Mr. Best, on the radio-telephone and sound him out . . . cagily of course.

Meanwhile, by November 15th, *Teignmouth Electron* had logged about 1,300 miles and was near forty degrees north latitude, about midway along the Portuguese coast. Much of this sailing—especially since November 8th—had been indirect and meandering. Along his direct route of thirty thousand miles, Crowhurst had made good only 800 miles or 2.6 per cent. All the other contestants had done better. At this rate it would take him seventy-five weeks or almost a year and a half to get around the world.

The next day *Teignmouth Electron* made good time to the southwest. Crowhurst had bailed out the generator compartment and had gotten the machine going after stripping and drying the magneto. Again he had electricity for the radio, so he called Rodney Hallworth, his press agent, and told him that he was "going on towards Madeira" which was really 200 miles to the south. That night with the radio playing and milder weather, he felt better, especially after a hearty supper of paella.

On November 17th Crowhurst searched the yacht for the missing bilge pump hose but it wasn't on board. On the following day he looked into the forward compartment of the starboard float and found it flooded. His instant coffee had been stored in this area, and the coffee-seawater mix had become an unholy mess. Crowhurst climbed into the float naked and bailed out the compartment, emerging covered with comical splotches of brown coffee stains that made him look like "something terrible from the deep" until he washed himself. He also bailed out seventy gallons from the main hull. He worried a lot about the leaks in all three hulls and the lack of a proper pumping system, something Nigel Tetley had anticipated and made provision for aboard *Victress*. Obviously in bad weather it was dangerous to unscrew a hatch because a wave might flood the open compartment. How could he possibly take such a vessel to the Southern Ocean?

Crowhurst made a careful list of crucial points to discuss with his wife and Mr. Best, but when he got them on the radio on November 18th he lost his nerve and said nothing of substance. The next day he heard on the radio that Knox-Johnston had passed New Zealand. By now *Teignmouth Electron* was going around in a slow circle north of Madeira in bad weather. In seven days the captain had made only 180 miles to the south. He thought of putting in at Funchal, Madeira and spent hours reading about the port and making a sketch chart. Again he called Mr. Best. Crowhurst wanted to talk about abandoning the race but he was only able to bring himself to discuss pumping difficulties.

On the 22nd he replaced a broken servo blade on the self-steering gear. The weather got better. *Teignmouth Electron* was almost into the northeast trade wind zone which meant one thousand miles of fair and warm winds. Crowhurst's spirits improved and he headed southwest again at 100 miles a day. He went up the mast to clear a knot in the jib halyard. His remarks were almost jaunty: "This mast climbing is good exercise—I feel exhausted. 'I'll take my constitutional now,' says he disappearing up the mast twice daily!"

On November 26th Crowhurst started a new type of logbook entry. Though he had ample logbooks, he began to conserve them by doubling up on his writing lines, which enabled him to squeeze one thousand words on a single page. He wrote with a new and chatty style: "Chicken Capri is quite nice with a fresh onion, extra dried peas, and cheese added."

He began to drop bottles with messages into the ocean. The idea was for publicity, of course. The Teignmouth city officials had given him printed forms that read:

> FROM DONALD CROWHURST, SAILING ALONE,
> NON-STOP AROUND THE WORLD
>
> > The bottle containing this message
> > was placed in the sea at . . . . .
> > hours on . . . . . . 196 . . my
> > position being . . . . . . and my
> > log reading . . . . . . miles.
> > Signed . . . . . .
>
> The finder of this message will be rewarded if he sends
> it to Mr. D. H. Sharpe, Bitton House, Teignmouth
> England

Crowhurst was full of ideas for publicity, for new devices on the yacht, for new ways to sail. Unfortunately his facile mind was faster than his ability to put his ideas into practice. With Crowhurst the problem wasn't the idea, the concept, or the notion, but the execution and application of the new plan, the ideal scheme, or the perfect solution. He should have been working in an idea factory or a think tank. If something didn't work or go according to plan there had to be a way around the difficulty. . . . While he sped southward he scratched his head.

Alex Carozzo had officially left on October 31st, as we have seen. He anchored his giant ketch *Gancia Americano* at Cowes off the Isle of Wight in southern England for a week in order to rest, to sort out his gear, and to hoist his various sails. Although he hadn't gone anywhere he was technically at sea in the race.

After the Italian sailor had satisfied himself that all was in order aboard his sixty-six-foot vessel, he sailed west down the English channel and into the Bay of Biscay where he soon encountered his first gale. ("The roaring forties are not only in the Southern ocean," he reported.) The big ketch handled the heavy weather with ease, and Carozzo sometimes touched nine knots as the racing machine knifed through the seas. On November 14th, the captain radioed that he was at forty-four degrees twenty-five minutes north and twelve degrees ten minutes west, or about 190 miles wet–northwest of La Coruña, Spain.

The cold weather and gales were behind him, but the Italian complained about heavy rain and low clouds. "What I need is some sun," said Carozzo. "The tomatoes on board are going bad. Unless the sun shines, mould will start growing on me too."

The captain of the shiny new ketch found that he was able to sail his enormous vessel very well in spite of the doubts of many people. As far as Carozzo knew, no single-hander had ever tackled such a large vessel before. *Gancia Americano*'s motion was much easier than his earlier smaller yachts and Carozzo hoped to be able to log 200-mile-plus days when things settled down and he found steady winds.

Carozzo's big problem was not sailing or handling his giant entry, but terrible stomach pains. He had been vomiting blood, and with a history of ulcer problems his prospects were grim. It seemed a pity when the new yacht was going so well.

The Sunday Times called in a doctor to advise Carozzo by radio-telephone. After a consultation on November 14th, the doctor duly recorded that his seaborne patient had a record of ulcer trouble. "The symptoms indicate that it has blown up again," said the doctor. "I advised him to follow a strict simple diet and to take any alkali medicines that he had. I told him that if he was still bleeding, he should give up. There's always the risk of an enormous haemorrhage." The doctor added that the bleeding had stopped, however, and that Carozzo was feeling better after keeping to a simple diet and drinking no alcohol.

In spite of the ulcer diagnosis Carozzo stubbornly refused to give up. "I'll sail on," he declared.

By November 23rd, in spite of his earlier brave words,

Gancia Americano

Carozzo's condition had worsened and the desperate captain was limping toward Lisbon for emergency medical treatment. A Portuguese Air Force P2V5 rescue plane was dispatched to search for the Italian mariner. "I do not know if we will be able to do much for the sailor," said the Secretary of State for Air, Brigadier General Fernando de Oliveira, "but the sight of a plane searching for him should cheer him up and make him aware that help is at hand."

Carozzo was determined to sail in by himself, but when the plane located him becalmed fifteen miles from the Coast he signaled for assistance. A pilot launch from Oporto hurried out and towed *Gancia Americano,* her mizzen and staysail still hoisted, into the Portuguese seaport.

"When you are alone at sea in a big yacht and the weather is poor, then it is bad enough. But when you are ill it is terrible," said Carozzo to a reporter in the hospital a few days later. "When the seas were rough in the Bay of Biscay all I wanted to do was sleep and be sick. I was vomiting blood and felt terrible. I was very weak but I had to keep control of the yacht. No one can understand what it was like for me.

"To make things worse the thought kept pounding through my head that I would have to retire," he continued. "All the preparations that I and so many other people had made would be wasted. I greatly admire mountaineers and the men who are crossing the Arctic at the moment but they always have companions. Out at sea, I had no one to help me, no one to talk with me."

Carozzo's undertaking had been prodigious. Not only had he dealt with the design and financial aspects of his big vessel, but he had supervised the rushed construction. Every day he had been obliged to solve a hundred large and small problems. With no time for sea trials he left immediately on the race. Alas, the slim, lion-hearted man from Venice had undertaken too much. The strong and powerful yacht didn't fail; it was Carozzo's health that collapsed from the strain.

From his hospital bed the patient explained his decision to the reporter: "I am a bloody fool to try to sail round the world alone, but I am not a complete idiot." While still at sea Carozzo had begun to feel a little better but he knew that he was still seriously ill. Worse yet, he had used up all his injections. Fortunately he was near land instead of being out in the middle of the Atlantic. "I decided I must retire and make for port," he said.

Now there were four men left in the race: Knox-Johnston, Moitessier, Tetley, and Crowhurst.

14. "Come On God"

ON ROBIN KNOX-JOHNSTON'S ONE HUNDREDTH DAY from England he was fourteen hundred miles east of the Cape of Good Hope, far out in the Indian Ocean, a little more than one-quarter of the way between the tip of Africa and the west coast of Australia. *Suhaili* hurried eastward near the 40th parallel of south latitude, with both the current and the great westerly winds pushing the yacht along.

The mileages between land masses in the Southern ocean are enormous. From Africa to Australia is 4,660 miles of ocean, a forty- or fifty-day sailing proposition for a small vessel.

The weather had been wretched, with gale after gale. Now, however, Knox-Johnston was west of the turbulent area around the tip of Africa and for a few days he found lighter winds and even sunshine. Soon *Suhaili* looked like a floating laundry with pants and shirts and sweaters and towels and underwear and even a sleeping bag flapping in the drying wind.

Knox-Johnston had plenty to do. The self-steering gear had given endless trouble. The problem was simply that the device wasn't strong enough for the hard sailing conditions in the Southern Ocean. The captain had two choices: either reduce *Suhaili*'s speed (in a race?) or strengthen the gear somehow. Otherwise the pipes and arms and brackets and auxiliary rudders would be bashed to pieces.

Even in a shipyard, however, such repairs are awkward because these devices are made and fitted, removed and modified, and changed and improved after trials—perhaps many trials—and the expert services of welders and machinists. Out

on the ocean any modifications are extremely tedious and perhaps impossible. Just drilling a single hole in a piece of metal is
a big job with the vessel rolling all over the place. And such jobs—
even if you have the tools and materials—must be fitted in
between eating and sleeping and watchkeeping. Fortunately most
sailors are perserving types. Knox-Johnston combined the talents of an engineer and a metal worker and he managed to put
his wobbly self-steering back together.

> The repairs took me three days [he wrote]. The old rudder blade
> was hopelessly split, so I made a new one out of one of the teak bunk-
> boards. The bar had broken by the middle of the blade, and to rejoin it
> I cut the handle of a pipe wrench and then filed it down until it fitted
> inside the bar, like an internal splint. I put the two broken ends of the
> bar together and then drilled through the bar and wrench handle, riv-
> eting them together with pieces of a six-inch nail, heated on the primus
> stove. The final job looked pretty strong, but to make sure of it, I bound
> it with glass fiber.

So far on the voyage Knox-Johnston had taken his drinking
and cooking water from plastic jugs that he had brought from
England. He had managed to refill these at various times from
rainfall in the tropics and hadn't touched the eighty-six gallons
in his main tanks at all. Now he was into his fourth month at sea
and had eaten a lot of his food stores. In addition he had used
up a good deal of gasoline in his battery-charging engine, and
had thrown various bits of unwanted junk over the side. *Suhaili*
was a bit out of trim—down in the bow—so the captain began to
pump drinking water from the forward tank to shift a little
weight. The water that flowed from the hand pump was foul-
smelling and brown. When Knox-Johnston slid aside the tank
inspection plate he found that all the water was contaminated
and undrinkable. The after tank was the same. All eighty-six
gallons were useless.

This was bad news. He still had ten gallons in the plastic jugs,
enough for forty days, plus 300 cans of fruit juice and beer. By
an end-of-the-world effort he could distill fresh water from salt
by making a still and using his kerosene stove. A more realistic
possibility was to continue catching rain—there was often plenty

with the gales—and to overlook no chance to fill the water containers. In any case he would keep going to Australia and see how things looked.

One day the captain stood in the cabin repairing his blue spinnaker. He was sewing rope around the edges of the sail and he braced himself against the motion of the yacht with one hand while he sewed with the other. His technique was to stretch a light rope between two points—say six feet apart—fold the edge of the sail over the rope, and then sew the material to the rope. Knox-Johnston was making good progress, but after a while he ran short of thread.

In order to tie a new length of thread to the old, he used his fingers and teeth. When he started to sew again he felt a terrible pain in his upper lip. The more he moved the more his mustache hurt. He had somehow sewn his mustache to the spinnaker rope! He groped for the near end of the rope to untie it, but he was too far away. He grabbed for his knife. It was just out of reach. What to do? In desperation he jerked his head back and ripped off part of his mustache.

"It hurt like hell and tears filled my eyes, but it soon passed off and at least, as I rushed to the mirror to reassure myself, the symmetry of the mustache was not badly upset," he said.

Suhaili's radio transmissions were a problem. Knox-Johnston was able to hear Port Elizabeth in South Africa, but the station had difficulty receiving *Suhaili*'s signals. The ship's batteries were low so one night the captain made a determined effort to repower them by running the charger for hours. During the night Knox-Johnston went into the engine room to check the batteries with a hydrometer. As he leaned over the batteries, however, the yacht broached before a wave and the sudden roll knocked acid from the hydrometer into the captain's left eye. Knox-Johnston rushed on deck and splashed water in the eye which had begun to throb and ache.

The poor captain was terrified. It was a disaster. Would he lose his eye? He put in antiseptic eye drops but the throbbing continued. Should he turn back for Durban? Would it be worth an eye to carry on? Where were the other contestants? What should he do? After a harried debate with himself, Knox-John-

ston continued toward Australia. At the end of a week the eye
was okay.

September 22nd. Awoke to find us heading north so got up and
gybed [wrote Knox-Johnston]. I banged my elbow badly during the night
and what with that, numerous other bruises and an eye that throbbed,
I felt as if I had just gone through ten rounds. . . . As the wind was
down I let out some sail and then went back to bed. It's warm and
reasonably dry there and I feel very tired. I awoke at 1400 to another
gale building up, this time from the S.W. so I had to start taking in sail
again. Reefing is no longer an easy business. My hands are very sore
and covered with blisters, and whirling the handle is sheer hell. I noticed
today over seven sail slides . . . loose or missing on the mainsail so there's
the first job when the wind goes down. I got up at 2000 and made a
risotto which I followed with a tin of fruit. . . . then I turned in again.
This may seem very lazy, but I wanted to rest my eye as much as possible; also to give some idea of how tired I have become, each time I
turned in I fell asleep at once and it was the alarm that woke me.

By September 30th, *Suhaili* had logged more than three
thousand miles in the Southern Ocean. The South African radio
stations gradually faded out. Knox-Johnston tried to speak to
Perth in western Australia but *Suhaili*'s transmitter had stopped
working when the yacht had broached. The captain tried repairs, but nothing had any effect. Not only was the radio transmitter dead, but *Suhaili*'s main engine would not turn over and
appeared to be frozen up from corrosion. This was disappointing, because Knox-Johnston had 100 gallons of diesel fuel on
board and had planned to generate electricity for the radios and
to power through the doldrums in the Atlantic on the way home
to England when the bottom of the yacht would be especially
foul with weed and marine organisms.*
     Again and again the twenty-nine-year-old captain watched
the sea birds, as do all sailors. The small dark-gray Wilson's storm
petrels (wingspan: one foot or less) flitted around the yacht in
bad weather, their delicate, pattering legs nearly touching the
water. The storm petrels were so frail-looking that they seemed

*This was not outlawed in the rules of the race.

to have no business at all on a stormy ocean; yet they always appeared during gales—from where, nobody knows.

There were two kinds of albatrosses, both large and formidable. The black-browed albatross had wings that spanned six feet. The wandering albatross, *Diomedia exulans,* the largest of all ocean birds, possessed magical wings that stretched to twelve feet or more. Up close the albatrosses were comical-looking birds with squat, pear-shaped bodies that appeared quite incapable of flight. It was only when you watched the perpetual soaring and gliding and wheeling of these incredible birds from a distance that you began to appreciate what they were: and to consider the legend of motion that never stopped.

The way the long, narrow, grayish-white wings supported these aerial magicians in their sweeping circles around a vessel at sea was forever a marvel. For it's the wings of the albatross that are its passport to magic—slender high-aspect knifeblades dark on top and white on the bottom with black leading edges. When an albatross flies around a vessel at sea, the bird's circles are large and leisurely, with scarcely a flap of the long wings. The bird usually climbs in a slanting direction against the wind, turns slowly across the wind, and finally rushes rapidly downwind before heading again into the wind. Additionally, the troughs and crests of the waves on the irregular surface of the sea appear to produce small air currents which the bird uses in some fashion. The albatross often flies very low and sometimes completely disappears behind a swell. A viewer is sure that the wings will have touched the water and the bird has toppled into the sea, but in fact this never happens. The bird always appears a few moments later flying at high speed, circling around and around with great banking and wheeling motions, a creature that has hypnotized sailors for centuries and seems a true perpetual motion machine.

Sometimes *Suhaili* was surrounded by a dozen dolphins which raced alongside and rolled and splashed under the bowsprit for a quarter of an hour. Occasionally the white ketch was passed by a blowing whale. "I always felt a little lonely when the whales left," said Knox-Johnston. "Even if we could not communicate, I felt that we shared the same difficulties."

At 0130 on October 6th the main gooseneck—the metal pivot holding the main boom to the mast—broke with a loud bang. The foot of the mainsail sagged and the roller reefing mechanism was no longer usable. The weary captain managed to lash the boom to the mast and once again got out his tools. Knox-Johnston spent two days drilling and filing out the broken jaw, which he hoped to reuse by putting in a new bolt that he would secure to the two mast jaws. The only suitable large-diameter bolt was too short, however, so the captain had to compromise by fastening the gooseneck jaw to a single mast jaw, which he hoped would be strong enough.

While he was dealing with these repairs, another Force ten gale swept down on *Suhaili*. The fifty-knot winds soon made the sea all white. The air temperature was thirty-eight degrees Farhenheit but with the addition of the wind the thirty-eight degrees seemed much colder to the captain, who nipped from a bottle of brandy to keep warm and to build up his resolve a little. As the wind increased, the triple-reefed mainsail began to come apart. Added to all this was a vicious cross sea. Knox-Johnston took down all the sails except a tiny storm jib and streamed eight lines astern to slow and steady the yacht before the storm. During the morning of October 8th the barometer began to rise rapidly. As Knox-Johnston was eating a little breakfast, a cross-sea rolled the ketch to ninety degrees for a few moments. There was nothing to do except to wait out the storm, so the captain crawled into his sleeping bag and tried to doze. By midday the wind had eased to thirty knots, so Knox-Johnston pulled in the warps, hoisted the staysail and reefed mizzen, and was on his way westward again. He sewed the torn mainsail, but while hoisting it later the halyard winch brake failed and he got a frightful blow on his right wrist from the wildly spinning handle. Fortunately the wrist bone did not break.

On the 13th I thought we'd had it [he wrote]. The wind was blowing a good Force ten and we were running under the storm jib when really big waves started to come up from the south and hit *Suhaili* with stunning force. This was by far the worst weather I had ever encountered and the terrifying shudder and cracks every time a wave hit the hull convinced me that the boat would not last long. I did not see how anything could stand up to this sort of continual punishment. Water was coming into the boat as if out of a tap from leaks all round the coach-house I had never known before.

Knox-Johnston panicked a bit and thought of getting out his liferaft and a few supplies, abandoning his yacht, and drifting to Australia. He came to his senses, however, climbed on deck and began looking at the ocean to see if he could do something to minimize the beating the waves were giving *Suhali.*

There was a huge swell from the southwest plus a system of dying swells from the south. The ketch was lying beam-on to the large southwest swell. If the captain could get the yacht to present her stern to the southwest swell instead of her side she would perhaps stop taking such a terrific pounding and ride better. After some trial and error, Knox-Johnston found that if he streamed a very long floating line—600 feet of ⅝-inch diameter—in a U-shaped bight over the stern, the line would hold *Suhaili*'s stern nicely up into the wind. The ketch yawed back and forth a bit and snapped the storm jib from one side to the other, but the captain stopped this by centering the jib and pulling the sheets very tight. The sail steadied the little ship and the result was that even in a sustained Force ten storm the foredeck sometimes remained dry.

The self-steering began to get stiff and unresponsive, so the captain did a little hand steering to help out. "We were about 500 miles from Australia by this time," he wrote. "Although the weather had been rough and uncomfortable, progress had been excellent, and I was beginning to pick up local radio stations in Western Australia. This kept me abreast of the news and the Albany wool sales; every time I tuned in, it seemed, I picked up the latest market report, and after a few days I could have given anyone a full run-down on every aspect of them."

A few days later the self-steering gear broke again and various parts were lost in the sea. Knox-Johnston managed another marginal repair but this was clearly the last because there were simply no more parts. On October 25th, *Suhaili* sighted the Australian ship *Kooringa* and hoisted signal flags requesting that she send a radio signal to England. Captain Joseph Scott recognized the white double-ended ketch from newspaper publicity. He gave her a whistle blast and acknowledged the flag signal with an answering pennant. Knox-Johnston was overjoyed.

The weather in the southern spring improved and became quite balmy as *Suhaili* slowly sailed eastward toward Bass Strait, the 125-mile-wide waterway between Australia and Tasmania. Though the yacht was sixty miles south of the coast, a large butterfly fluttered on board and fascinated Knox-Johnston. The weather was pleasant and the captain thought about his suntan. Poor *Suhaili* continued to fall apart. On November 2nd the tiller head sheered off where it entered the rudder. Knox-Johnston managed to get the broken tiller head off and fitted the spare, but he was afraid to drive it on properly because the rudder bearings were worn and loose and any hammer blows might have weakened them further. He put lashings on the rudder to take some of the load from the bearings. The next day a key part of the self-steering gear sheared off and the important underwater parts disappeared into the sea.

What next? The engine was ruined by corrosion. The self-steering gear was gone. The water tanks were foul. The rudder didn't look too good. A jury gooseneck rig held the main boom to the mast and might go at any time. The cursed halyard winch brakes were so dangerous that the captain had to tie the handles in place. Two sails were finished. The radio transmitter was dead. Only half of his stove worked. In heavy weather the yacht leaked everywhere. Not only was the captain bruised and scarred from the voyage, but he was exhausted and fed up. Even his seaboots were falling to pieces. And ahead lay six thousand miles more of the Southern Ocean with Cape Horn at the end! "Come on God— give me a break" he wrote in his diary. "It's been nothing but calms or gales for weeks. How about some steady winds for a change?"

Suhaili had already set a record for the smallest yacht to have come so far without stopping. With the vessel in such abysmal condition Knox-Johnston certainly would have been justified in stopping at Melbourne. Besides, a soft, unmoving bed, a hot bath, a large steak, humans to talk to . . .

But no! *Suhaili* was leading the race. Maybe she could make it all the way around the world nonstop. Wouldn't that be something! He was already halfway and still ahead of the French. Why stop now? He'd never forgive himself if he did. The big problem was the self-steering. With the mechanical gear sprinkled across the bottom of the Southern Ocean the only way left was to somehow contrive a balance between the rudder and the various sails. Or if that wasn't possible, he could steer for sixteen hours a day and then stop the yacht while he slept—like the Argentine sailor Vito Dumas a quarter of a century earlier. Self-steering would be easier and infinitely less boring, however, so the captain began to experiment with the sails.

A little before midnight on November 6th, Knox-Johnston made his landfall in southeast Australia when he picked up the lighthouse signal on Cape Otway, seventy-five miles southwest of Port Phillip Heads, the entrance to Melbourne. Just after lunchtime on the following day, *Suhaili* arrived at Port Phillip Heads and sailed up close to the pilot vessel *Wyuna*. "I'm nonstop from the U.K.," shouted Knox-Johnston to a startled man on the bridge. "Will you please take my mail?"

The pilot vessel lowered a launch and the coxswain hurried to *Suhaili*. After 147 days on his own, Knox-Johnston passed a waterproof box with mail, films, track charts, and various writings to the coxswain. He also handed across a radio message for his family and friends in England. At ten minutes past four in the afternoon he waved goodbye to the pilot vessel, hardened in the sheets, and began tacking into the southwest wind to get back out into Bass Strait before night fell. He was not quitting. He was going on.

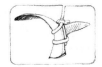

15. *South from Trindade*

ON NOVEMBER 7TH, THE SAME DAY that Robin Knox-
Johnston had watched the dark land mass of Australia
gradually recede behind Suhaili's port quarter, Nigel Tetley
hurried toward the Cape of Good Hope in the South Atlantic
on his big blue and white trimaran. Three days earlier, Tetley
had photographed himself on Victress's port foredeck with the
rocky mass of Ilha Trindade only a mile or so in the distance.
Moitessier had slipped past the same island thirty-five days earlier and was far ahead in the Indian Ocean. Tetley was sailing a
little faster now, however, and began to make up time on the
leaders because the trimaran was getting lighter and was more
responsive to weight changes.

The passage through the 1400 miles of the southeast trades
north of Ilha Trindade had taken ten days. *Victress* had headed
a little west of due south, closed-hauled on the port tack. The
winds had been remarkably steady between twelve and fifteen
knots. The yacht sailed well, but Tetley worried about the water
that he had found in the forward compartments of the trimaran's port and starboard floats. Thirty gallons in one two-day
period was not too good. The captain was able to pump out the
water quickly enough, but there should have been no leaks at all
in these easy waters. After the radio stations in England had faded
out, Tetley tried to speak to Cape Town, but although he tried
a dozen times he was unable to make contact. He eased his
uncertainties by listening to music—Irish ballads, Boccherini,
Delius, and Beethoven's *Eroica*.

As mentioned earlier a through-hull fitting had gradually corroded away and one morning Tetley discovered water flooding in. He bunged the hole with a cork and pumped out the water. The engine was partly submerged and the starter motor was flooded with salt water. After a few days, Tetley managed to get the starter going and the engine working, but then he noticed something wrong with the stern gear or propeller. One calm afternoon the captain dived over the side into the tropical water and found that both the propeller and the bracket for the propeller shaft were broken. While he nervously watched for sharks, Tetley removed the stern bracket and damaged propeller and fitted a spare propeller, a big job at sea. Without a bracket to support the propeller shaft the engine could only be used at low revolutions. In truth, the engine was finished.

Machinery at sea is troublesome to maintain on a long voyage. The constant enemies are corrosion from salt air and salt water and long periods of inattention. Almost no marine engine on a sailing yacht ever wears out; its innards get destroyed by corrosion. King and Moitessier—the old sea dogs in the race—preferred to sail with no engines at all. Knox-Johnston and Tetley had nothing but trouble, and might as well not have had engines considering the amount of annoyance and complication. In addition the machinery was heavy, took up space, and was costly. The drag of the propeller was another factor. Knox-Johnston and Tetley would have been better off to have taken their engines apart piece by piece and to have tossed the scraps over the side. Knox-Johnston, Tetley, and Crowhurst all needed to generate electricity for their big radios. Knox-Johnston and Tetley carried small air-cooled gasoline engine driven generators; Crowhurst had a large inboard diesel generator that suffered greatly from salt water.

Now on November 8th, Tetley was in the southern horse latitudes, or variables, which lay between twenty-three and forty degrees south. Both the variables and the doldrums are difficult for sailors because the wind often blows from one direction for a few hours, dies away, and then starts up from a new point on the compass. You get the vessel going nicely, spend half an hour trimming the sails and adjusting the vane and various lines, make good time toward your target for two hours, and then the wind collapses to a whisper and stops. The next morning the wind is blowing from the opposite direction with whitecaps in the water. Seas begin to build up. By the time you reef and get going again, the wind has faded away to a breeze that barely ruffles the water. . . . Sailors find the variables and doldrums two whirlpools of frustration.

Tetley was two thousand miles west-northwest of the southern tip of Africa. A fresh wind from the north pushed *Victress* directly toward Cape Town. The next day the wind dropped, rain came, and the wind swung around to the southwest. Then came calms, followed by light airs from the southeast. The daily run on November 11th was a miserable twenty-four miles—not all in the right direction. By evening, however, a fair wind pushed hard against Tetley's sails.

"I ate the last of the apples," wrote the captain, hoping that the steady wind would last. "The stock had kept very well considering the heat in the tropics: only two or three had gone rotten. The oranges have ripened nicely and are now in perfect condition. Eggs are down to half a dozen, but there are sufficient fresh onions for a month."

On November 16th, Tetley had been at sea for two months— some sixty days of solitude. Except for the radio problems, he was in good spirits and generally pleased, particularly after three days of fair winds during which he logged 500 miles toward the tip of Africa. In the evening the wind died. It was suddenly calm. Tetley was in a reflective mood.

"Two months at sea!" he wrote in the ship's logbook. "I now feel I have settled down, if that is the word, and [have] become conditioned to a solitary existence. This way of life no longer strikes me as novel or strange; the days go by more or less on a framework of routine. This is through necessity; I could give it all up gladly. I do not think Eve will find me much changed when it is all over.

Victress has traveled 6,100 miles along the clipper route, less than a quarter of the total distance, so far [said Tetley]. But having reached the region of stronger winds, and the yacht being that much lighter, I anticipate a significant improvement in the average daily run. Working to a target of 120 miles a day, the trimaran is twelve days behind at this point; but barring some misfortune, I believe most of this can be made up over the next three months. *Victress* herself has given me little cause for worry. Bits [of trim] have dropped off her, it is true, leaks have developed, a mast stay has parted, but such minor troubles are to be expected. She is an excellent sea-boat; the self-steering works effectively and, from the sailing point of view, she is a very easy craft to handle."

The next day Tetley checked the bilges in the floats. The port float had ten gallons of sea water in it—not too bad—but the starboard float had seventy gallons; *Victress* was carrying almost 700 pounds of extra weight! Tetley worried about the continual leaks so while the wind was light and the sea calm he cleared the stored gear from the floats and cut limber holes in the various compartments so all the water would drain to a central place in each float. He then ran a bilge hose from each float into the main hull and pumps so he could handle any bilge water from a convenient, protected position. All this was a tedious job at sea, but the captain felt that he had made a major improvement to safety. With the stormy Southern Ocean and the roaring forties ahead who knew when there would be another chance to do such work?

Tetley used his spare hours to read a book called *Lord of the Flies* by William Golding, a somewhat morbid bestseller (1962) about the behavior and savage decline of a gang of young boys on a remote island. "Whether or not . . . my emotions have grown more responsive through solitude, they have been well and truly wrung by this tale," wrote Tetley.

During the afternoons when the wind was light and *Victress* slowly glided along, the captain often sat on deck in the sun, listening to the tinkling piano refrains of Chopin and watching the birds. Now on the fringes of forty degrees south, there was usually an albatross and a petrel or two circling the trimaran. The black-and-white-checked pintado petrel (or cape pigeon) had a wingspan of two feet or so—long narrow wings with pointed tips. It was a fast flyer that went around the yacht quickly in small circles, sometimes coming in close for a look or occasionally landing on the water alongside.

On November 19th, Tetley finally made radio contact with Cape Town on 17 megacycles. He was immensely relieved to get a message off to his wife and the newspapers. He was concerned that his long radio silence had caused fears in England. When people expected you to call on schedule and you weren't heard, there was a nagging uncertainty all around. In many ways it was easier on everyone not to have a radio and schedules on such ventures.

The weather grew cooler and Tetley began to put on warmer clothing and to think of sweaters and long underwear. The main battery charger had given out weeks before. Tetley had been using a spare, but now it developed problems as well. Fortunately, the captain was able to get the spare charger working again. He had some anxious moments, however, because no battery power meant no radio communication and no electric lights.

Tetley became aware of increased activity in the cooler ocean. One morning he found two twelve-inch squid on deck. There were more sea birds and he sighted two sperm whales. A radio exchange with Cape Town on November 21st brought the news that Bill King had been rolled over in a severe storm near Gough island and was out of the race. King had been towed into Cape Town three days earlier. Robin Knox-Johnston was reported to be in some sort of trouble off New Zealand. What would happen next? Who was left?

As Tetley neared the Cape of Good Hope, the winds continued light and fitful—even in the same area where Knox-Johnston had met his big storm. When it rained, the temperature sometimes dropped surprisingly and the captain began to wear his polar suit. He felt quite mellow and content and on November 22nd he wrote: "While in the trade winds I had often towed a fishing line and spoon astern hoping for a tuna or bonito. Now, when I saw a small tuna jump near by, I left the fishing line in its box: I felt too much at peace with all God's creatures."

Because of the north-flowing current up the west coast of Africa, Tetley was careful not to aim for the continent itself but a little to the south. When possible, therefore, he steered south or southeast. The winds remained erratic and the sea calm with fog and light drizzle. If the sun appeared for a few minutes, Tetley hurred out on deck with his sextant for a celestial observation.

He had plenty of sail drill in the fluky winds. One day he broke a spinnaker pole when lowering a poled-out jib. He was anxious not to use his two three-hundred-square-foot headsails for running in the Southern Ocean because these large sails were unmanageable in strong winds. Nevertheless in winds under fifteen knots he needed both these sails and more. The problem was running in light winds that increased rapidly. "Leaving a lot of sail up is like playing with dynamite," said Tetley, "and yet, I will have to learn to do just that to get anywhere in the race."

The captain of *Victress* began to get moody and depressed and didn't feel well. "The further I go, the madder this race seems," he wrote on November 27th. "An almost overwhelming temptation to retire and head for Cape Town is growing inside me. The cold finger of reason points constantly in that direction."

Tetley thought that his melancholy outlook might be due to missing nutrients in his diet. He looked at Eve's food recommendation sheet and began to take a daily drink made from dried milk, dried cream, vitamins, yeast, and fruit juice. He reported that he felt better and claimed that his depression vanished in a few days. Cape Town radio informed him that Alex Carozzo had been forced into Lisbon by illness. Moitessier was making the best time and was three weeks ahead of *Victress*. Tetley decided to drive his vessel a lot harder.

Though the trimaran was almost even with the Cape of Good Hope, the winds were light and sporadic. The barometer began to fall, however, and there was an ominous ring of heavy cirrus clouds around the sun that suggested a storm was coming. While it was still calm, the resourceful Tetley made a replacement spinnaker pole from a spare aluminum tube he had on board. Being a sailor in such a race wasn't enough; one needed to be an inventor, an engineer, a mechanic, and a squirrel who kept endless spare parts hidden in a burrow somewhere. On December 1st, the following day, Tetley's sun sights and calculations confirmed that he was east of the tip of Africa, which lay 300 miles to the north. Now it was the Indian Ocean and the roaring forties. Sure enough by the next morning the first gale was shrieking out of the northwest.

16. *Across the Indian Ocean*

LONG-DISTANCE SAILORS WITH AN EYE ON THE PAST often speak of the *Southern Ocean,* but today you seldom find mention of this great sea in encyclopedias. Indeed it's rare to discover the Southern Ocean on a map or in a world atlas. Yet the boundaries are simplicity itself: the Southern Ocean is the great world of water below forty degrees south latitude that runs around the planet south of the continents of Africa, Australia, and South America. The southern boundary is the ice cap of Antarctica.

The Southern Ocean includes:

The South Atlantic—85° of longitude or 3,619 miles from Cape Horn to the Cape of Good Hope (measured along 45°S.)

The Indian Ocean—120° of longitude or 6,034 miles from the Cape of Good Hope to Tasmania (measured along 39°S.)

The South Pacific—146° of longitude or 5,652 miles from Tasmania to Cape Horn (measured along 50°S.)

The islands of Bouvet, Kerguelen, McDonald, Heard, Macquarie, Auckland, Campbell, Diego Ramirez, South Georgia, South Sandwich, and so forth—all remote, obscure, and mostly uninhabited except for birds, penguins, and seals.

The Southern Ocean is really an anachronism, a term that dates from the days of square-rigged sailing ships, when captains ran down their easting in the high latitudes where the west winds and east-setting currents were strong and the diameter of the earth was less. In the days of wind ships the Southern Ocean was the fastest and most direct way to get around the world. The weather was often severe, and ice was a hazard; celestial navigation was chancy with overcast skies and uncertain chronometers. The ships were sometimes leaky and short of supplies, but the men pushed on anyway and usually made it back home where they laughed about it all. Now a century later the big wind ships were gone. The Southern Ocean remained the same treacherous place, however, patrolled only by the birds and the whales.

October 24th was Bernard Moitessier's sixty-third day at sea and he headed south–southwest to get away from the dangerous swells stirred up by the wind and converging currents near the Cape of Good Hope. As Africa fell astern, the French sailor calculated that he had logged 7,882 miles from Plymouth, England, one-quarter of the total distance of the race. Almost twenty-four thousand miles lay ahead as he pushed ahead into the Indian Ocean.

Moitessier was still mentally and physically weary from the strain of getting past Africa after the terrible collision with the freighter and the bent bowsprit. In truth, it was a miracle that *Joshua* was still in one piece and fit for the race. At the moment the steel ketch was fully reefed and plowing along at six knots before a fresh westerly wind. Moitessier could have changed up to larger headsails from the tiny jib and staysail and picked up another 15 per cent in speed. He was exhausted, however, and realized that he needed food and rest.

"My motions were clumsy and inefficient [last night]," he wrote. "It took me three times longer than usual to secure gaskets and reef points. And my reflexes were dangerously slow: somehow, I got caught with water up to my knees at the end of the bowsprit, without having seen it coming. The mounting fatigue and under-nourishment of these last days may be to blame."

In the evening the wind eased off. The captain hoisted more sail and *Joshua* hurried through the night. At noon the next day, Moitessier had logged 164 miles and had reached the latitude of forty degrees south, seventy miles into the iceberg zone. Now he believed that he was well clear of the problems off the Cape of Good Hope, so the French sailor steered northwest to get away from the ice dangers. His general strategy was to sail roughly eastward, but because of first the current and then the ice, the captain had elected zigzag tactics. Finally the route ahead was clear all the way to Australia.

The sky was decorated with fair-weather cumulus clouds that alternated with patches of blue. The pointer on the barometer hadn't moved for hours and the wind stayed at about twenty-five knots from the west–northwest. Big seas rolled up past *Joshua* in a steady procession. Moitessier had spent most of the last two nights in the cockpit drinking coffee and smoking cigarettes. On the first night he had worried about the sea conditions; on the second was the danger of icebergs—marked by an ominous dotted red line on the pilot chart. In spite of his tiredness, the captain was exhilarated.

"I wonder if my apparent lack of fatigue could be a kind of hypnotic trance born of contact with this great sea, giving off so many pure forces, rustling with the ghosts of all the beautiful sailing ships that died around here and now escort us?" wrote Moitessier. "I am full of life, like the sea I contemplate so intensely. I feel it watching me as well and that we are friends."

A lone sailor at sea needs to be as cautious as a cat crossing an alley patrolled by fierce dogs. Danger is on every side, yet the path down the middle is safe. If he lets his guard down or becomes careless he is liable to get into trouble that lurks only an eyelash away.

A seaman's best defense is routine, *the ship's routine.* The same way of doing each action, practiced until the behavior is almost automatic. He hoists a sail from a certain position. He belays a reefing pendant on a special cleat. He ties a bowline, a clove hitch, a reef knot, or a sheet bend with the same practiced motions. He holds on to a lifeline or a grab rail with one hand as he goes forward. He coils lines clockwise and puts each coil away in an orderly manner. His oilskins hang on the same hook. The winch handle is stored in a favorite place. His hand closes easily around his knife in a certain pocket. The sailor uses the same line for the same job week after week and becomes friendly with that certain well-worn three-strand line with the blue thread. The hauling part of the main halyard goes on the starboard side of the mast; the jib halyard lives to port. And so on. His routine, his practiced certainty, is the sailor's protection from danger. His actions all have a marvelous, essential simplicity.

The sailor is intensely conservative. He will change from his practiced routine, but only if the new way can be demonstrated to be better—infallibly better. He has a preferred way of doing each thing. If something fails he has a second scheme, and then a third, each carried out in methodical order. The seaman checks and rechecks in a patient, logical manner—probing, trying, testing. He is not perfect, of course, but the best sailors are orderly and deliberate. Sloppiness has no place on board.

Each sea-going vessel is different; nevertheless the sail and anchor handling are standardized to a surprising degree and a seaman can move easily from one yacht to another.

Sometimes when a sailor is tired he tries to deviate from the routine he has established. This almost never works. Moitessier took a noon sight of the sun. Instead of stowing his sextant in its box below in the usual safe place, he thought he could save a trip, so he put the boxed sextant in the cockpit for a few moments while he adjusted the sails. Just then a large sea broke on board, filled the cockpit, and almost washed the sextant overboard. Moitessier managed to grab the sextant before it floated away, but he was obliged to spend hours cleaning and drying the precious instrument and its box. So much for departing from a well-established routine!

After the sextant episode an enormous breaking sea hammered into *Joshua*'s port side and rolled the yacht far over to starboard; the yacht was knocked flat for a few moments before her ballast keel rolled her back upright. From the impact of the sea and the crashing noise Moitessier thought that all the portlights on the starboard side had been smashed when the ship was slammed downward.* Fortunately the portlights were okay. The vessel wound up headed into the wind with her sails flap-

---

*As Adlard Coles has pointed out, the damage is seldom on the side of the breaking sea but on the downside—the lee side—where the water is as solid and unyielding as a concrete blockhouse.

ping and the wind vane blade broken. Moitessier got back on course, fitted a spare wind blade, and replaced the mizzen boom preventer line.*

During the big roll, the poor sextant—undergoing drying out—was hurled from the port berth to the starboard berth. "Poor little pal," noted Moitessier, "if this hasn't done you in, there really is a guardian angel for sextants, and morons too. First I leave it in the cockpit, then on the *windward* berth. . . . It took an eight foot free fall through the cabin when *Joshua* went over."

An hour later *Joshua* was knocked down again. The wind had moderated to twenty knots or so. "The sea had become strange, with peaceful areas where it was very heavy, yet regular, with no dangerous breaking waves," wrote Moitessier. "In those areas I could have walked blindfolded twenty times around the deck. Then, without any transition, it would turn jerky and rough; high cross-seas overlapped to provoke sometimes very powerful breaking waves. It was probably one of these cross-seas that hit us earlier. Then *Joshua* would again find herself in a quiet area for ten minutes or more, followed by another rough one."

The flow of water around the Cape of Good Hope was a confused mess. The warm southwest-flowing Agulhas current running up to five knots along the *west* coast of Africa collided with the cold northwest-flowing Benguela current going up the *east* coast. Some of the Benguela current came from a northwesterly diversion of the east-flowing current of the Southern Ocean. The meeting of these huge masses of water of different temperatures, salinities, speeds, and directions churned the ocean into confusion and uncertainty. When strong winds blew across these upset seas the sailing conditions became unpredictable and horrible. The best thing was to get away from the southern tip of Africa as quickly as possible.

Once again—in only twenty-five knots of wind—*Joshua* got

---

* A *preventer* is a line from the end of a boom taken forward to a strong point to keep the boom under control (particularly when running). The preventer line also helps to stop chafe. In *Joshua*'s case the preventer line on the mizzen boom kept the boom from striking the steering vane blade if the yacht gybed or if the yacht was rolling about in light airs.

knocked down and her mast and sails and spreaders shoved into
the sea by an exceptionally high overtaking wave. This one did
not break but picked up the steel ketch and scooted her forward
and down. It was almost as if a giant's thumb had pushed on her
coachroof and had pressed the yacht down into the water for
four or five seconds. The mast and sails and rigging held.
Moitessier had seen the wave coming and embraced the chart
table with a death grip until the yacht righted herself.

Finally on October 26th, the next day, *Joshua* got away from
the upset seas. The Indian Ocean weather turned fair. The captain relaxed, cooked himself huge meals (fish soup with rice and
butter), and slept and slept. The daily runs totaled 117 miles and
then 68 in calms and light airs. It was time for sail sewing and
dealing with worn places on the staysail and mizzen halyards.
While the yacht drifted slowly eastward she was festooned with
damp sweaters and trousers and blankets drying in the sun.
(Moitessier noted that flapping and furious shaking and brush-
ing loosens and drives out the salt crystals.) The wind came back
on October 28th and the ketch made a marvelous noon-to-noon
run of 188 miles.

Moitessier thought of the enormity of the challenge of trying
to sail around the world alone. It was madness, impossible, much
too much for anyone. You had to work into it little by little. It
was like when he had built *Joshua*. In the beginning the project
was too big to even think about. He had put the whole building
job out of his mind and had concentrated only on an immediate
detail—one frame, one steel plate, one deck fitting. A single step
at a time. The rest would follow. Sailing around the world was
the same. No one could do it at the start but had to work into
the project with faith, hope, and patience.

The first gale came on October 30th. The wind rose to a little
less than forty knots, but the storm blew from the southeast and
was hardly worth slamming into. Moitessier hove to under
reduced sail. By the following morning the wind had veered to
the northeast and finally to the northwest before dropping away
to nothing. First the seas were steep, then white-streaked and
choppy as the sky cleared and the barometer climbed. The
Frenchman rested and read in his bunk. He wondered about the

other contestants in the race and was disappointed that neither Radio Cape Town nor the BBC had any news. Moitessier often thought of his sailing friends with affection.

Was Loïck Fougeron growing his seeds in the plastic saucers the two sailors had bought together in Plymouth? "Very easy: you take seven saucers, punch a few holes in them, and line them with cloth," wrote Moitessier.

Fill with wheat grains, soybeans, and watercress seeds. Stack them one on top of the other, and moisten with a little water. After a few days, the sprouts are long enough. Remove the bottom saucer, and boil the sprouts or make a salad. Refill the saucer with fresh seeds, put it on top of the pile and sprinkle; next day, remove the bottom saucer, eat the sprouts, refill with seeds, put it on top, sprinkle, etc. and you have perpetual motion!

Nigel [Tetley] laughed at our germination experiments" said Moitessier. "He thought we were going to a lot of trouble for nothing, and he was probably right. Where is Nigel? How far will he get with his trimaran? And Bill King, where is he? Perhaps far ahead, perhaps behind if he got hung up in the doldrums. . . . It is surprising that I did not hear about anyone on the BBC or elsewhere, since Bill and Nigel have weekly radio contact with their sponsoring newspapers. Maybe they just chucked it . . . transmitter, batteries, heave-ho!—the whole bloody lot overboard, for a little peace and quiet.

Soon a quarter of the Indian Ocean lay behind *Joshua*. The birds fascinated Moitessier. Not solitary fliers or half a dozen, but *hundreds* of birds. There were the two albatrosses, the colossal wandering albatross with its twelve-foot wingspan, thick downy covering, and commanding performance. There was the six-foot black-browed albatross ("All display an attractive almond-shaped pattern around the eye, like a vamp's make-up.") Next came the small black-and-white-checked cape pigeon or pintado petrel. The French captain watched chocolate-brown shearwaters that glided along in teams of eight to fifteen with hardly a flap of their slender, high-aspect wings. There were the diminutive, scampering, butterfly-like black and white storm petrels. And hundreds of unidentified tiny birds the size of robins with silvery plumage, white undersides, dark grey tails, and a big W on top of their wings (perhaps Wilson's storm petrels, a second variety).

Fresh water was a nagging problem for the round-the-world sailors. Moitessier needed two liters of water a day. His tank held 400 liters and was still half full, so he had enough for more than three months. One night rain fell steadily and rinsed the sails. Moitessier added forty liters to the tank, a bit of a relief because *Joshua* had sailed through very little rain since the Canary Islands two months earlier.

The French captain felt tired. He had lost a few pounds and was a bit underweight so he began taking vitamin B complex tablets. He made an effort to cook better meals and began to exercise regularly.

Onward across the Indian Ocean he went, taking in reefs, shaking them out, and putting them in again, as the winds from the west rose and fell with the passage of the east-going weather systems. As he crossed the Indian Ocean, the French captain thought of the beautiful tropical islands far to the north. He recalled the three years he had spent on Mauritius and all his friends there. Was he mad not to head north at once and to forget the race, this stupid chase around the world?

During the first seventeen days of November, *Joshua* logged 2,114 miles, an average of 124 miles every twenty-four hours. But the average masked a phenomenal run of 183 miles on November 14th and nothing at all on the tenth and eleventh when Moitessier hove to because of adverse winds. Now *Joshua* was nearly halfway between the Cape of Good Hope and Tasmania. The captain drew a long line on the little world globe he carried to mark his progress.

On November 17th Moitessier ate the last of the 100 grapefruit he had put aboard in England. In three months only five or six had gone bad. The garlic was keeping perfectly and the lemons—each wrapped in paper—were good too. The little purple Morocco onions were in excellent shape; a few had sprouted but Moitessier plucked off the sprouts and put them in his rice. The big white onions were all rotten, however, and the captain heaved the whole bag into the sea.

Now, like Vito Dumas, the Argentine singlehander who had come this way in *Lehg II* in 1942—26 years earlier—Moitessier was becalmed. *Joshua* drifted slowly eastward in the grip of the current of the Southern Ocean. When you sail on the sea during a brisk wind the surface is upset by waves and swells. The world beneath is lost. It's only during calms that you begin to get an idea of the teeming life under the surface.

Absolutely flat calm [wrote Moitessier]. Sunshine everywhere, above and below. Filling a bucket with water for the dishes, I noticed that the sea is covered with plankton. It is made up of tiny animals smaller than pinheads, zig-zagging along the calm water. Scooped along the surface, the bucket harvests a good hundred of the living mites; a foot or so deeper it only brings up three or four.

There is also a carpet of pretty, flat jellyfish the size of a penny, that I do not recognize, and a few Portuguese men-o'-war, lovely in the sunlight. They look like blue-tinted oval balloons.

The calm and quiet gave the French captain time to rest and to reflect on his early days: "When I was a child, my mother told me God had painted the sky blue because blue is the color of hope," he wrote. "God must have painted the sea blue for the same reason."

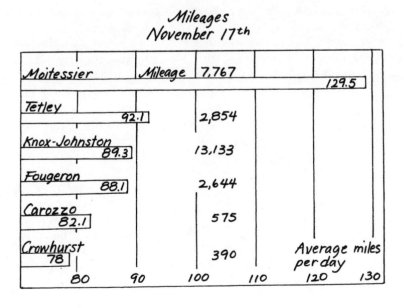

Mileages
November 17th

	Mileage		Average miles per day
Moitessier	Mileage	7,767	129.5
Tetley		2,854	92.1
Knox-Johnston		13,133	89.3
Fougeron		2,644	88.1
Carozzo		575	82.1
Crowhurst		390	78

The wind finally returned; Joshua was soon sailing fast on a flat sea. Moitessier added sail after sail and eventually flew eight sails that totaled 1075 square feet "I gaze at my boat from the top of the mainmast," he noted.

Her strength, her beauty, her white sails well set on a well found boat. The foam, the wake, the eleven porpoises on either side of the bowsprit. They are black and white porpoises, the most beautiful I know. They breathe on the fly, almost without breaking the surface, without wavering from the course, towing *Joshua* at nearly 8 knots by invisible bonds. Climbing down to fetch the Beaulieu [camera] is out of the question. I would lose everything, and what they give me is too precious; a lens would spoil it all. They leave without my touching them, but the bonds remain.

The albatrosses, malamocks, and shearwaters flew round and round *Joshua* as she surged eastward with the new wind. Light rain alternated with a hot sun; with each rain, the captain bucketed a few gallons of water into the tank. He listened to the radio in vain for news of the round-the-world race.

Moitessier was born in Saigon of a French colonial family and now as he twisted the radio dial he turned to programs from Vietnam. After twenty years away from his native land, however, he was barely able to understand the language that he had spoken as a child and young man. He thought of the native junks he had once sailed and the fifteen to twenty-five tons of rice he had taken from Cochin-China to Cambodia. Then back to Rach-Gia with a load of wood or palm sugar. Lug-rigged with stayed masts that held fan-shaped sails of woven palm fronds. But the chafe on the rig was terrible and the sails and sheets were forever sawing themselves to bits.

From November 18th to the 24th, *Joshua* logged another 1,064 miles, a superb run. If we surmise that the east-running current ran at 1.5 knots, however, then 252 of those miles or about 24 percent of the total was due to natural causes in the Southern Ocean. During the week, Moitessier collected another sixteen gallons of fresh water. Then as he neared the edge of an atmospheric high pressure area that reached westward from Australia, the wind dwindled and stopped. *Joshua* drifted slowly toward southwest Australia while birds landed around the red ketch. A dozen, then more. Soon there were sixty shearwaters. Moitessier fed them cheese, butter, and paté, which they relished, scrapped over, and deviously stole from one another. The French captain watched the birds closely. They became almost tame and Moitessier felt a great kinship with these wild, feathered sailors of the Southern Ocean.

The wind returned and blew steadily once again. *Joshua* crossed the 113th meridian of east longitude. Now the French entry was south of Cape Leeuwin at the southwest corner of Australia. The plan was to sail south of this great land that measures 1,680 miles from top to bottom and 2,160 miles from west to east. Moitessier wanted to give word of his progress to a fisherman or a ship in Bass Strait, the 110-mile-wide waterway between the southeast corner of Australia and Tasmania, the island to the south. In truth the captain was leery of another encounter with a ship after his disastrous collision off the Cape of Good Hope. But he wanted to let his family and friends know that all was well. During the long calm Moitessier had built two little model sailboats. Now he put letters on board and launched them.*

The wind remained fair and *Joshua* made runs that averaged better than 165 miles a day. The sky was full of signs of weather disturbances, but they didn't come. The southwest swell remained constant. Moitessier thought of his early sailing days:

> When I was sailing with the fishermen of the Gulf of Siam during my childhood in Indochina, the taïcong would tell me, for example, "Keep the swell two fingers off the quarter, and you should always feel the wind behind your left ear, looking forward. When the moon is one big hand plus a small hand from the horizon, or when that star is one arm from the other side (in case the moon is hidden by a cloud) then the sea will become a little more phosphorescent, and we will almost be in the lee of the island to set the first lines."
>
> There were no compasses on the Gulf of Siam junks, and I did not want it used during my sailing school cruises in the Mediterranean. Instead of bearing 110° from France to Corsica my crew had to steer

---

*Both models were found more than a year later. One on a beach in Tasmania and the other in New Zealand. The letters arrived intact.

with the *mistral* swell very slightly off the port quarter. At night, it was the Pole Star one small hand abaft the port beam, And if there was neither distinct swell nor star, we made do with whatever we had. I wanted it that way, because concentrating on a magnetized needle prevents one from participating in the real universe, seen and unseen, where a sailboat moves.

In the beginning [my students] could not understand my insistence on getting away from the compass, that god of the West. But in exchange, they began to hear the sky and sea talking with the boat. And when blue-tinted land appeared on the horizon, looking as it did to the mariners of old, all nimbed with mystery, a few of them felt that our rigorous techniques should leave a door open to those gods which the modern world tries so hard to exclude.

Cape Leeuwin lay far astern. Bass Strait was ahead in the distance, but the area was full of rocks and problems. The French captain decided to skip Bass Strait entirely and to go south of Tasmania. On the night when *Joshua* started her fifth month at sea it began to rain and the captain soon collected enough drinking water to last until the Atlantic doldrums.

Moitessier reached the mouth of the D'Entrecasteaux Channel in Tasmania before dawn one week before Christmas. The weather was squally. There was a new moon, but the sliver of light was scarcely enough to illuminate the dark sea. The Frenchman stopped his ketch by backing the staysail. In the morning he spotted a fishing boat in the distance and signaled to her with a mirror. The boat motored alongside and stopped thirty yards off. In it were Varley Wisby and his two sons from Launceston.

Moitessier passed his films and letters to Wisby who said he would give them to the commodore of the Hobart yacht club. Did the Wisbys have any news of the round-the-world solo race? Had any of the sailors passed this way? One of the men had heard something about an English yachtsmen who had rounded New Zealand without stopping. The fisherman was uncertain, however, of the man's name or the date. The crews of the two vessels chatted for a few minutes and then parted, one resuming fishing and the other an endless course eastward.

Tasmania and the sea around it seemed colored an enameled

green. Everything was green. The land, the sea, and the wake of the ship all reflected a marvelous, incredible green. Only little by little as the land slipped astern did the green fade and turn to the familiar blue. Ahead lay the mighty Pacific.

When the news of Moitessier reached England, excited murmurs of surprise rippled through sporting circles. Knox-Johnston had told his sponsor that he expected to round Cape Horn during the first week in January. This would put him back in England about April 10th. However Moitessier was picking up thirty miles a day on Knox-Johnston. It looked like a close contest.

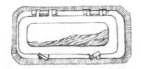

17. *The Documented Liar*

Of the four men still in the race, Donald Crowhurst was in last place. On December 10th, after forty-one days at sea, his Victress trimaran *Teignmouth Electron* was 240 miles south of the Cape Verde islands off the bulge of West Africa, roughly 2,800 miles from England. He had been averaging about 68 miles per day, a long way from the 220 miles he had once hoped to achieve on a daily basis.

Crowhurst had been sailing fairly well in a southerly direction with the steady northeast trade wind behind him. However, instead of concentrating on sailing, navigation, eating, and resting as a solo sailor should, he had been spending a lot of time on fraudulent logbook entries, the first of which claimed a record run of 243 miles on December 8th. He had radioed his claim to England where it was duly reported and published. Both Sir Francis Chichester and the navigational consultant for the race, Captain Craig Rich, were surprised at such a fast daily run. The average mileage of the other contestants had been remarkably consistent; Crowhurst's daily runs, by contrast, were erratic and suggested problems other than weather. Whatever was going on aboard *Teignmouth Electron?*

Crowhurst was evidently ashamed of his progress so he decided to give a boost to his ego and to reassure his backers by showing that he could sail fast and still had a chance to win the race. His true course was roughly south with the northeast trade wind blowing across his port quarter. Crowhurst began preparing a series of bogus positions. In order to do this and to keep an accurate series of navigational fixes and noon positions in his logbook he had to invent a series of fake sunsights. Normally a navigator works from a sextant angle of the sun at a certain moment of Greenwich time. He enters the figures in the Nautical Almanac and navigational tables to get a *calculated* sextant angle, which he compares with his *observed* sextant angle. He then establishes his location somewhere along a position line.

Crowhurst, however, had to work *backwards*. That is, from a bogus position he worked out a phony dead reckoning latitude and longitude, an ersatz intercept, false calculated and true sextant angles, and all the rest. Doing this sort of mental hocus-pocus while rolling around at sea is extremely difficult; yet the brainy Crowhurst worked it all out and wrote down the final figures in his falsified logbook.

He knew the previous record for a twenty-four-hour run by a singlehander was 220 miles so he exceeded it by just 23 miles. He added various details to round out the deception ("Boom guy parts, and jib pole folded up on shrouds".)*

You get the feeling from all this that Crowhurst was a character in a novel that had come to life. A fictional deception that had burst onto a nonfiction scene. A piece of brass in an iron world. We know that in a seaman's day almost every moment is documented. Crowhurst was a fraud who now invented his own documentation. Henceforth his whole existence became one of tragic make-believe. The truth was somehow unfair; therefore it had to be bypassed.

The trouble with lying is that once you begin a deception you create a monster that can hardly be stopped without destroying yourself. In order to protect himself a liar must constantly compound his falsehoods. He needs a phenomenal memory. Eventually he becomes so involved in deceit that his false tower crashes to the ground. The only uncertainties are how high the tower will climb and how long it will stand. Few people have compas-

---

*If a boom guy parted while running with a favorable wind, the pole might fold up and break if it slammed against a headstay. This is unlikely, however, because only the tip portion would strike the headstay. A pole generally breaks by being winched aft against the shrouds.

sion for liars; the pity is reserved for the innocent who are caught up and victimized. The round-the-world race was so unique, the sailing demands so unusual, and the physical and mental requirements so daunting that no one dreamed that any of the contestants would attempt to cheat. Indeed the men out there had so much to do that there was no time to cheat. Or was there?

On Thursday, December 12th, Crowhurst began to keep a new logbook of his actual progress. He used a large blue exercise book into which he entered his courses, the winds, mileages, sail changes, and so forth. In case he were to continue with his fraudulent logbook he would need a *true* logbook from which to work.

As Crowhurst's biographers point out, however, faking a one-day speed record is very different from faking an entire round-the-world voyage. It had taken Crowhurst hours to falsify his logbook when he claimed the one-day record run on December 8th. If he were to counterfeit his entire voyage he would need the creative abilities of a Tolstoy plus the navigational background of a Sir Francis Chichester. How could Crowhurst possibly know the weather off the Cape of Good Hope or New Zealand or Cape Horn at some date in the future? How would he explain his failure to be sighted? Or worse yet, suppose after radioing a spurious position he was seen and reported elsewhere by a ship? What if he—as a monstrous thought grew in his brain—what if he returned to England before the others after marking time in the solitary backwaters of the South Atlantic? Suppose he sent false messages from time to time to suggest that he had rounded South Africa, that he was near Australia, and that he was passing Cape Horn? In each case he could arrange his progress to indicate that he was gaining on the leaders and finally had passed into the lead. He would arrive home ahead of the others and be the winner!

Could he pull off the radio and television interviews, the speeches at the banquets, and the yarning with other sailors without tripping himself up? He would need the skill of a Shakespeare repertory actor and the factual grasp of an encyclopedia editor.

To phony up a logbook was one thing. To be a false national

hero was quite another. The humiliation of exposure could be disastrous. What would his friends say? How could he face his wife and his children? He would be denounced as a hoax and a fraud and a humbug. Yet the scheme was unique and had a certain fascination.

Crowhurst was full of indecision. He was like a child running back and forth on a teeter-totter, not sure which way to go. He considered three choices:

1. The round-the-world deception was tempting and a possible way out, but the problems were horrendous.

2. He could simply withdraw from the race. By doing this he would admit failure. His sponsor, Mr. Best, had the right to demand that Crowhurst buy back the yacht, which would mean bankruptcy. This might not happen, but it could.

3. He could continue in the race and get down to the business of necessary repairs and honest sailing. If he were the last to finish at least he would complete the competition honorably.

Instead of making a choice, Crowhurst tried to juggle all three options. He postponed what should have been a simple decision of right and wrong. He was weak and vacillating and seemed almost afraid.

On an Admiralty planning chart he began to sketch a schedule for a false voyage:

DATE	FALSE POSITION	TRUE POSITION
December 18th	3° south of the equator	2°N
December 22nd	10°S; off NE Brazil	2°S
December 24th	15°S; NE of Rio de Janeiro	6°S
January 5th	35°S; between Buenos Aires and Cape Town.	17°S
January 15th	42°S; 12°W; SE of Gough Island in the roaring 40's	22°S; 33°W

Crowhurst studied the pilot book for Brazil in case he decided to withdraw from the race. He made a detailed sketch chart for Rio de Janeiro just as he had done earlier for Funchal, Madeira.

If he continued around the world he would need to make a number of repairs. Crowhurst wrote out a list of sixteen projects, including repairs to the self-steering gear, which had become damaged, the masthead buoyancy bag arrangement, which had never been completed, and work on the generator to make it less susceptible to salt-water damage.

While he was thinking about the three choices, Crowhurst continued to send misleading telegrams to Rodney Hallworth, his press agent, who was doing his best to present his client favorably. On December 17th, Crowhurst tapped out a message in morse code that read: "Through doldrums. Over equator. Sailing fast again." At this time he was really 180 miles *north* of the equator, still in the doldrums, and was scarcely making any progress at all. On December 20th he radioed that he was off Brazil and averaging 170 miles daily. On this day he actually covered only 13 miles—his slowest twenty-four hours so far—and was only a little south of the equator at thirty degrees west, a position about 390 miles from the Brazilian coast.

Although he was leaning toward the false round-the-world voyage, Crowhurst still hadn't made up his mind definitely. He continued to draw up lists of work necessary to get the trimaran into shape for going on. He was also still thinking of putting into Rio de Janeiro. On December 21st, Crowhurst received a new blow when he discovered that some of the plywood on his starboard float had begun to split. This discouraged him further.

Three days later he sent a telegram to Hallworth claiming that he was near Ilha Trindade. In truth *Teignmouth Electron* was at six degrees south and thirty-three degrees west: a little west of Natal, Brazil, where the shoulder of the South American continent pushes furthest east into the Atlantic. Ilha Trindade lay 900 miles away to the south-southeast.

The deceit was growing. Crowhurst's real world was crumbling. The repairs were beyond him and he was afraid to put into Rio de Janeiro. The decision had been made.

18. *A Hell of a Prospect*

WHEN ROBIN KNOX-JOHNSTON HAD A BIG JOB AHEAD of him he always liked to split it in two and make the first part as difficult as possible. He was then able to reward himself with an easier second half. For the round-the-world trip the logical half-way point was Melbourne at the southeast corner of Australia. From this point on, Knox-Johnston marked his daily log *Homeward Bound* (underscored several times). As his personal halfway mark, however, he chose the international date line—east of New Zealand—which he was not to cross for another three weeks.

From Bass Strait, *Suhaili* sailed southeast and passed the northeast corner of Tasmania via Banks Strait. The early November spring weather was calm and sunny, a good time for sail repairs. There was scarcely any swell and Knox-Johnston got lots of sleep. *Suhaili*'s course lay to the east-southeast to pass south of New Zealand, a distance of 960 miles. By now Knox-Johnston had broken Chichester's nonstop sailing record of 15,517 miles.

Since the mechanical self-steering devices aboard *Suhaili* had fallen to pieces and there was nothing more on board from which to make parts, Knox-Johnston began to experiment with the sails to see if he could get the thirty-two-foot wooden ketch to steer herself. This is a tricky business because wind seldom blows steadily from exactly the same direction. It changes slightly in force and direction. In addition a vessel at sea is pushed from side to side by the waves and swells of the ocean which tend to disturb a ship's balance and heading. Also a nicely working arrangement can be upset by all sorts of things—more wind, less wind, bigger seas, momentary calms, reefing the sails, and so forth. A really effective self-steering arrangement needs to be dynamic, that is, something based on wind direction that will exert a positive, course-correcting force. This can be linked to some part of the running rigging, utilize the wind pressure on a sail, centerboard balance, a plywood blade that weathercocks into the wind, and so.

As *Suhaili* headed toward New Zealand, the wind was from ahead and the yacht steered herself close-hauled. On the third day, however, the wind changed to a fair breeze from the northwest—behind the vessel's port quarter. Knox-Johnston tried easing all the sheets, putting the sails on the starboard side, and lashing the tiller. The vessel kept swinging into the wind. The captain then lashed the tiller a little to port to give more corrective weather helm. This resulted in keeping the ship from turning into the wind. Now, though, she began to swing the other way and gybe; that is, to turn the stern of the yacht through the eye of the wind so that the wind blew on the other side of the sails.

Knox-Johnston kept adjusting the tiller, moving it a fraction of an inch at a time. The wind picked up, however, and obliged him to shorten sail which made the vessel easier to steer. Obviously the self-steering problems were not going to be solved on the first day.

One night the wind increased and the yacht gybed. When the captain attempted to put his ship back on course, the tiller broke off at the rudder head. While Knox-Johnston was lashing the shortened tiller back on the rudder, he dropped the mainsail and most of the mizzen. To his surprise, with a jib set forward, *Suhaili* tended to run off before the wind right along on course. Knox-Johnston eventually found that if he sailed with the full mizzen and three reefs in the mainsail, his vessel would go along nicely at five knots.*

---

*Evidently the yacht was set up to run with lee helm and, if she bore off, the jib would be partially blanketed by the mainsail and the mizzen would push her back on course by increasing weather helm—the force that heads a vessel into the wind.

With *Suhaili* now steering reasonably well, Knox-Johnston was heartened. His spirits went up and he began to think that maybe he would get across the Pacific yet. At one time he had considered steering by hand for sixteen hours a day and then stopping for eight hours to eat and sleep. The actual work this involved did not bother him; what oppressed him was the boredom of months of sixteen-hour steering watches.

On Sunday, November 17th at 2100, Knox-Johnston switched on his radio to get the weather report from New Zealand. The weather had been good for several days and the captain hoped it would continue until he got through Foveaux Strait, a fifteen-mile-wide passage that lay between New Zealand's main South Island and smaller Stewart Island. The weather forecast mentioned unsettled conditions for the next twenty-four hours and a deep low pressure area forming south of Tasmania, which could mean a gale from the west. At the end of the forecast the announcer read a special message that took Knox-Johnston's breath away:

MASTER *Suhaili*. IMPERATIVE WE RENDEZVOUS OUTSIDE BLUFF HAR-
BOUR IN DAYLIGHT. SIGNATURE: BRUCE MAXWELL

The man on *Suhaili* was overjoyed. Obviously his mail and messages from Australia had gotten through. He looked forward to news from home and a chance to find out how the race was going. The New Zealand radio station thought that he might be listening and had read the message for *Suhaili* with each broadcast.

Bluff Harbour was on the north side of Foveaux Strait, about 160 miles from *Suhaili*'s position. The ketch was running at five knots before a fair wind under a large jib and the mizzen. When Knox-Johnston awoke at 0500 the next morning he saw South Island to the north and tiny Solander Island away to the east, which gave him his position. Bluff was still 90 miles away, too far to make it by sunset, so Knox-Johnston hove to near Solander island, 72 miles from Bluff, to use up a little time. He wanted to sail the remaining miles during the night so he would arrive at Bluff in the early morning hours. Then he could see what he

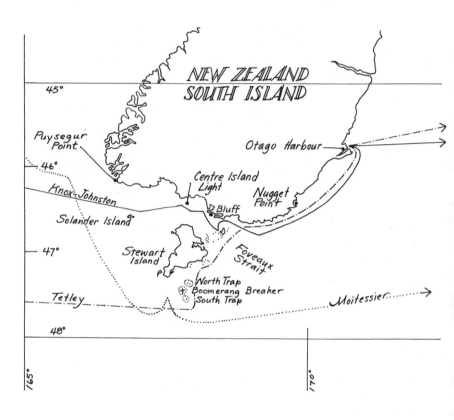

45°

NEW ZEALAND
SOUTH ISLAND

Puysegur
Point

Otago Harbour

46°

Knox-Johnston

Centre Island
Light

Nugget
Point

Bluff

Solander Island

47°

Stewart
Island

Foveaux
Strait

North Trap
Boomerang Breaker
South Trap

Tetley

Moitessier

48°

165°

170°

was doing and would have some extra daylight hours available in case of delays or problems in sailing and maneuvering. One is seldom ahead of time in a small vessel.

The barometer had fallen and the wind freshened. The sea got rougher and Knox-Johnston had to steer by hand because the ketch was being tossed about too much for her to manage by herself. The predicted weather low had moved quickly to the east; obviously the front itself was not far away.

The situation was ominous and reads almost like the prelude to a shipwreck. Because he wanted to keep the rendezvous at Bluff, Knox-Johnston found himself sailing toward a lee shore in a gale. Foveaux Strait appeared to be a trap—a narrow passage impeded with islands and shoals and unknown currents and tidal streams. The visibility was getting worse. The yacht was in poor condition. The one-man crew was tired and had only limited reserves of energy. All told, it was a hell of a discouraging prospect. The prudent course would have been to have sailed southeast and to have left all the land to the north. Now, however, it was too late because *Suhaili* was already into the strait. The vessel was committed and running eastward with a tiny storm jib and a double-reefed mainsail. The only thing to do was to press on and try to avoid the hazards of the land and somehow get through. Knox-Johnston cleared his vessel for action.

He went below and switched on the evening weather report. He felt like a prisoner before a judge who is delivering a sentence. The words came in calm, methodical, passionless phrases:

The cold front is 80 miles away and is moving at 40 knots. Winds of Force nine are expected. The gale will increase to Force ten, with very heavy rain and poor visibility.

Knox-Johnston listened to his special rendezvous message read out again and wished that he had never heard it. If he hadn't slowed down he would have been clear of the strait and islands by now.

In the early evening of November 18th, he sighted the Centre Island lighthouse ahead. This gave him a course to steer. Shortly afterwards, however, the light disappeared when the wind changed from north-northwest to west, freshened appreciably, and rain began to pour down. Knox-Johnston streamed a warp and sea anchor to slow his progress as much as possible. By 0230 the wind was shrieking at gale force. The captain gulped a little brandy and handed the mizzen and sheeted the storm jib amidships. The visibility was appalling. Clouds of spray from the wind-lashed waves streamed into the air and shattered into horizontal streaks of needle-like hail. Knox-Johnston climbed above the cockpit on the remnants of the self-steering gear and looked for the Centre Island light. It was bitterly cold and the captain's hands grew numb. After an eternity he spotted a whitish glow with the time interval of the Centre Island light; so he adjusted his course thirty degrees to the south, needed to clear some rocks southeast of the lighthouse. He watched for breakers until he was past the rocks and went below for an Irish coffee and a cigarette.

In the early dawn the visibility was still abysmal because of the wind-driven spray. Knox-Johnston changed his course back to the east. He was worried that he might run past Bluff and on to a mass of shoals and small islands. Finally at 0730 a dim outline ahead straightened into land. *Suhaili* was being set directly down on it. There was no recourse except to set the main and reefed mizzen quickly and to take in the sea anchor and the 720-foot warp. The sails went up okay, and *Suhaili* started to head up, but the warp and sea anchor had gotten hopelessly tangled, and pulling in the mess was a frightful job. Knox-Johnston wondered if this was going to be the end of his voyage. With strength born of desperation the captain somehow hauled all the lines aboard. Waves battered the ship and water flew everywhere as *Suhaili* labored to claw up to windward a little. She inched past the land.

It had been a near miss. Suddenly Knox-Johnston realized how cold, wet, and tired he was. His hands were red and raw from the exertion of pulling and the cold. And the day was only beginning! He thawed out his aching hands around a cup of coffee. The barometer had begun to rise and although the wind was still a full gale the seas were smoother in the strait. At 0900 an island appeared. Then a second. Knox-Johnston tacked around the second island and headed north toward where he thought Bluff might be. A little later a local ferry, the *Wairua*, appeared, madly rolling. The people on board seemed to recognize *Suhaili* and told Knox-Johnston that Bluff was nine miles north.

At 1030 Bluff showed up ahead, but the tidal stream was pouring out of the channel into the harbor. *Suhaili* was now out of the protection of Stewart island and was rapidly being shoved to leeward by the force of the storm. The water was shoaling so Knox-Johnston turned downwind again, streamed his various warps to slow the vessel, and went forward to drop the mainsail. When he threw the winch brake and the sail did not come down, his heart sank. The main halyard had somehow jumped off the masthead sheave and had jammed alongside. The sail could be neither hoisted nor lowered. What a time for this to happen!

The resourceful Knox-Johnston slacked off the reefed sail by unrolling three turns off the boom. He then topped the boom up and lashed the sail to the mast and boom. The job was not perfect by any means but it was better than nothing. The wind was still shrieking at more than fifty knots. By 1300, however, it had eased a little. By this time *Suhaili* was north of all the small islands that lay across Foveaux Strait. The captain continued his watch until dusk when he spotted the light signal on Nugget Point, which meant that he was well clear of danger. He went below and collapsed.

The next morning the wind was only twenty knots. *Suhaili* was alone on the ocean with no land in sight. Knox-Johnston took a number of celestial observations to establish his position and set a course for Otago on the southeast coast of New Zealand's South Island. Land appeared in the early afternoon and the wind dropped off. With the jammed main halyard, however, only the reefed mainsail could be set which was inadequate for the light weather. Knox-Johnston finally slipped around the cliffs of Tairoa Heads at 1840. The wind had fallen still lighter, was fluky, and a strong tidal stream ran out of the harbor against *Suhaili*. Knox-Johnston didn't have the proper chart of Otago harbor and attempted to tack along the south shore where the strength of the tidal stream was less. While maneuvering in a little bay near Tairoa Heads he ran aground on a sandy bottom.

The tide was dropping so the only thing to do was to carry

out an anchor to deeper water and to wait for the flood tide to float *Suhaili*. When Knox-Johnston took out the anchor and turned to swim back to his vessel he got quite a shock. His home for the last five months looked ghastly. No longer were *Suhaili*'s topsides white and glistening. She was tousled and dirty. Ugly brown rust stains ran down from various pieces of ironwork along the hull and masts. The once-white Dacron mainsail was streaked and tired. The yacht certainly needed a refit but it would have to wait.

A voice shouted down from the cliffs above *Suhaili*. Knox-Johnston asked the caller to please contact Bruce Maxwell in Otago. The captain declined any help, however, because he was afraid of being disqualified from the race. He thought he could get off by himself.

A launch and the crayfishing boat *Anna Dee* came to see him and offer assistance. Knox-Johnston politely rejected help but was overjoyed to talk to people after having been by himself for 159 days. While the talk continued and various people came and left, Knox-Johnston hoisted himself aloft and dealt with the jammed masthead sheave. While he worked, he kept talking to his visitors. It was lovely and peaceful in the little bay, some contrast to the day before when *Suhaili* and the captain had been in a desperate fight for their lives.

About an hour before midnight on November 20th *Suhaili* began to lift on the rising flood tide, Bruce Maxwell, the chief reporter of the *Sunday Mirror,* finally arrived from Bluff. Knox-Johnston was keen for mail and news from home. The rules of the race had been changed and no material assistance of any kind was now allowed. Maxwell had decided this included mail so he had brought none. This infuriated Knox-Johnston, who thought this was a petty and childish restriction. Nevertheless Knox-Johnston was brought up to date on the race by Maxwell who told about Fougeron and Moitessier and King. Knox-Johnston was disappointed to hear that King's *Galway Blazer II* had been forced out of the race with broken masts.

"If only [King] had had a conventional rig," lamented Knox-Johnston. "A junk rig may be the easiest to handle, but junks have huge masts and even then are constantly breaking them.

The whip on a mast in a small pitching boat is terrific, and this has to be restrained by shrouds."

Knox-Johnston was told about Tetley and Crowhurst and Carozzo. The race authorities predicted a close finish between Moitessier and Knox-Johnston if both kept going at the same rate. This news excited *Suhaili*'s captain and made him more determined than ever to win the race.

A little after midnight, a dangerous northwest wind began to blow into the anchorage. Knox-Johnston decided to leave. He hoisted the mainsail and mizzen. Then he went forward and set the jib. When *Suhaili* swung onto the port tack the captain pulled in the sheets from the cockpit. As the ketch picked up speed she headed for the rocks along Tairoa Heads to the north. Knox-Johnston tacked quickly, rushed forward as *Suhaili* sailed over her anchor, and picked up the anchor and some of the line. He tacked again, cleared the rocks, set the staysail, and hauled the anchor on board.

The crayfishing boat *Anna Dee* had stood by just in case, and now Knox-Johnston threw across a completed diary, some letters, and charts to be sent to England. The Pacific and Cape Horn lay ahead.

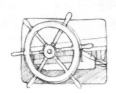

19. *"Nasty Hissing Seas"*

NIGEL TETLEY WAS THE THIRD MAN IN THE RACE to sail across the Indian Ocean. Though the weather was sharp and overpowering at times, he managed to keep his trimaran flying along eastward in pursuit of the leaders. Each day Tetley ate into his stores and used up various supplies a little more. The multihull got a bit lighter and faster, and the bearded naval commander nursed a faint hope that he would slip ahead of the others. At least he was getting closer to the leaders. In the meantime every twenty-four hours that passed was a small battle in itself. Tetley had heard so much about the roaring forties and the great westerly winds that he presumed he would have constant winds behind him. In truth what he found was a never-ending series of east-moving weather depressions—some to his north and some to his south—whose winds boxed the compass as they overtook *Victress*. All this meant endless sail drill to keep the vessel going at her fastest. Yet Tetley had to be careful or else he would overpower his ship and drive her to destruction.

The great virtue of multihulls is speed, which exercises an almost hypnotic fascination for some men. Tetley had already logged almost 200 miles in a single day and in theory could go a good deal faster. A monohull with a displacement hull, by contrast, has its maximum speed precisely dictated by its waterline length. The monohull *Joshua*, for example, had a maximum hull speed of 8 knots or so which could not be exceeded under any circumstances except when running before big waves that might sweep the vessel forward for a few seconds. In theory the multihulls could go much faster and win the race—*if* they weren't capsized and *if* the three hulls could be made to stay together. In a short race in England a multihull sailor named Bill Howell had pushed his catamaran *Golden Cockerell* up to twenty-two knots. She had capsized, however, and finished the race with her spars pointing downward before being towed into port. There were neither ports nor friendly rescue crews in the Indian Ocean where *Victress* was speeding eastward.

"The multihull sailor must be more skilful, more vigilant, and must work harder than his singlehull rival," wrote *Sunday Times* reporter Murray Sayle in a highflying story on November 24th. Unlike the other reporters Sayle had actually accompanied another man on an Atlantic crossing in a multihull.

"The nervous strain is tremendous," said Sayle. "The compensation is speed. Tetley now has before him 14,000 miles of a multihull sailor's paradise, with the relentless following winds of the Roaring Forties, all the way to the Horn," continued the reporter, repeating the myths and fantasies about the Southern Ocean and its steady following winds.

> If his nerves hold out, 200 or 250 miles a day is possible. . . . Sailing the Atlantic . . . this summer, we did 1,000 miles in four and a half days, but we found the self-steering wildly erratic. . . . A couple of hours at the wheel at speeds of 16 to 18 knots, wildly skating down waves and pulling up with the bows buried in a smother of foam, was like riding the Wall of Death. No one really knows whether a singlehander can keep a boat like *Victress* under control from Good Hope to the Horn, because Tetley is the first man to try it. His attempt has has given the race a new fascination.

Tetley had already sailed a solo trimaran much further than anyone else and had set a record for long-distance multihull travel. It was obvious that it took great talent and determination to keep the light, powerful vessel going at high speeds week after week. A monohull with its heavy ballast keel is infinitely safer and easier to sail because the hull design is stable and forgiving. No matter what happens—unless she is holed—a monohull with a fixed lead or iron keel will always return to an upright, stable position. A multihull that is once upset and is upside down, however, will stay upside down. No one knew this better than Tetley.

When the wind began to moan and hum in the rigging he had learned to:

1. reduce sail quickly;
2. to run dead downwind with a small jib sheeted amidships;
3. or to take down all the sails and drift before the storm and hope that a breaking wave didn't get him.

During the first two weeks of Tetley's run from the Cape of Good Hope to New Zealand, he experienced four gales, three near gales, and one spectacular broach. On two days he was set backwards by the ocean current. Another day *Victress* heeled enough so that all the dishes on the sink drain crashed to the cabin sole (for the first time on the voyage). Yet there were times when the wind was so light that the sea birds gave up flying. And there were moments when Tetley was lyrical about the sunsets of the Indian Ocean. "This evening's was no exception," he wrote one night. "A beautiful matrix of indigo, blood red, bright gold, and cerulean blue."

Tetley's major problem was how long to hang on to his big sails when the wind increased. He needed large sails for speed, but in strong winds they were a risky business. The basic running sails were two 300 square foot jibs, each hanked to the headstay and held at the outer lower points—the clews—with long spinnaker poles that were inclined slightly forward. One sail was poled out to port and the second to starboard. *Victress* went fast with these big running jibs and also steered herself very well. When the wind increased quickly, however, it was a hair-raising game for one person to get the big sails and long poles safely down on deck. On a crewed ocean racer, for example, generally three or four men dealt with the running rig. Tetley was a clever and resourceful master mariner and did manage by himself, but the job was scary. He wanted *Victress* to fly as fast as was reasonably safe; yet if he waited too long he was liable to get into trouble unhooking the unwieldly poles, lowering and lashing them on deck, and then letting the halyards go and doing a dance to capture the slippery jibs, which were full of wind.

With gale or near gale force winds coming from astern, Tetley's first plan was to put up tiny forty-square-foot storm jibs.

Victress

He did not pole out these sails, so the yacht did not steer herself downwind. In order for the yacht to run unattended the captain had to adjust his course so the wind was on the quarter. This system seemed good in theory but did not work out because the sails were too small and flogged terribly when the yacht yawed from side to side. Tetley happened to read an excerpt from Joshua Slocum's *Sailing Alone Around The World* in which the shrewd Nova Scotian had run before a frightful storm on the west side of Tierra del Fuego by sheeting a jib amidships. Tetley tried this scheme, which worked so well that he adopted it at once.

During the night of December 14th, Tetley hung on to full sail before a twenty-two-knot northwest wind, and when he worked out his position the next day he was delighted to find that he had run 202 miles noon-to-noon, a new record. In the afternoon the wind dropped to five knots and *Victress* glided slowly along while the captain played classical music, cooked his evening meal, and used a bit of extra fresh water for a bath. The calm weather lasted for three days.

Although he had just completed a marvelous run, Tetley decided to make a larger rudder for his self-steering unit ("The present one is designed for high-speed sailing and can hardly be expected to cope with the trimaran moving slowly under the heavy conditions of the Roaring Forties."). Albatrosses paddled up to *Victress* on the quiet sea and Tetley fed them bits of home-made bread that he baked once a week. He thought of Samuel Taylor Coleridge's poem *The Rime of the Ancient Mariner* as he fed a big bird:

> It ate the food it ne'er had eat . . .
> And every day, for food or play,
> Came to the mariner's hollo!

On December 17th the project of the day was to repair a sheet winch that had seized up. Tetley had tried hammers, wedges, penetrating oil, and even a blowtorch, but the recalcitrant winch drum wouldn't budge. Finally he got the idea of drilling and tapping two holes in the top of the drum. He then bolted on a long piece of wood and with the leverage of length managed to twist the drum off the winch base. The grease had evidently failed so Tetley resolved to use oil to lubricate his winches henceforth.

The wind returned on December 18th and by the following noon, *Victress* had run 183 miles. On the next day Tetley managed a marginal radio contact with Cape Town and was pleased to get Christmas greetings from his family, his Music for Pleasure sponsors, and *The Sunday Times*. On December 20th a mizzen shroud parted ("over-strong wire for the job too, and the sail was not even hoisted at the time. Metal fatigue."). Three squid landed on board during the night and were tossed into the pot for breakfast. The wind died away in the afternoon so Tetley inflated his rubber dinghy, put it in the water, and began to scrape away a crop of fat, speed-robbing goose barnacles that he had noticed along the waterline of *Victress*. As Tetley worked around the hull he looked into the water and saw a seven-foot shark beneath him. When he finished with the barnacles and got back on board he baited a giant shark hook with a can of corned beef and hoisted the shark on board. Tetley kept the tail, which he decided to display on the bow of *Victress* if she should complete her trip around the world. To finish the day the captain repaired the broken mizzen shroud.

On December 22nd the wind got up to twenty-five knots but by the following morning had dropped to fourteen knots or so. At noon Tetley discovered that the steering wires had broken. He had put on new wire near the Cape Verde islands—eight thousand miles ago—and now fitted more new wire. This time a bit heavier. He sometimes wondered whether he could keep ahead of the problems that appeared each day.

"The wind continued to increase and I lowered the second jib and sheeted the other fore and aft," wrote Tetley the next day. "Before long it was blowing Force 8–9 [about forty knots] with snarling crests flinging themselves at *Victress*'s stern—trying to slew her round. These conditions are typical of the Roaring Forties and I will have to learn to live with them. Towards dusk, when the sea had grown longer, though higher, she seemed a lot happier."

On Christmas eve the wind blew hard all day, but eased off

at nightfall. Tetley had decided on a mushroom sauce to go with his Christmas bird so he marinated some first-quality dried mushrooms in red wine. He made bread, tidied up the cabin, and got out the Christmas presents that had been put on board before he left England.

Tetley started Christmas day by playing carols from Guildford Cathedral. When he opened his presents he found a handsome pewter tankard from his wife Eve, a stainless steel comb from his son Mark, and a dictionary from his son Phillip. Tetley had only seabirds for company; so he made up an offering of bread and tinned fish for his flying friends. The wind settled down in the afternoon and the yacht steered herself nicely while the captain had a few glasses of sherry and prepared his holiday meal.

"The dinner table was made as attractive as possible with the last of the oranges, the only surviving packet of nuts, and raisins and sweets displayed," wrote Tetley. "The pheasant, on the verge of falling to pieces, was carved with due solemnity; and to toast the family a bottle of champagne. . . . I felt very festive for a time with my favourite music playing—afterwards very lonely . . . then I fell asleep."

Tetley took several photographs of himself seated before his Christmas dinner in the cabin and eventually—as we shall see— the films were tossed on the deck of a fishing vessel and flown to England and developed. Of all the photographs to come out of the round-the-world race none is more poignant than the sight of Nigel Tetley raising his new pewter tankard to the camera while his elaborate Christmas dinner and bottle of champagne and loaf of bread sit on the table in front of him. The photograph reaches out and touches you, demonstrating at once the paradox of the singlehander: the battle to prove his strength of purpose and resourcefulness, and his need to be with his friends and loved ones. Obviously Tetley's carefully arranged picture and his salute to the camera with his brimming tankard reflect a terrible loneliness and a longing for his wife and sons. We see a plucky naval officer on a tour of duty that turned out to be a hundredfold more demanding than any military maneuvers. We see a remarkably capable man on a voyage that hadn't been tried

The Sunday Times

NIGEL TETLEY

before. We see a shy man in a stripped naked moment of uncertainty and doubt, of longing and hope, of comradeship and
joie de vivre, of wretchedness and desolaton.

The picture was so strong and powerful that even the flint-
hearted editor of *The Sunday Times*, a man used to news of a
thousand crises, horror stories, and troubles, immediately
printed the photograph in an eight-column cut across a full page
that his 1,413,847 weekly buyers and their families would see
and understand. Tetley had the champagne and pheasant, but
he had no one with whom to share it. What could be worse? It
was the dedicated hermit writhing on a bed of loneliness.

Of course, trying to generalize about singlehanded sailors is
like trying to generalize about the human race. Each of the four
men still in the round-the-world competition were as different
from one another as a butterfly is different from a bluebird. The

dogged and persevering Knox-Johnston was busy worrying about defeating the French and winning the race to uphold the honor of the British. He was also occupied trying to keep his small vessel together. Moitessier, with the best ship in the race and the most sailing experience, was happy communing with nature and the sea and recharging his spiritual batteries. Crowhurst was a pathetic mental case. Tetley couldn't wait to finish the wretched race and to be done with it. In the meantime he was perfecting his wine sauces and listening to Beethoven.

By January 1st, *Victress* had passed tiny Amsterdam and St. Paul islands in the south Indian Ocean where Tetley had listened to some "nasty hissing seas." He had done more sail sewing (after first gluing on patches) and had gone through yet another gale. The captain ate the last orange and had ceremoniously sacrified the final onion for a special spaghetti sauce. During calms, whales swam past the trimaran while Tetley worked on his lifeless main engine, which had developed its fifth major defect since England and which apparently had gone to sleep for good. On January 2nd, Tetley spoke on the radio to Australian operators who were surprised at the strength of *Victress's* transmission.

During the afternoon of January 5th, the wind shifted to south by east. Rain thundered down and Tetley collected several gallons of drinking water from the runoff on the wheelhouse roof. In the evening the wind backed to the south and quickly increased to gale force. After two hours of sail shortening, Tetley finally put all the sails down and laid beam on to the storm. The wind blew fifty knots, the rain continued, and the temperature plummeted to forty degrees Fahrenheit. There was a steep cross-swell and several waves banged hard against the yacht. Water worked into the wheelhouse and even squirted past the usually impenetrable cabin skylight. Tetley finally got tired of the storm and tried sailing with one of the tiny storm jibs. But when the yacht got hit by a big wave and knocked half over, he quickly returned to lying to before the storm without any sails up. By the evening of January 6th, however, the wind had eased off, and on the next morning was only eight knots from the west.

Tetley spent the day opening up and drying out the trimaran and his wet clothes and bedding, a sailor's usual move after a nasty storm.

On his January 7th call to Australia, Tetley learned that Moitessier had been sighted off Tasmania on January 2nd (the actual date was December 18th). Knox-Johnston's last known position was along the east coast of New Zealand's South Island on November 21st, six weeks earlier. Knox-Johnston's radio was out of order so no one knew where he had gotten to since then. Donald Crowhurst's radio was also silent, but the race watchers postulated that on the basis of 100 miles a day (Crowhurst's reported average) *Teignmouth Electron* should be in the Indian Ocean.

During the next three days the wind blew at gale force, although not steadily. *Victress*'s course was erratic until the captain discovered that a control line had come off the self-steering unit. Tetley experimented with a sail set athwartships behind the mast for more speed but took it down quickly when the trimaran started to run downwind at high speed with a wild, corkscrewing motion. Two days later three blowing whales startled Tetley while he was on the foredeck hoisting a sail. The captain wondered if the whales mistook his three-hulled vessel for three other whales. The daily celestial observations put *Victress* 400 miles south of Cape Leeuwin, Australia's southwest corner, so Tetley—ever the epicure—celebrated passing the second of the great southern capes with a roast duck and a bottle of sherry.

As Sunday, January 12th began, the wind blew hard from the north. *Victress* steered herself until 0200 when Tetley took over. He managed a southeast course until 0400 when all he could do was to run south—downwind. By dawn the wind was shrieking at fifty knots again. Tetley took down all sails. "As the front passed at noon, the storm culminated in a very heavy squall which blotted out all visibility. It was followed by a wind shift to the northwest," he wrote, "and I plucked up courage to get underway again. The wind had moderated to Force 8, but there were periodic squalls, making it unwise to carry more sail than a single jib sheeted flat. My opinion of the Southern Ocean stood at zero, and I tried to forget that there were 7,000 miles more of it still to cross."

At midnight another gale started up, this time from the west. Tetley raced before the storm until 0330 when he took down his single sail. Most of the bronze hanks had been torn off the luff of the jib and the captain had a lot of trouble throttling the sail and getting the flapping mess down on deck. At 0500 a large sea slammed on board. "A battering ram," said Tetley. Cold water shot into the wheelhouse, cascaded below into the cabin, and poured over Tetley, who was drinking a cup of coffee. The force of the sea knocked the mainsail boom loose from its crutch and bashed in the side curtain and coaming board of the wheelhouse. All sorts of loose gear rocketed across the cabin. By 0700 the wind had risen to Force eleven (fifty-six to sixty-three knots) and the entire sea was covered with white foam. Tetley watched nervously as an army of huge waves advanced relentlessly toward *Victress*. Was the enemy force going to batter him to death and march right over him? The bearded naval commander concluded that this was his last battle, that he was losing, and that his end was near.

"The sea, covered entirely in foam, seethed round . . . [*Victress*] and yet she remained undismayed, bobbing here, curtsying there, but always eluding the massive crests. Repeated squalls of hurricane force only helped her slip sideways out of their reach. And despite my doubts, so it continued, with only an occasional wave hitting the side. The barometer, which had fallen half an inch, steadied at noon and began to rise. The wind continued at Force 11 all afternoon. Then [the weather] gradually started to ease."

The next morning Tetley decided to give up the race and head for Albany, Australia, 450 miles to the north. He had been shaken to the roots by the storm. "Had God first shown me his strength and then spared my life for some special purpose?" he wondered. "To warn other yachtsmen not to be such fools? Then I realized that such conditions can be regarded as relatively commonplace in the Southern Ocean. . . . When I got under way at sunrise I headed her bows eastwards once more. I would endeavor to get as far as New Zealand."

Tetley sorted out the damage. The battery charger had been flooded and would need attention. A breaking wave had smashed the glass shade of the hurricane lamp. He began repairs to the wheelhouse coamings and side curtains.

By the next day, January 15th, the wind had worked around to the west. The terrible seas had eased off. Tetley set a small jib athwartships and once more sped eastward at six knots. His sole source of electricity was the flooded battery charger. If it failed there would be no radio, no lights, no power tools, and no instruments. He would not be able to listen to his beloved music. . . . Tetley held his breath while he worked on the charger. To his delight it began to work. The next day the barometer began another weary plunge and the wind backed to the north. Tetley stopped *Victress* for a few hours until the wind veered to the northwest when he got going again. "The seas were steeper than usual and gave me some anxious moments," he said. "*Victress* plummeted down the faces of the waves, her stern cocked high in the air." Toward evening more storm clouds hove into sight and some wretched-looking seas began to slide up behind the dark blue trimaran.

Gales and frightening seas continued on and off for the next three days. The trimaran ran hard and at times turned sideways to the seas and rolled wildly. Once the captain feared that she was burying her bows and about to somersault. Finally on Sunday, January 19th, the waves began to hiss less loudly and the needle of the barometer moved to the right. In an effort to keep the bows from plunging, Tetley tried setting a small lifting sail forward of the jib as a kind of spinnaker. This seemed to work satisfactorily. In the meantime the captain was doing more sewing on sails that were getting thinner and thinner. He was certainly trying hard.

At two o'clock in the morning of January 22nd, the yacht rolled heavily in a violent rain squall. The captain rushed on deck to reef the mainsail further. The wind was shifting so Tetley stayed on watch, kept company by the music of Boccherini and Delius. By the end of the day the weather front had passed and *Victress* ran eastward under full sail while the captain repaired a corroded navigation light. Tetley was now south of Tasmania and not far from Hobart, the capital, so his sponsor chartered an airplane and tried to locate the trimaran. The captain tidied up his vessel for photographs, but the plane wasn't able to find the yacht.

During the following week the weather alternated between good and bad. On favorable days Tetley washed clothes and attempted to get his pathetic main engine to run again. On stormy days the captain grimly hung on to his small sails and tried to make as much mileage as possible. By January 26th, the 132nd day from Plymouth, Tetley had logged 14,250 miles, the halfway mark of the round-the-world voyage. Sometimes the motion of the yacht reminded Tetley of a carnival ride ("the trimaran made good speed close-hauled under mizzen and jib but did everything but loop the loop.") The captain noticed that additional pieces of moulding had been torn off the starboard side of the hull by the battering of the waves.

Finally on January 30th, as *Victress* hurried along a little below forty-seven degrees south latitude, the yacht drew even with 168 degrees east longitude, the meridian of New Zealand (see map on page 180). Tetley decided to head a little north to see if he could drop off mail and films with a fisherman. On February 1st he passed close to Stewart island and was thrilled to glide along close to land that reminded him of Scotland. He sailed near Waikawa harbor, Long Point, and Newhaven harbor on the southeast coast of New Zealand's South Island. Then on February 2nd, as Knox-Johnston had done seventy-four days earlier, on November 20th, he headed into Otago harbor. It was Sunday and Tetley found a fishing launch whose owner, Keith Reid, motored alongside the multihull and took off films, a journal, tape recordings, and a letter for Tetley's wife. Reid offered Tetley some crayfish but he declined because of the rules of the race. Tetley then tacked out of the harbor against an adverse wind. Once at sea he set a course eastward toward Cape Horn.

Since the start Tetley had picked up twenty days on Knox-Johnston, not unexpected because *Victress* was longer and faster. Tetley had also gone further south where the mileage was less but the weather was stronger. What was surprising was how well Knox-Johnston was doing in his smaller vessel.

In six weeks, the tail of the shark that Tetley had caught had shrunk to half its original size. The captain wondered whether he would get a chance to display the tail on the bow of *Victress* in the Atlantic or whether the tail would find its way into the sea earlier.

20. *A Slice of His Soul*

ON CHRISTMAS DAY Donald Crowhurst sailed southward along the Brazilian coast, near the great reef that forms the harbor of the old Portuguese city of Recife. The tropical weather was hot and sultry and a weak southeast trade wind blew lightly across the baggy sails of *Teignmouth Electron,* which were sheeted in tightly as the trimaran loped along close-hauled on the port tack. The sleek, streamlined, two-masted white yacht with light blue decks was only three months old and her paint still had the shiny gloss of Eastwoods shipyard where she had been built. An officer on a passing ship might have sighed at her sight and wished that he, too, could have possessed such a fine yacht and a chance to sail on a warm and calm sea. After all, to be the captain of a new yacht and to sail on tropical oceans were foremost in the dreams of many men.

Teignmouth Electron had a few problems, it is true, but the main difficulty was the troubled mental state of her captain. Crowhurst had started late with a new and untried vessel of radical design. He had exaggerated his sailing experience. He had bragged about the electronic miracles he was going to perform. Once in the race, however, Crowhurst should have gotten down to business and solved his various technical problems as the rest of the contestants did. He should have chased and overtaken the other yachts as he had boasted he would. Instead Crowhurst effectively withdrew into a pathetic and hopeless inner shell and did nothing constructive at all.

A rather fiendish plot hatched in his troubled mind. He planned a fraud that was breathtaking in its dimensions. Instead of sailing south of the Cape of Good Hope, Australia's Cape Leeuwin, and Cape Horn as the rules of the race dictated, Crowhurst's scheme was to mark time in the South Atlantic. He would send out a few vague radio messages and complain of electrical problems that might stop further transmissions. His sponsor, his press agent, *The Sunday Times,* and presumably the public would assume that during his radio silence he was crossing the Indian Ocean and making for Cape Horn. After a suitable interval he would then reappear in the South Atlantic near the leaders. His radio—somehow repaired—would again issue position reports

DONALD CROWHURST

and terse bulletins from the intrepid Crowhurst. Finally he would pull ahead into first place. He would return to England triumphantly, collect his prizes, write his book, and be acclaimed as his country's (and the world's) hero. He would do all this if he could stay out of sight and fake his logbook entries for three or four months in a way clever enough to defy detection.

In order to fill out his fraudulent logbooks, Crowhurst began to take detailed notes from marine radio broadcasts. He wrote down thousands of words of weather reports, routine messages to and from ships, accident summaries, requests for tugs and pilots, military traffic—any and all bits of miscellaneous information that he might be able to enter in his fictional logbooks.

Weather forecasts from along the course of the round-the-world
race were especially important and Crowhurst carefully under-
lined all of his longhand transcriptions of weather data for Tristan da Cunha, Cape Town, the Indian Ocean, and other points.
Crowhurst's messages to England were hard to compose. He
wanted to send something concrete but not to give away his true
position. His precise location, however, was exactly what his con-
tacts in England wanted and asked for again and again. What
could he do? It was similar to the lost sailor's game of stopping
a fishing boat or other vessel along an unknown coast and trying
to find out where he is without humiliating himself by admitting
that he is lost.

On January 3rd Crowhurst tapped out a morse code message to his agent Rodney Hallworth:

> STRICKEN GOUT FOLLOWING NEWYEAR SHERRY PARTY NOW EQUAL
> FOOTING MERMAIDS STOP ALMOST INTO FORTIES

The message was jaunty but said little of substance. Hallworth radioed back the positions of the three leaders. He mentioned that *The Sunday Times* reckoned the winner to be home
April 9th and suggested this date as a target for Crowhurst. A
second cable pleaded for weekly positions and mileage. How
could Hallworth possibly write stories with no information?

On January 19th Crowhurst sent:

> 100 SOUTHEAST GOUGH 1086 GENERATOR HATCH SEALED TRANS-
> MISSIONS WHEN POSSIBLE ESPECIALLY 80 EAST 140 WEST

Such messages echoed the craftiness of a wily courtroom law-
yer. Crowhurst had radioed a false position 1,670 miles from his
true location and claimed 1,086 miles a week or 155 miles every
twenty-four hours. Gough island was far away in the South
Atlantic, fourteen hundred miles west-southwest of Cape Town,
South Africa. At that moment *Teignmouth Electron* was only 640
miles east of Rio de Janeiro, Brazil. In other words Crowhurst
was really in the shadow of South America but he claimed that
he was one thousand miles further south and far to the east. He
suggested that his radio messages might stop because of generator problems. Finally, to get everyone looking for him further

east, he suggested that the principal coastal radio stations tune their aerials to eighty east and one hundred forty west, meridians of longitude that lay between the middle of the Indian Ocean and the central Pacific.

On January 19th Crowhurst also sent a cable to his sponsor in which he exaggerated the problems from the split plywood on the starboard float. He asked for release from the buyback scheme. Mr. Best replied that any decision to withdraw was Crowhurst's business. With regard to the contract, Best generously offered to cancel the repurchase clause.

Crowhurst prepared other complicated and bizarre radio messages but he did not send them. Even in the transmissions that did not go out, Crowhurst pleaded with other people to make up his mind for him. In any conditions of strain, his will collapsed. After the cable to Mr. Best, Crowhurst closed down his transmitter for the next three months. He continued to receive messages perfectly.

In the meantime Hallworth tried to write bulletins for *The Sunday Times* based on the sparse information in the January cables and on a radio telephone call between Crowhurst and his wife on Christmas eve when the captain had vaguely mentioned Cape Town. "Almost into forties" became "in roaring forties" in Hallworth's story. In the January 12th issue this was changed to an actual position: "Latest reports put him 200 miles southwest of Cape Town." On the following weekend *The Sunday Times* speculated further: "If Donald Crowhurst has kept up his recent record-breaking runs in his revolutionary trimaran *Teignmouth Electron* he should now be well into the Indian ocean and sailing hard for Australia."

If Crowhurst wasn't moving at a suitable rate, it was easy for the newspapers to speed him up. Hallworth looked over part of one of Crowhurst's January 19th cables that read: "generator hatch sealed" and decided to provide a reason. In the January 26th issue (page two) the weekly story brazenly stated: "A giant wave smashed over the stern of his trimaran *Teignmouth Electron,* damaging the cockpit and causing splits in the superstructure. He was delayed for three days repairing the rear cockpit compartment." Not only were the newspaper people inflating Crowhurst's progress and daily mileage, but they were inventing problems, solutions, and parts of the trimaran ("the superstructure") that did not in fact exist.

Crowhurst's January 3rd cable had an error in transmission in which GOUGH was changed to TOUGH. Hallworth assumed that his client was having a *tough* time near Cape Town which further advanced even Crowhurst's fanciful position by an additional fourteen hundred miles. Not only was Crowhurst moved bodily east to near Cape Town, but he was presumably averaging 1,086 miles per week or 155 miles every twenty-four hours. Henceforth the newspaper calculations used this figure. The published estimates of Crowhurst's weekly position got further and further exaggerated and *Teignmouth Electron* was said to be zipping along eastward far out in the Indian Ocean toward Australia when in truth she was marking time near Brazil.

The word *extrapolation* means to infer or estimate unknown information by extending or projecting known information. Crowhurst's biographers wryly suggested that the newspapermen were "extrapolating on the extrapolations." Certainly the newsmen did not allow any common sense or journalistic skepticism to temper their optimistic stories and calculations.

During Crowhurst's long and meandering sojourn in the southwestern Atlantic he spent days and days at his radio taking notes and working on his logbooks. During these months he sailed slowly without pushing the yacht very hard. *Teignmouth Electron* was in the trade wind zone off the Brazilian coast where the winds were light, warm, and steady, which meant that the trimaran didn't require much attention, especially under reduced sail.

To fill his days Crowhurst played his mouth organ (badly) for his BBC tape recorder, wrote poetry (poor to appalling), and tried his hand at creative writing (no better). He showed a surprising talent for shooting motion pictures of himself with the 16mm camera the BBC had given him. Crowhurst clamped the camera to various strong points around the yacht and used a self-timer on the shutter release to shoot sequences of his sailing and living duties. Because of his mathematical interest the captain studied a book titled *Relativity* by Albert Einstein. Crowhurst spent a great deal of time observing fish and birds that appeared around him. He often drew pictures of these creatures, gave them childish names, and constructed complex stories in which his characters generally met violent ends.

The deceptions that Crowhurst was trying to invent seemed to parallel the collapse of the confidence and breezy self-esteem that he had shown in England before the start of the race. He began to cultivate a pity for himself based on feelings that he was brighter than other men. The general mass of society somehow didn't appreciate him. It was unfair because *he* represented the true light, the spirit alone, the difficult way. Nevertheless, he was rejected and pushed aside. He was a misfit. At some level, however, he realized that he was guilty of a grievous deception in the race and that a penalty of one degree or another would be sliced from his soul as recompense. It was the old Anglo-Saxon guilt complex: you get what you give.

Crowhurst's complex mental capacity had unfortunately taken a morbid turn. In one story that he wrote he compared himself to a stray land bird lost out on the ocean and "destined like the spirit of many of his counterparts to die alone and anonymously, unseen by any of his species, yet accepting that one chance in a million of knowing things unknown." In spite of this Crowhurst still had a streak of common sense. He somehow managed to put aside all his mental turmoil and confusion and began to concentrate on a practical problem that demanded attention. The split in the plywood on the outboard side of the starboard float was getting worse. Already the split was three feet long. In addition a frame on the inside of the float had pulled away from the plywood. Crowhurst tried to sail on the starboard tack as much as possible to keep the float out of the water, but heading south in the southeast trade wind meant that he was on the port tack. This pushed the damaged starboard float into the water and flooded it, which in turn lowered the float even further and made the problem worse. Something had to be done.

What Crowhurst needed were sheets of plywood and screws and nails. A patch or two could be fixed in place at sea if the weather was calm and the swell was down. What Crowhurst had in mind, however, was a quiet place ashore. Also he had neglected to take repair materials with him, so he had neither the plywood nor the fastenings. Where could he go? If he selected a large city like Salvadore or Rio de Janeiro or Santos or Buenos Aires he would be discovered in short order. These cities had yacht clubs and boating enthusiasts and nosy reporters and officials with forms to be filled out. What Crowhurst didn't want above all were people with questions. He needed an out-of-the-way place where he could beach the trimaran for several days. A quick repair and then back to sea.

Crowhurst made his usual thorough study before doing anything. After a long session with the Admiralty sailing directions for the east coast of South America he decided to go to a place called Bahía Samborombón. It was located in Argentina near the southern entrance to the great estuary of the Rio de la Plata about eighty miles southeast of Buenos Aires. The landing place had a small stream called Rio Salado with a shallow bar at the entrance.

After Crowhurst had made his choice, he sailed slowly southward along the Brazilian coast and into the waters of Argentina. He used up the month of February working on his logbooks and various creative pursuits while he poked along toward Bahía Samborombón. When the weather was bad he sometimes took down all his sails (like Nigel Tetley) and drifted before the wind and sea. On March 2nd, he was close to his target and spotted the various landmarks mentioned in the Pilot. For some reason he sailed back out to sea again and returned four days later. On the morning of March 6th he headed in toward Rio Salado where he promptly ran aground in the brown, silt-laden waters of the Rio de la Plata.

The tiny settlement in front of Crowhurst didn't amount to much. There was a scattering of houses and crude buildings on low land along the coast, which was marked by trees and shrubs and tall grasses. One dirt road led to the world beyond. The area was too rough for cattle or farming. A few hunters sometimes came to shoot deer, ostriches, or wild pigs, but in truth people seldom came to Rio Salado or knew that it existed. The place didn't even have a telephone.

A fifty-five-year-old fisherman named Nelson Messina looked

out from his house and saw *Teignmouth Electron* aground. It was certainly a strange looking vessel. Messina went next door to the three-man outpost of the Argentine coast guard where he rounded up Santiago Franchessi and a young conscript. The three men jumped into Messina's fishboat *Favorito de Cambaceras*, motored out, and pulled the trimaran into the channel and up the river to the coast guard wharf.

The three Argentines were surprised that only one man was on the yacht. He seemed extremely thin and had a scraggly beard. Franchessi spoke to him in the harsh local dialect of Spanish. Crowhurst answered in English, then French, and finally in sign language. The Englishman got the trio to understand that he was in a race of some kind. He had had to stop because he couldn't go on until he had repaired the damage to his right-hand float. Crowhurst showed the men the split plywood and used gestures to explain what he proposed to do. He also wanted some electrical parts. The men had difficulty understanding the technical details so they loaded Crowhurst into the coast guard jeep and drove seventeen miles to a store where a former French army sergeant named Hector Salvati lived with his family. Crowhurst spoke excellent French and explained to Salvati what he wanted. He also said that he had rounded Cape Horn as part of a five-month sailing race from England. Crowhurst would be back in England in a month or so if only he could get his ship repaired. He accompanied his explanations with three quick sketches on wrapping paper.

Salvati translated Crowhurst's information to Senior Petty Officer Franchessi. Salvati and his wife also noticed that Crowhurst seemed extremely thin and that his trousers were floppy and loose. When Franchessi went to telephone his superiors for instructions, Crowhurst got very upset and began to talk loudly and irrationally. He needn't have worried. Franchessi spoke to a junior midshipman in La Plata who decided the problem was a trifling matter. The young officer told Franchessi to give Crowhurst what he wanted and to send him on his way.

While Franchessi was on the telephone, Crowhurst kept talking to Salvati and his wife in an exaggerated, bizzare manner. Crowhurst repeated over and over "Il faut vivre la vie" (life should be lived). The Salvatis didn't know what to make of such a strange person. "He laughed a lot, as though he were making fun of us," said Rose Salvati. "We thought that something was wrong, that he might be a smuggler."

The coast guard men and Crowhurst returned to Rio Salado in the jeep. Crowhurst—who had no money at all—was given what he needed. He immediately made two small plywood patches which he screwed in place and painted white to match the rest of the float. That evening Crowhurst shaved off his beard and ate beefsteaks with the two unmarried coast guard men who lived at the outpost. Because of the language problem there wasn't much talk during dinner. Crowhurst again slept on board his trimaran.

The next morning Nelson Messina was asked to tow the trimaran out to sea. Once again the towline was attached and *Favorito de Cambaceras* pulled the strange ship with the three hulls down the Rio Salado and across the bar. Crowhurst's mission had been accomplished. He had repaired his vessel. But when Franchessi had stepped on board to secure the towline on the day that Crowhurst had arrived, the Argentine's action had disqualified the Englishman from the race. The only catch was that no one connected with the race knew about the unscheduled stop in Argentina.

21. *On to Cape Horn*

KNOX-JOHNSTON WAS THE FIRST MAN to sail into the
Pacific and he ran into a terrible problem right away.
Instead of strong westerly winds to push *Suhaili* toward Cape
Horn, the English captain found easterly winds that forced him
to tack back and forth. Since he no longer had his mechanical
self-steering gear, each tack and each change of wind required
complicated sail balancing to get *Suhaili* to steer herself. The wind
often blew from the southeast, which favored the starboard tack.
The best that *Suhaili* could do on starboard, however, was a
northeast heading: which meant that Knox-Johnston was aimed
toward Alaska instead of Cape Horn. The captain wept with
frustration at the persistent adverse winds and the constant upset
seas that slapped at *Suhaili*. Sometimes the seas were quite short
from crest to crest and caused *Suhaili* to pitch up and down.
Then she scarcely logged any miles at all. "A few extra feet in
length would have made all the difference," wrote Knox-Johnston. He gritted his teeth while the yacht hobby-horsed and went
almost nowhere.

When the wooden ketch had left New Zealand on November
21st she had been at forty-seven degrees south latitude. During
the next three weeks *Suhaili* slammed into easterly winds on all
but one day. By December 12th, the captain was half out of his
mind. He figured that the easterly winds had delayed him at
least a week and he feared that Moitessier would overtake him
for sure. By this time Knox-Johnston had slogged northward to
thirty-seven degrees. Obviously he was out of the westerlies and
into the zone of variables so he tacked to the south and deter-

mined to hang on until he found the westerlies, icebergs or no icebergs. "After three days of heading slightly west of south I ran into . . . [the westerlies] again," he wrote, "but I had lost about ten days, and I seriously wondered if this had . . . [cost] me any chance of winning the race."

Knox-Johnston's radio transmitter had not worked for a long time, so he began taking it to pieces. He discovered a broken wire which he resoldered. Although *Suhaili* was 900 miles east of New Zealand, the English merchant marine officer managed a faint radio contact and was pleased to know that his radio was in order. Further east he was out of range and had trouble getting radio time signals which were the only way to update his chronometer error. Although there were regular time signals broadcast from Hawaii, Argentina, Australia, various BBC repeater stations, and elsewhere, Knox-Johnston had no luck receiving them and was obliged to rely on his chronometer for longitude sights for the next four weeks.

The captain dreamed a lot on his Pacific crossing. Many dreams concerned the race, hot baths, and spectacular meals ("The cook immediately took a huge steak with fried eggs, mushrooms, peas and chips and threw it overside. This outrage woke me up"). Sometimes Knox-Johnston dreamed of people he had not seen in years. He was amazed at the recall powers of the mind and he marveled at the capacity of the brain to store astonishing amounts of obscure information. Perhaps dreams should be taken more seriously by the public at large. Modern society is so busy and materialistic that it forgets to look at dreams and their meanings. In many rural societies in Africa and Asia men often meet and talk of their dreams and what they represent. Knox-Johnston's more abstract dreams seldom made sense, but he continued to recall long-forgotten people and to speculate on the remarkable contents and depth of a person's mind.

Suhaili had found westerly winds, but the lack of a self-steering gear was a problem. In order to sleep, Knox-Johnston often shortened sail to achieve a steering balance. The reduced sail drive meant slower daily averages, which were disappointing. The bottom of the yacht was getting foul; but the weather and frigid ocean prevented any in-the-water scraping; nevertheless

Suhaili

the captain leaned over the side and used his kitchen spatula to clean off the stringy weed that grew along the waterline. This was only one problem. There were lots more. In truth after six months of continuous hard sailing, much of the gear and equipment was wearing out and Knox-Johnston was forced to spend two or three hours a day on repairs and upkeep just to stay even. Some of the running rigging began to look ragged and frayed. More and more frequently, the captain had to lower a sail and to run a row of hand stitches along a seam between two Dacron panels or slap a patch over a weak place. Maintenance was a never-ending task; the saving graces were Knox-Johnston's handiness with tools and facility for quick thinking.

Moitessier was a constant worry. *Suhaili* had been going poorly. To make up time, Knox-Johnston decided to chance the danger of ice and to sail further south where the west-to-east distances were shorter and the winds hopefully steadier and more westerly. In addition to the problem of cold, navigating near ice was lethal, especially for a singlehander who had to sail blind in order to sleep. Knox-Johnston discovered that the advice in his Admiralty Pilot book differed from the information on his Admiralty chart. So instead of taking the more northerly ice limit warning in the Pilot, he used the chart, which showed the ice a bit further south. He realized his action was not wholly prudent but he was desperate to get east.

By December 19th, *Suhaili* was at one hundred nine degrees west and forty-four degrees south and had made good about 2,280 miles or roughly 43 per cent of the 5,340-mile New Zealand-Cape Horn run. The yacht's daily average from New Zealand had been only 81.4 miles per day. The winds began to get more favorable and steady, however, and *Suhaili*'s average began to increase appreciably.

Sometimes while the captain fixed something or steered during changing weather he sang songs or recited poetry. He wondered whether the long solo voyage had changed him. Knox-Johnston felt sane and he thought that his powers and faculties were as good as ever. Once in a while he got out his tape recorder to check his speech delivery. He especially enjoyed learning new stanzas of poetry and decided that the mental discipline was good for him.

Severe squalls often swept down on *Suhaili* and heeled the little vessel as if a giant hand were pushing on the sails. The captain learned to watch the clouds to windward and to shorten sails whenever he saw a low line of dark clouds advancing toward him—especially clouds with ragged bottoms.

For several days Knox-Johnston's eyes itched. He immediately thought back to the mishap he had had with the battery acid months before. Now, however, both eyes bothered him. He eventually traced the problem to a can of disinfectant that had somehow leaked into the bilges. The smell spread all through the yacht and it wasn't until the captain tossed the leaky can overboard that the fumes began to ease. Knox-Johnston poured buckets of seawater in the bilges and pumped out the water to flush out the horrible chemical. He then opened up both hatches to air out the cabin. Unfortunately just when he had the hatches open a large wave bounced on board and a great deal of water cascaded below into the cabin. Knox-Johnston immediately closed up the yacht, jumped below, and began pumping out the water. In twenty minutes he had the bilges emptied, but his clothes, the galley, the charts, and his radio were soaked. In his entire voyage only three waves broke on board and this had to be one of the times!

Knox-Johnston's clothes and bedding had been damp for a long time but he had managed to keep them reasonably dry by airing them when he could and letting the warmth from his body help dry his things. To wash his clothes the captain soaked them in sea water and detergent and then dragged them astern on a bit of line for a rinse. If he was lucky there would then be rain to rinse his clothes; otherwise he wrung out the seawater and hung the clothes next to the heater. Unfortunately clothes with salt in them never really get dry because salt is hygroscopic and absorbs moisture from the atmosphere. In addition, any water that fell on the captain while he was working on deck and ran underneath his oilskins made things worse. After a while the clothes got so salty that a soak in sea water was an improvement.

When Knox-Johnston slept, he generally stripped off his damp clothes, took a slug of brandy, and climbed into his damp sleeping bag which gradually warmed up from the heat of his body. He longed for the warm freshwater rains of the tropics.

Forty-eight hours after the wave broke on board, *Suhaili* sailed into fog. She was at forty-seven degrees south latitude and some two thousand miles from Cape Horn. Knox-Johnston thought of ice at once, and took the air and sea temperatures, which were colder than he had expected. The cold could have been caused by an upwelling of ocean water from the depths or by ice. The water was blue and devoid of plankton and fish and there was no bird life around *Suhaili*. Upwelling water is often greenish and full of plankton and small and large fish with bird life overhead. Knox-Johnston concluded that since the sea was blue, the cold was caused by ice. He climbed into the cockpit and kept watch, with naps when the fog cleared somewhat. After forty-eight hours the sun appeared again. The captain hurried below, climbed into his sleeping bag, and sacked out for eighteen hours.

On Christmas eve Knox-Johnston thought of his family back in England. He felt very lonely so he poured himself a few glasses of whisky, climbed out on deck, and sang all the Christmas carols he knew. His solo vocal performance managed to cheer him up. On Christmas day *Suhaili*'s captain woke up with a wretched hangover, but he made a big effort with his holiday meal. Stewed steak, potatoes, peas, a special currant duff, and a bottle of wine that his brother had sent along. He drank a toast to the queen of England and solemnly hoped that he—a Briton—would be the first man to complete the race. He also admitted that he was thoroughly enjoying himself.

During the next few days the winds turned easterly again and soon *Suhaili* was banging along on a south-southeasterly course. The fat ketch did not sail well in lumpy head seas and when the course made good fell to due south (180°), he tacked but could only make north-northeast 020°). The wind kept its easterly component day after day. Sometimes the course improved to northeast or southeast, but when the yacht pounded hard into head seas the captain felt that he had to steer by hand to ease his vessel through the waves. Years before, in the Arabian sea, when *Suhaili* was on her first long voyage, a seam in the hull had opened up and the three men on board had bailed for their lives for thirty hours. Knox-Johnston had no wish to duplicate that experience. Steering by hand near the ice zone was a cold business, however, and the captain's hands soon got numb. The easterly winds continued. Knox-Johnston got madder and madder. "I'm not the sort of person who takes adverse conditions calmly and my mood at present is murderous," he said. Seas swept over *Suhaili* until the captain felt that he had to bear off to ease the pounding. When the wind shifted and Knox-Johnston tacked, he was left with the slop from the old sea. The wind rose and fell; the rain turned to hail; the barometer rose and fell and rose again. In the meantime, Knox-Johnston sewed split seams on the sails that weren't in use.

Even in midsummer at forty-eight degrees latitude in the Southern Ocean the weather was bitterly cold. During gales *Suhaili* pitched and rolled. Knox-Johnston wondered whether his home afloat could withstand the swirling tempests around him. Sometimes the only recourse was to hoist the tiny storm jib, stream the long warp over the transom, drink a hot whisky and water, and turn in.

Finally on January 1st the easterlies—the winds that did not blow according to the pilot charts—shifted to the west. The messy, leftover seas hindered *Suhaili* at first but soon the wooden ketch was hurrying toward the tip of South America. The English captain realized he would soon see Cape Horn, so he looked over his vessel with an eye to extra severe weather. He had already gone through so much, however, that he was reasonably prepared. The only thing he did was to hack off the remains of the iron self-steering vane structure and toss it over the side. He feared the legs of the framework might tear up the deck or endanger the mizzen mast.

At 0430 on January 10th, the captain felt *Suhaili* head into the wind and straighten up. He looked out and saw that the mainsail had split in two. Knox-Johnston furled the remains and went back to sleep. Later in the morning, while preparing breakfast, he spilled boiling porridge on his wrist as the yacht took an unexpected jump. A burned wrist on a hand that was in constant use was awkward, and it was only a short time until the cuff of his oilskin jacket broke the blisters. Knox-Johnston removed the torn mainsail and bent on his old one, which surprised him by its relatively good condition. The torn mainsail had deteriorated so gradually that he hadn't realized how worn it had become.

On the next day Knox-Johnston steered by hand for twelve hours and made excellent mileage with a fair wind. He tried various radio calls but got no response. Now he steered southeast to get down to the latitude of Cape Horn—fifty-six degrees four minutes south. January 12th was relatively clear and the sextant sights showed 480 miles to go. The weather was squally with a high sea and swell. The captain had trouble steering and was obliged to shorten sail. His burned wrist hurt a lot. He was short of matches and cigarettes and began to ration both items. At noon he made the dreadful discovery that *Suhaili*'s jibstay wire had three broken strands and was unraveling. There were still sixteen strands left but the signs were bad. Knox-Johnston clipped on his safety harness for the first time in three-and-a-half months, crawled out on the pitching bowsprit, and made a temporary lashup.

He surveyed his liquor stock and found that he had ten bottles left. So far he had drunk thirteen bottles and spilled one. His consumption was about one bottle every two weeks.

By January 14th, the captain was very tired because of the long watches and never-ending repairs. His trials weren't over, however, because the gooseneck on the main boom broke again. This time the brass casting sheared in two. Poor Knox-Johnston had been plagued with junky Sunday afternoon yacht hardware since the race began, but the two worst items were the wire halyard winches and the main boom gooseneck, both of which had apparently been designed by fools for a fool's market.

"So, now, there is no jibstay, the jib is damaged, the main gooseneck has gone, and the new mainsail which has rope at its reefing points, is split," wrote the captain. "Not to fuss, I've put the kettle on, and I shall settle down and try and work out a way of fixing up a jury gooseneck."

All throughout the long race Knox-Johnston exhibited marvelous patience and an incredible perseverance to go on in spite of a marginal yacht and one frustration after another. To deal with the broken gooseneck he took a long piece of metal from the remains of the self-steering apparatus, cut a slot down the middle of the wooden boom, bolted three-quarters of the long dimension of the metal piece into the boom slot, and then fitted the forward one-quarter of the metal piece to the remains of the fitting on the mast. He put fiberglass material over the metal plate-boom joint and followed this with two strong rope seizings. The repair took two days. In the meantime Knox-Johnston set the spare mizzen as a loose-footed mainsail and logged another 90 miles.

The barometer took a mighty plunge, the wind increased, and Knox-Johnston reefed the mizzen he had set as a mainsail. Dreaded Cape Horn was only 200 miles away. "I don't mind admitting I feel a bit scared tonight," wrote the captain as he thought about the evil reputation of his approaching goal. During the night, the cold front advanced from the west and soon it was blowing fifty knots. *Suhaili's* master dropped the sails, streamed his long warp over the stern, and turned in. By the middle of the next morning—January 16th—the weather was easing as the barometer began its usual dance upwards. The yacht was soon plowing along eastward with more sail up. Later in the day, *Suhaili* was bombarded with hail that rattled on deck like stones falling on a snare drum. In the squally weather, Knox-Johnston had to shorten sail, but every change was now a problem because of the raw and painful burned place on his right hand and wrist.

An hour after midnight the captain tried to steer through a squall, but part of a wave broke over him from the port side and as *Suhaili* rolled, the remainder of the wave sluiced over the helmsman from the starboard side. He was soaked. Between the squalls the weather was reasonable and except for the cold wind and the burn on his hand—now bandaged—the captain thought it "enjoyable on deck." Although he was still taking a dollop of whisky now and then, he began to prefer hot coffee and cocoa, which he found warmed him more.

On the morning of January 17th, the visibility was excellent. At 0500 he saw the tiny islets of Diego Ramirez—sixty miles southwest of Cape Horn—bearing south of his vessel. During the day the wind eased off, so Knox-Johnston hoisted more and more sail. *Suhaili* ghosted along in five knots of wind while her captain watched heavy clouds rolling up in the west. Rain fell on the land in the distance and Knox-Johnston sat in the cockpit almost holding his breath while he looked at the marvelous scene before. It was almost a make-believe dream. Was that long island really Tierra del Fuego? Were those mountains the southern end of the mighty Andes? Somewhere in that maze of geography lay the Strait of Magellan. The rain shower to the north moved away and as the air cleared, Knox-Johnston could plainly see steep cliffs at the southern end of a small island. It was Cape Horn at last. A little after seven o'clock in the evening the stern black islet was abeam and the long crossing from New Zealand was over. Knox-Johnston drank a bit of whisky and broke open a fruit cake that his aunt had sent along for this moment. In his log book he wrote YIPPEE!!!

22. *The Gentle Philosopher*

BERNARD MOITESSIER HAD LEFT THE INDIAN OCEAN and Tasmania behind him and had sailed into the Pacific on December 19th, about a month (twenty-nine days) before Knox-Johnston reached Cape Horn. Neither man had any idea where the other was, although each thought about his fellow competitor from time to time. Both men knew that *Joshua* was faster and more suitable for the race. Both also knew that Knox-Johnston had started the race sixty-eight days before the French sailor and that the Englishman was fiercely determined to be first.

Moitessier started off well and logged 642 miles during his first five days into the Pacific. He looked forward to celebrating Christmas east of New Zealand. On December 24th, however, after a brief gale from the southeast, the wind fell away to nothing. A warm sun beamed down and *Joshua* rode easily on gentle swells in the Southern Ocean near the southern tip of New Zealand's South Island. Moitessier watched small seals swimming around his red ketch. "These seal families sleeping in the sun will be my Christmas present; especially the little ones—they're so much nicer than electric trains."

For Christmas the French captain unwrapped a specially prepared York ham given to him by friends in England. "The ham is perfect, without a trace of mould after four months in a humid atmosphere," he wrote. "Hey! What's happening to me? I suddenly start drooling like a dog with a choice bone under his nose. I must have had a long-standing ham deficiency. . . . I snap up a piece of fat the size of my wrist; it melts in my mouth."

For lunch, I fix a sumptuous meal. I pour a two-pound can of hearts of lettuce, well rinsed in seawater, into a pot where a piece of ham has been simmering with three sliced onions, three cloves of garlic, a little can of tomato sauce, and two pieces of sugar. Jean Gau was the one who explained that you should always add a little sugar to neutralize the tomatoes' acidity. Then I take a quarter of a canned camembert, cut it into little cubes, and sprinkle it over the hearts of lettuce, along with a big piece of butter. The aroma wafts all through the cabin as the pot simmers very gently on the asbestos plate. Cook it very, very slowly, because of the cheese. That is another secret.

The mountains of New Zealand—some fifty miles away— chopped dark blue notches into the sky above the horizon to the northeast. As the Christmas sun set, the flimsy breeze died, and *Joshua* floated quietly on the silent ocean. The only light was from pinpricks of white from the stars far above the quiet sea. Moitessier had given up listening to the radio because he was sick of the endless commercialism of Christmas. He hated the sleazy huckstering and the radio advertisements which in essence chanted that if you didn't buy buy buy you would go to hell hell hell. Where in the Bible is it written that a person has to spend money with merchants at Christmas? Did God require you to buy expensive presents? "How could we so lose our sense of the divine and the meaning of life?" the French sailor wondered.

The wind returned the next day and *Joshua* again churned a white furrow eastward. The first problem was to get past the tip of Stewart Island, a forty-mile-long bit of hilly land that extended southwest from South Island, the main mass of New Zealand. In addition to Stewart Island itself, south of the island were three nasty breaking ledges: North Trap, Boomerang Breaker, and South Trap (see map on page 180). The day was overcast, which made it hard to catch the sun with the sextant. Nevertheless Moitessier waited patiently on deck and followed the bright places in the clouds where the sun was trying to peek through. Suddenly the sun appeared for a few moments. The captain quickly raised the sextant to his eye and carefully twisted the micrometer screw to bring the reflected image of the sun down to the horizon. Then he glanced at his watch, wrote down the time and sextant angle, and hurried below to work out the calculations. Hooray! The job was done. *Joshua* was forty miles west of Puysegur Point, the southwest corner of South island. Moitessier steered south to give Stewart Island and the rocks as wide a berth as possible.

By noon the next day *Joshua* had logged another 100 miles and was thirty-two miles southwest of Stewart island; South Trap

BERNARD MOITESSIER

lay ahead to the east. While a good sailing breeze strengthened from the southwest and then west, Moitessier navigated carefully. Once South Trap was abeam, the ocean was clear for 4,635 miles—all the way to Cape Horn.

Suddenly the captain heard familiar whistling and squeaking sounds. Dolphins! Moitessier hurried on deck to find a hundred dolphins swimming alongside, rushing around and around in tight formations like ballet dancers, splashing, cutting from port to starboard and back again, whipping the water white, then submerging, zigzagging upwards again—a wild exhibition of exuberance and power. Moitessier had seen thousands of similar creatures during his years at sea but these dolphins seemed different. These dolphins were nervous and agitated beyond normal. They jumped and beat the water with their flat tails and kept making massed turns to the right.

Moitessier glanced at the compass and froze. The west wind had shifted to the south, and the yacht—under the guidance of the steering vane—had obediently followed the shift. With the sea so smooth and the sky overcast, the French captain had not realized what had happened. *Joshua* was running straight toward Stewart Island and South Trap at seven knots! How long had this been going on? Moitessier immediately dropped the mizzen staysail, hardened in on the sheets, and adjusted the vane for a closehauled course to the southeast to get away from the land and rocks. After the course change Moitessier again watched the dolphins. Now their movements were different: more subdued, with the customary rapid swimming at the bow. The dolphins rushed along from port to starboard and back again, but their violent antics had stopped. An exception was one big black and white porpoise that leaped entirely clear of the water and rolled over and over. Had these creatures been trying to tell *Joshua* that she was headed for trouble? Or were these nautical acrobats merely crossing the sea and showing off? Or had the captain imagined the whole thing?

The porpoises stayed with the yacht for five hours instead of the usual ten or fifteen minutes. Moitessier was wonderstruck. He was tempted to go back on the course toward South Trap to see if the porpoises would resume their violent behavior, but his better judgment told him to keep headed away from danger.

Initially *Joshua* found light winds from the west. The mileages of the daily runs were irregular—80, 20, 63, 55, 130, 140—but the red ketch kept going in the right direction. Even at forty-eight degrees south latitude the days were mild and sunny. Where were the gales and the terrible seas? And the icebergs? Icebergs? Moitessier knew almost nothing about the hazards of ice. Today's pilot books have little to say on the subject because all big ships carry radar. As part of his preparations for the voyage, therefore, Moitessier had written personal letters to fifteen French captains who had rounded Cape Horn under sail in the old days. Were there any ways to predict icebergs other than by visual sightings? Which routes across the Southern Ocean were the most dangerous? Had any of the captains encountered ice near the Falkland Islands after rounding Cape Horn?

Captain François Le Bourdais said not to worry. Icebergs exist and can be fatal but are usually not seen at all. The other captains agreed. In fact only three of the Cape Horn veterans had ever seen icebergs along the route. Captain Georges Aubin had come upon ice east of the Falklands in the South Atlantic but not elsewhere. Captains Francisque Le Goff and Pierre Stéphan had sailed near icebergs in the Southern Ocean only twice in eighteen voyages.

Le Goff wrote that the ice was clearly visible. Once in a fog bank his crew had seen little floes. A short time later his men sighted icebergs ahead. Captain Stéphan's sole sighting was a stranded berg on Falkland bank, south of the islands. This berg was enormous, some 240 feet high and 2500 to 2700 feet long, a colossus of flinty ice. The men on board had felt no temperature change when they passed the ice.

The letters did not give Moitessier much specific advice. Nevertheless they were full of comradeship, hope, and encouragement. The retired master mariners may have been old and feeble (some were in their eighties; one was almost blind) but their spirits and memories were as sharp as fresh winter breezes.

The stars blazed in the night sky and *Joshua*'s weather continued clear, even at forty-eight degrees south, near the broken red ice line on the chart. After passing New Zealand, Moitessier had planned to head up to forty degrees where the weather might have been easier. However, as the weather continued fair where he was, he stayed eight degrees further south. He logged daily runs of 130, 146, 148, 143, 149, and 148 miles. He was almost to the middle of the Pacific and still the hatch was open. Scarcely any spray had fallen on the decks. "[I] breathe peacefully and thank heaven for its gifts," wrote the Frenchman.

Of the nine men who started the race Moitessier was by far the most experienced in sailing small vessels across oceans. In previous voyages he had sailed tens of thousands of miles through the Indian Ocean, the South Atlantic, the Mediterranean, and the Pacific. He had left the bones of two yachts on remote shores, but he had learned much and had become a master mariner. Three years earlier he had taken *Joshua* from Tahiti to Spain via Cape Horn on a trip with his wife. Although not a fancy yacht by any means, *Joshua* was strong, fast, and sailed to the limit by the French captain, who put up lots of canvas and drove his vessel as hard by himself as an ordinary captain would have done with a crew of four or five. The lofty ketch rig could carry clouds of sails, and when the weather was light *he carried them*, not only the ordinary working sails, but two or three or more extra sails. Depending on the wind and its steadiness, he chose from among a mizzen staysail, a watersail slung beneath the main boom, an extra jib to fill up the space to leeward behind the eased mainsail when running with a poled-out headsail carried to windward, a bonnet or extension to the foot of the largest genoa, and a light-weight storm jib hauled up as a second main-staysail. Such a collection of sails and their halyards and sheets was mind-boggling for a singlehander. In smooth weather, however, the rig picked up the slightest breeze.

When the wind strengthened, the sails were arranged so they could be easily shortened. They came down one at a time or were reefed to smaller and smaller sizes. Through the years Moitessier had perfected his handling techniques so that it was easy for him to have the right sail area for the corresponding wind. Coupled with a fast hull whose underwater parts he endeavored to keep clean by occasional scrubbing, he often chalked up 160 and 170 miles a day, astonishing runs by a singlehander in a thirty-nine-foot vessel.

Now with moderate winds in the mid–Southern Ocean he averaged 144 miles a day for the next six days. The good weather held. On his earlier voyage from Tahiti to Cape Horn, Moitessier and his wife had had to close the companionway hatch when they had passed forty degrees south. They had not only closed the hatch but they had been obliged to *gasket* the hatch with a heavy towel to keep the icy water from gushing in. On that trip Moitessier seldom went on deck without a safety line around his waist. It was double-thick woolen socks and seaboots and mittens and gloves and heavy sweaters and fishermen's trousers and oil-skins just to survive. On this voyage so far, however, except for a long southwest swell, the sea stayed relatively calm. At dawn the temperature of the unheated cabin was fifty-five degrees; at noon seventy-five degrees. The captain seldom dressed during the day and he was as tanned as he had been in the tropics. Sun bathing at forty-eight degrees south? It was positively immoral!

The Frenchman had plenty of food on board. Enough for a year in case of dismasting or being stranded on an isolated island. The only thing the captain lacked, he complained, was talent as a chef. "Cooking reminds me of beautiful music: I can appreciate it, delight in it, but not produce it."

Before the start of the voyage, Dr. Jean Rivolier, the head doctor of the French Polar Expeditions and a man who knew much about short-handed enterprises, had counseled varied and appetizing meals. He said not to eat the same things too often or cooked the same way or not cooked at all. Michael Richey, another prominent singlehanded sailor echoed a similar thought: "It seems important to eat well, to prepare the food with care, and even to serve it properly: one could be reduced to gnawing in one's bunk."

Finally the needle on the barometer began to creep to the left. Five miles up in the sky a high altitude wind was shredding feathery cirrus clouds into mares' tails. Heavy weather was on its way. Moitessier changed sails: a fifty-four-square-foot storm jib, a reef in the staysail, two reefs in the small mainsail, and a close-reefed mizzen. He put up a half-size steering vane blade in place of the regular blade and set the steering to head east-northeast to get away from the approaching weather depression and any possible icebergs.

The gale turned the sea white with foam. Moitessier dropped his reefed mainsail entirely and then the mizzen. *Joshua* raced along under two tiny headsails. The captain had the yacht under careful control. His mind, however, raced far ahead and considered incredible decisions.

Moitessier had a wonderful communication with the sea. The link was almost a spiritual thing, a semireligious appreciation of the sun and wind and clouds. He was attuned to the creatures of the sea and sky, and came close to talking to the seals and dolphins. He treated the albatrosses and petrels as welcome friends. He loved the cloud forms and was fascinated by the changing moon.

At an earlier date, a friend and his wife had noticed that the frantic pace of ordinary life in Europe was making them nervous and tired. Modern "civilization" was too demanding and hectic. The friend and his wife turned to yoga, which helped them to regain their equilibrium. Before the race, Moitessier showed the same symptoms of being upset and frantic so the friend sent Moitessier a book on yoga. At first the book was set aside, but in the Indian Ocean, Moitessier began to look at it. His ulcer pained him and he suffered from lumbago. Both his energy and spirits were low.

"When I first leafed through the book in the Indian ocean, I felt it emanating all the values of my native Asia, all the wisdom of the old East, and I found a few little exercises I had always done instinctively when I was tired. My ulcer stopped bothering me, and I no longer suffered from lumbago. But above all, I found something more. A kind of undefinable state of grace."

What Moitessier had discovered in his long solitary hermitage of the sea was a philosophy of peace, a mystical, oceanic experience that seemed better than all else. Land and people were foreign and alien. The sea was his friend. At sea, Moitessier's mind and spirit were at ease and he was filled with a marvelous tranquility. After almost five months, his hair had grown to shoulder length, and with an enormous beard he took on the outward appearance of a Hindu swami. As his solitary sailing continued, he became so at one with the sea that he found it hard to imagine any other life.

When this gentle man thought of Europe and all the people and business and commerce and automobiles and industrial smoke and the noise of machinery and screaming children and bank payments and scheming attorneys and parades with booming bass drums and growling helicopters and shrieking jet airplanes, he rebelled. He just couldn't return to Europe. "Man has been turned into a money-making machine to satisfy false needs, false joys," he wrote.

He would not go back. Any life other than the present one was a desecration. He knew he would eventually have to stop his marathon voyage because of supplies and food; still there was plenty of stuff on board for a long time yet. He thought of the seals and their friendly simplicity. Yes, he would sail back to the Galápagos islands off the coast of Ecuador where the seals were the friendliest anywhere. Or return to French Polynesia where the dark-haired people accepted you simply and whole-heartedly.

To get to the Galápagos all he had to do was to turn gently to the left and head north. He could be there in a few weeks. A run north in the beautiful southeast trade wind. . . . In spite of these thoughts he had to round Cape Horn first. He still had bridges to cross in his soul. "If I hold on, if *Joshua* holds on, then we will try to go further. Round Good Hope again, round Tasmania again, across the whole Pacific again . . . and reach the Galápagos to add things up." Moitessier was determined to ignore Europe. He would "forget the world [and] its merciless rhythm of life. Back there, if a businessman could put out the stars to make his billboards look better at night, he just might do it."

The gale passed over in one day. Soon the bigger sails were up again. Moitessier washed out his heavy woolen socks with rainwater. Now he wore more adequate clothing because it was cold. The sea felt icy and he seemed to have slipped into a zone of real Cape Horn weather. Another gale passed going eastward, and the sea rumbled continuously. He had days of 152, 166, 158, 147, 162, and 169 miles—a thousand miles a week. Neither Moitessier nor Knox-Johnston knew it, but *Joshua* was gaining steadily on *Suhaili*.

The cabin hatch was shut. Rain and low clouds swept across stormy skies. Cross-seas slammed on board. Now, when Moitessier dealt with sails, he kept himself tied to his vessel with a safety harness snapped to a $3/16$-inch diameter wire that stretched along each side deck from bow to stern. The harness clip slid along the wire and the captain was able to do deck work with both hands. A bucket hung from the main boom to collect rainwater. So far in the Pacific, Moitessier had poured nineteen gallons in his tank, only a little less than he had used (he needed 2½ quarts a day). During the fifty-six-day Indian Ocean crossing he had collected forty gallons and used thirty-five.

After four peaceful days (130, 111, 147, and 142 miles), more sunbathing, and a lot of drying and airing of bedding, all the signs pointed to another big gale: a wind shift, heavy swell, and a falling barometer. *Joshua* was dropping down toward Cape Horn and she crossed fifty degrees south as she angled toward the tip of South America. The wind rose to thirty knots and then eased. The sky cleared partially, the heavy northwest swell lessened, and the barometer steadied. There was no gale.

Moitessier took stock of himself and felt that he was working within the limits of his strength. Compared with his first Cape Horn trip he was ahead, both in miles covered and in energy saved, because he flew small sails with lots of reefs that were easy to handle. On the first voyage he had had no winches; now he had excellent winches that made pulling down a reef a cinch. Every action—trimming, reefing, unreefing, or dealing with halyards had to be easy; otherwise it was dreaded and avoided.

This French philosopher of the sea savored the magic moments. It was the spirit of Melville and Ahab, the whale and the eternal quest:

A moonbeam bounces off a cloud far to the south, becoming a slender spire of softly glowing light rising straight up in the sky. . . . How did the moon pull off such a lovely trick?

The spire widens, glows very brightly. It looks like a huge spotlight searching among the stars. . . . A chill comes over me. It isn't the moon playing with a cloud, but something uncanny I don't know about. Could it be the white arch of Cape Horn, that terrifying thing Slocum mentions, the sign of a big gale? The stars shine with a hard glint and the sea looks menacing beneath the icy moon.

A second spire rises next to the first. Then a third. Soon there are a dozen, like a huge bouquet of super-natural light. And now I understand . . . it is an aurora australis, the first I have ever seen, perhaps this voyage's most precious gift to me.

Later *Joshua* sliced through thin banks of fog. Four small sails and a thirty-knot wind drove her at hull speed. The Southern Ocean scarcely rumbled; perhaps the closeness of land to the east had eased the discontent of the ocean. With hazards getting ever closer, sextant work was critical. Too far south risked ice; too far north meant the peril of land. Moitessier wanted no surprises while he was asleep. *Joshua* hurried ever eastward and a bit south under her little sails, scudding and surfing while the captain stalked the elusive sun with his sextant. Sometimes the sun appeared for a few moments. On other days the cloud cover was too heavy and he had to make do with dead reckoning—advancing his compass course and recorded mileage.

Now he was up at night, watching and looking ahead, trying to drive *Joshua* past Cape Horn before a new gale erupted from the west. In the darkness the sea sparkled with bits of blue-green. "The lower part of the staysail is full of living pearls," he wrote. "They reach almost a third of the way up, then run off along the bunt of the reef. They come from the phosphorescent foam picked up by the bow and shattered by the whisker stay."

The wind increased a little so Moitessier put the third reef in the mainsail, which meant its area was only sixty-five square feet. *Joshua* logged forty-eight miles in six hours. The captain stood by the mainmast hypnotized by the speed and the rushing water. He thought of dropping the mainsail altogether. But no! *Joshua* was going too well to be disturbed, surfing forward on each overtaking wave in a swelling whoosh of white. . . .

Down went a sail, another pot of coffee, a wind drop, a reef out, a nap, a noon sight (171 miles), a heavy sea, forty-five knots of wind, a hunt for the tiny islets of Diego Ramirez (the western outpost of Cape Horn), sunset, less wind, a clear night, twinkling stars, another sleep (dreams of youth and adventure), an alarm clock that rang but was not heard, and moonlight through a portlight on the captain's face. Up again. Less wind. A careful look in the moonlight. A black hillock that climbed above the sea and did not move. Cape Horn. February 5th. *Joshua* had crossed the Pacific.

23. *The Battered Trimaran*

AFTER THE DETOUR TO OTAGO HARBOR on February 2nd
to hand across films and letters, Nigel Tetley steered
his big blue and white trimaran eastward. The radio crackled
with reports of Hurricane Carrie whirling closer and closer to
New Zealand from the north and crushing and demolishing
everything in sight. Down at the south end of New Zealand,
Tetley hurried east to get as far away from the land and storm
as he could. The wind drove the yacht so hard that he finally
pulled down the sails and stopped in order to get something to
eat and to rest. By the afternoon the wind had lessened so he
got underway again, but during the first few hours some nasty
waves slammed into *Victress* and heeled her alarmingly. It was a
hell of a way to start across the Pacific.

Tetley soon neared 180 degrees east longitude—the international date line—where his clock read twelve hours more than
Greenwich time. Going eastward, this meant that he would have
two days with the same date. Two February 5ths. He toyed with
the idea of delaying the time change for three days—to February 8th—his birthday and the date for his official retirement from
the Royal Navy after twenty-seven years of service. If there were
two February 8ths would there be two birthdays and two retire-
ments? It sounded like a children's game of riddles, so the captain settled the problem by writing two February 5ths in the log
and officially changing from east to west longitude.

sped onward. He was delighted to receive birthday greetings from Eve and his two sons. For his birthday lunch he baked white bread, uncorked a bottle of special wine, served himself prawns and octopus pilaf. He might have been behind the others in the race, but he certainly ate well and was the undisputed gourmet of the solo round-the-world fleet. He had also become quite a music lover. While Tetley cooked and ate and washed the dishes he played symphonies and choral music and concertos on his

NIGEL TETLEY

music system. Already the tapes seemed old, however, and he wished that he had brought twice as many.

On the evening of his birthday the wind settled in the northwest where it stayed for the next four days. The bearded lieutenant-commander kept plenty of sail up and during gusts and squally periods he took the helm to hold her steady while the trimaran planed ahead. He had no idea where the other contestants were, especially Moitessier, but Tetley hoped that *Victress* was pulling ahead in the race. A whale blew alongside and then blew again a little in front of the yacht before making off. Later the wind dropped to eight knots so Tetley checked the port float and pumped it free of water. He switched to a full bottle of cooking gas for the galley. He made efforts to caulk the skylight and cabin portlights with sealing compound. The leaks were so persistent, however, that to be sure he rigged a drip can inside the cabin over his bunk at the worse spot. He read a bit but he had been through all the books and wished for something new to lose himself in.

On the tenth day from New Zealand another gale developed. Tetley took down everything except two small headsails as the weather front passed. The battery charger needed new brushes. He had none, but after a lot of head-scratching and looking at everything electrical on board, he managed to rob the useless engine generator of one of its brushes, which he filed down to fit. Radios and charging plants certainly added to the complexity of a voyage.

From February 14th to 19th the wind blew lightly from the south and east. "One day when the surface wind blew gently, I noticed several spiral-like cloud formations first gathering and then whirling away at great speed, as if marshalled by some unseen hand," he wrote. "I had an uneasy feeling."

When Tetley next spoke with New Zealand he learned that Moitessier's red-hulled two-master had been sighted off the Falkland islands on February 10th. This meant that the Frenchman was two weeks ahead of *Victress,* which was a disappointment. There was no news of Donald Crowhurst or Robin Knox-Johnston.

On the afternoon of February 20th, *Victress* lay becalmed under a sunny sky on a quiet sea. "The ocean was almost asleep: even the swell had subsided. An intense feeling of loneliness swept over me. Time . . . seemed of no account and mortal man a brash intruder." To cheer himself up Tetley fired up his stove and cooked another spectacular: rice, runner beans, mushrooms, and crab and mackerel in a tomato sauce.

The next day the west wind was back and *Victress* hurried eastward again. The wind didn't rise above twenty-five knots, but he felt uneasy: "A heavy swell made me shorten sail after several alarmingly prolonged wave rides," he said. Tetley had begun to play his tape recorder in the wheelhouse because the acoustics were better than in the cabin. One evening at sunset he listened to a guitar virtuoso softly plucking the strings of his instrument while the colors of the sky shifted from whites to reds to grays. "The world seems to pause and catch its breath," he wrote.

On February 24th Tetley logged 156 miles. He had hoped for more and was disappointed. That evening the wave patterns were a mess; the swells banged into one another from three different directions. During the next morning while the English captain ate a lumberman's breakfast (to the strains of Bruch's violin concerto) the breeze picked up again. The problem was that when the wind increased, it often rose too fast and soon overpowered the trimaran. Then the sails had to come down. If not they blew away or threatened the trimaran's stability. This happened later in the morning, when the wind split the jib from luff to leech as a gale escalated to forty-five knots. Tetley stopped his vessel, but on three occasions the yacht was knocked completely around to face the storm. A sea slammed into the wheelhouse and swept a five-gallon jug of water into the cabin. The main engine was flooded again; this time Tetley gave up on it.

In the night the wind dropped to thirty-five knots. The captain doggedly hoisted the spare jib and got going again. By noon the wind was a little less and he had a second small headsail flying. The trimaran kept up good speed until evening; everything seemed to be all right when a breaking wave zoomed in from astern. "*Victress* all but capsized," wrote Tetley. "I felt her teeter at an angle of about 50 degrees in a half cartwheel; then she slowly righted. One of the self-steering lines had parted, the cabin was a shambles, and as usual I received a soaking. Later I discovered that a heavy steel box of tools in the after cabin had been turned on end."

Tetley reviewed the incident.

The yacht had accelerated on the slope of the wave, had broached, and had then been slammed over by the crest. A cross-swell had been running at the time. Was the boat or poor seamanship to blame? If the boat, then I should head north out of the Roaring Forties immediately. I came to the conclusion that it was the trimaran's great stability that had saved me. The extra weight in the stern had probably averted disaster.

I harbored few illusions about . . . righting *Victress* if she did capsize—though I had of course made some provision. Firstly, I always
carried at my waist a well-honed knife with which to slash a way out
through the side curtain. Stowed ready to hand in the wheelhouse lay
a zipper bag containing a frogman's suit and face mask. My plan was to
take this with me and, from the upturned side of the yacht, pull out the
life raft and other survival gear. . . . Dressed in the rubber suit, I would
deliberately flood one of the floats by boring holes in it; then launch the
big RFD life raft on the other side and, pulling on one of the masthead
halyards, try to lever the trimaran upright. That all this would need
calm weather and more than a little luck needs no emphasis.

At noon on February 27th, Tetley wrote forty-seven degrees
south latitude and 115 degrees west longitude in his logbook.
Cape Horn lay 1,860 miles away on a course of 107 degrees true,
a little south of east. Everything continued smoothly until the
afternoon of Sunday, March 2nd.

The wind increased to storm force [48–55 knots], [he wrote]. I hove-
to for a couple of hours until I thought the worst had passed. But within
an hour of getting under way it came on worse than before, and after
experiencing a wild ride on a giant breaker, I hove-to once more. I
particularly noticed one large overhanging crest as it broke near *Victress:* if she had been underneath, it would have smashed her open like
an egg box.

At 0300 . . . a sea climbed into the wheelhouse before I could
straighten out the course. Constant hand-steering was needed, and I
hove-to for breakfast and to pump out the floats. . . . During the night,
conditions worsened. . . . and I was quite happy to let the trimaran surf.
As a breaker passed beneath, *Victress* would bounce rapidly up and down.
On one occasion this was accompanied by the sound of wood cracking
below. A long piece of joinery had sprung away from the cabin side. . . .

I was in the cabin clear of the window when the wave struck. There
was a roar and the six-foot-wide starboard window gave way. Simulta-
neously the clear panel on the wheelhouse side curtain was punched
out, and I heard the familiar sound of water coming in. Jagged pieces
of perspex swept across the cabin; full paraffin containers were lifted
from the deck on to the settee; practically everything else found its way
into the bilges. There was no quick recoil this time, just a solid wham,
and the sea was in.

Tetley's life was suddenly filled with problems. He needed hose clamps for the hand bilge pump. Rice from the galley clogged the electric pump. A ton of salt water rolled back and forth in the bilges with his clothes floating around here and there. All of his precious musical tapes had been submerged and soaked. The lieutenant-commander bailed with a bucket and somehow managed to board up the enormous hole where the cabin portlight had been. The waves roaring past seemed enormous and irregular and often collided with big cross-seas, which caused acres of foam and several near misses. Each time, the force of the falling water was like an avalanche of giant boulders and he could feel the ocean tremble.

The wave that had burst against the cabin had been focused on a small area, and when Tetley later inspected the starboard float he found two split frames and the deck edging sprung. That night—March 4th, still summertime in the Southern Ocean—was long, miserable, and wet. At dawn the wind blew a little under forty knots; the sea looked grey and dismal.

The cabin top had given way at deck level, posing a tricky repair problem, [he wrote]. I could only hope to patch it up at best. My high regard for *Victress* as a seaboat remained unshaken. On the other hand . . . she was insufficiently robust for the Southern ocean. One thing was certain. I had to find better weather. . . . [He decided to sail northward.] I went forward to hoist the jib. While undoing a sail tie I was suddenly jerked off my feet and slammed into the safety net. I lay sprawled face downwards staring into the cold and restless water. If confirmation were still needed this was it. The sea was the victor. I would retire from the race, make for Valparaiso, put the trimaran up for sale, and fly home.

By evening the resourceful naval officer had bolted various supports to the broken portlight area and had covered part of the damage with a sheet of plywood. The cabin was reasonably watertight again. The storm had moderated; so Tetley set a reefed headsail and headed north. He was fed up with the Southern Ocean and the cursed race.

On the next morning—March 6th—he spun the wheel to the right and headed east-southeast for Cape Horn again. "Sheer obstinancy," he said. In fact Tetley felt groggy and staggered about with a headache. He had been drinking salt water that had gotten into his two rear tanks but he switched to a forward tank which luckily was full of good water. The English sailor, exhausted by all the extra work and nervous tension, uncharacteristically gobbled down food when he could. The next day he spent repairing his jib, which had two long rips in it. The spare jib was a terminal case; so he had to fix the original because a jib was absolutely necessary if he were to sail anywhere. His sewing wasn't over, however; on the following day the mizzen split in two places and a little later several mainsail seams let go. Things were going to hell fast. Fortunately, while Tetley sewed, he could be cheered by music from a Chilean radio station.

On March 9th he repaired the side curtain in the wheelhouse and pumped out the main bilges, which he was surprised to find held sixty gallons of seawater. The cabin was a mess. The flooding had ruined a lot of food and gear.

I was determined to keep *Victress* going at full tilt and had the mainsail and reefed jib set when, in the evening, with a heavier sea running, water began to spurt into the cabin from under the starboard wing. The side buckled each time she hit a large wave and slivers of wood dropped from the stringers. Fatigue had produced in me a terrible mood of pigheadedness and—even faced with this evidence—I might well have continued until the whole boat was in pieces, had not common sense finally prevailed and I lowered the mainsail. Both yacht and man were near the end of their tethers. Only the closeness of Cape Horn and the prospect of kinder weather beyond kept me going.

Fortunately during the next few days the winds blew easier. Tetley had a chance to rest and to eat reasonable meals. He screwed a board over the center of the undamaged cabin window on the port side to break the force of any future waves "rejecting the idea of strengthening the window itself, as the whole cabin might then go." The sails continued to fall apart and demanded daily sewing sessions.

Early on March 12th, Tetley dropped the mainsail because of rain and squally weather. He moved the radio batteries to a drier place because salt water coming in under the wings made the batteries fume and smoke. Later he hoisted the mainsail and sewed on the mizzen. The next day he contacted Buenos Aires on the radio. On Friday, he dreamed that *Victress* was an airplane; he awoke and rushed out to drop the genoa as squalls swept in from the west.

Now he steered directly southeast for Cape Horn. The mainsail was in appalling condition so he dragged the spare on deck and exchanged one for the other as he had done earlier (how long could this go on?). Tetley baked bread for the first time in two weeks. On March 16th, a spinnaker pole sheared at the deck fitting. While he limped along with another sail Tetley did a midnight repair in the wheelhouse by the light of a flashlight. He then set the twin headsails again.

On March 17th, thick clouds made sun observations doubtful, but the veteran naval officer waited patiently and finally got useful sights. That night he kept a careful watch. The wind faded and then sprang up from the south—a blistering breeze that seemed straight from the South Pole. Tetley sat huddled in thermal underwear, a polar suit, and sweaters. In addition he had a sleeping bag draped around his shoulders, but he still shook from the cold. In the early morning he passed several islets to port that showed him exactly where he was and gave him time for a nap. At noon he was close-reaching to the east under one thousand square feet of sails. At 1300, he saw land ahead and an hour later Cape Horn hove into view. The weary officer's spirits revived and he cooked a fancy celebration dinner and opened a bottle of wine. Tetley and the battered trimaran had rounded Cape Horn. It was the first time for Tetley and the first time that a trimaran had sailed across the Southern Ocean. Both were lucky to have gotten across this stormy polar sea and past Cape Stiff, the seaman's name for Cape Horn.

24. *Back to the South Atlantic*

IT WAS STILL NOBODY'S RACE. Robin Knox-Johnston somehow hung on to the lead, but his margin was slipping, and almost the entire South and North Atlantic lay between Cape Horn and his finish line at Falmouth, England. According to Admiralty chart #5309, the official distance for sailing vessels totaled 8,260 miles. By the time the mileage penalties for unexpected headwinds and storms were factored in, however, a ship would easily log more than nine thousand miles.

Knox-Johnston used all his talents to try to keep his thirty-two-foot vessel going at four knots. *Suhaili's* wooden hull seemed reasonably sound and only leaked a little, but the coachroof had shifted, some of the rigging had given way, the self-steering had crumbled before the force of the sea, and corrosion had ruined the engine. Not only was the roller reefing gear for the mainsail useless, but the main boom gooseneck had broken twice, the wire halyard winches could only be used by tying the handles in place, the tiller was secured to the rudder with lashings of line, and one sail or another needed daily attention with a needle and thread. The list of defects went on and on. Nevertheless the English merchant marine officer was a good mechanic and he attacked each problem with skill and energy because he was keen to win and wanted to get home.

At Cape Horn, the third mark of the competition and the turning point for the final dash to England, Bernard Moitessier seemed certain to win. He had already shaved forty-nine days from the sixty-eight-day lead of Knox-Johnston and was sailing about 20 percent faster than his English opponent. Could Moitessier continue to average 120 miles each day? With calms and times of poor winds this meant that he would need days of 150 and 160 miles. He was sailing *Joshua* all by himself and doing as well as with a racing crew. His yacht was in excellent order and except for the collision incident near South Africa and a few minor repairs he had had no equipment difficulties at all.

Moitessier was a master seaman with extensive sailing experience. Yet, he was also a visionary whose yacht was his magic carpet to a kind of heaven-on-earth. Consequently, he became increasingly unwilling to return to Europe. During the previous August in England he had seemed reasonably happy and full of confidence. He had shared his sailing knowledge with Nigel Tetley and had even given him a special leak-stopping compound made of cement and plaster of Paris. Moitessier had been on the friendliest terms with his pal Loïck Fougeron and had gotten to know Bill King. Now the race itself receded in importance and the Frenchman muttered about withdrawing and sailing on to the Pacific. Could the effects of almost six months of solitude and the demands of twenty-four-hours-a-day sailing have influenced his judgment?

Nigel Tetley had rounded Cape Horn on March 18th, forty-one days after Moitessier and two months after Knox-Johnston. Tetley was a hearty man who liked good food and drink and who clearly loved classical music. All three of these graces were firmly on board his experimental three-hulled yacht (the big wave of March 4th *had* soaked the music system). Unfortunately his chances of winning seemed small and his vessel was in poor condition and getting worse with each storm. One could never tell in a long race, however. The leaders might get dismasted or suffer collisions with floating wreckage or other vessels. Those ahead might get sick, decide to give up, have their important sails blown out—anything was possible. In a competition you were honorbound to do your best and an English naval officer would certainly do his utmost. There was no doubt that Tetley drove his vessel as hard as he dared. In any case, no one had ever sailed a trimaran around the world nonstop before and Tetley was well on his way to a new record, whether he won the race or not.

Donald Crowhurst was the fourth man still in the race, a shadowy figure lurking along the untraveled edges of the South Atlantic. He had left Rio Salado in Argentina on March 8th after patching the starboard float of *Teignmouth Electron*. It was hard to believe that no one had noticed his illegal stop except a few locals, who labeled him a harmless eccentric.

After his brief visit to Argentina in early March, Crowhurst zigzagged southward in the South Atlantic toward the Falkland Islands, which lay 450 miles northeast of Cape Horn. As he got further south and away from the radio shadow of South America he was able to monitor the distant New Zealand radio channels for information and weather reports for his false logbook. He thought of trying to make transmissions to Wellington. Crowhurst also wanted to sail in the Southern Ocean so his descriptions would have reality and substance; a few filmed sequences with his BBC motion picture camera would verify that he had actually been in the roaring forties. A few days north of the Falklands, *Teignmouth Electron* sailed into heavy weather and was blown more than a hundred miles to the west-northwest. Crowhurst had found the gale he sought. He also felt safer in these southern waters because if he were seen and reported by a ship it would be better to be close to Cape Horn.

Crowhurst arrived at the Falkland Islands—the southernmost point of his journey—on March 29th. He didn't stop at Port Stanley, the main settlement, but merely jilled around for a day a little offshore before heading east and north toward England. He had been aboard his white-hulled ketch for 150 days and now he headed toward home in earnest.

The distance from Gough Island in the South Atlantic—which he had radioed he was near on January 15th—to Cape Horn via South Africa, Australia, and the Pacific is roughly 13,500 miles. Crowhurst planned to emerge from radio silence on April 15th—ninety days after he wrote the Gough Island telegram. He hoped that people in the outside world would believe his announcement that he had averaged 150 miles a day during his supposed crossing of the Southern Ocean. An average of 150 was perhaps high and might be thought suspicious after his abysmal runs early in the race. If he used a lower figure, however, he would have to mark time in the South Atlantic even longer and the other contestants would all be back in England. His idea was to slip in just before the others and to scoop up all the prizes. Maybe even a knighthood!

In early April, while sailing northward, Crowhurst began to compose various veiled messages for the commercial radio stations in New Zealand and Cape Town. He decided to announce his presence, but he wanted to infer that he was in the Pacific *west* of Cape Horn without giving away his true position *east* of Cape Horn in the Atlantic. He had his old problem of transmitting "TR" messages: telegrams sent by ships to long range radio telegraphy stations that keep track of ships' positions and destinations. Naturally the first questions the radio operators asked were Where are you? What is your position? Even the clever Crowhurst had trouble being evasive. Finally on April 9th he sent a telegram to his agent Rodney Hallworth:

DEVONNEWS EXETER HEADING-DIGGER RAMREZ   LOG KAPUT 17697
28TH   WHATS NEW OCEANBASHINGWISE

Hallworth got the message on the morning of April 10th and immediately telephoned Crowhurst's wife. Then he began to try to puzzle out the cryptic telegram which was studiously imprecise as always. Digger Ramrez was Diego Ramirez, the outpost islands a little west and south of Cape Horn. *Teignmouth Electron*'s mileage log had stopped working on March 28th when it read 17,697. Crowhurst asked for news of other contestants.

Hallworth calculated that if Crowhurst could maintain his speed he might win the race for the fastest time. Again there was no position given. Just where in the hell was Crowhurst anyway? Getting around Cape Horn was certainly newsworthy, but a press agent needed details. Facts. Something to work with. Hallworth reread all the old telegrams, did a lot of figuring of mileages, gazed into his crystal ball, and finally decided that Crowhurst has accidentally left out the information that he was 300 miles from Cape Horn when he had sent his message. By now (April 10th) he was well around the tip of South America. Hallworth

hurried to his typewriter, and the English newspapers for April
11th carried stories that *Teignmouth Electron* had weathered Cape
Horn and was now speeding northeastward toward England.
The news reports worked faster than Crowhurst had planned.
Everything was one week ahead of schedule. The trimaran's time
was really too fast for credibility but in the usual press confusion
this was overlooked. Only Sir Francis Chichester, the old fox of
small-ship voyaging, was convinced that something was wrong.
He reported his doubts to the race committee.

Crowhurst's wife, Clare, dutifully tried to explain her husband's inconstant radio messages. "Donald has a great sense of
humor and would think it a big joke to suddenly appear out of
nowhere and surprise everyone," she told a reporter.

Who among us doesn't long for moments of quietness and
solitude? Time to be alone with our private thoughts, our inner-
most hopes, our secret longings. Time for thoughts on the blue
edge of our consciousness. Time to reflect on dreams so personal that we hardly dare open the door to them. Who doesn't
need time to think about what we've done (or not done), time to
consider what we'll do next week, time to make peace with our
souls? We all have these moments, but most of us also have spells
when we want to be with someone, to ask advice, to talk about a
problem. Often we like to share a special experience with a loved
one or just to laugh and be with friends. A man's mental health
is usually a shifty balance between aloneness and gregariousness.
Yet we vary hugely in our appetites for other people. Some individuals cherish a solitary walk; others want a party every night.

The nine men who sailed from England on the solo round-
the-world race changed suddenly from living in an ordinary
society with people, to a life with only one person. Each of the
solitary mariners had to run his vessel, draw courses on his charts,
keep an eye on the compass, and maybe catch a fish once in a
while. Each man diagnosed his ills and remedies, made up his
mind about the strength of the wind, and decided on his daily
menu, the number of meals, and when he would eat. He had to
determine when to sleep (and for how long), and how to pace
himself—that is, how to spin out his daily jobs so he didn't get

too tired. Should he fill a kerosene lamp now or later? Should he get up out of his comfortable bunk and check around the horizon? Should he do some extra navigation? If he got exhausted his mind wouldn't work properly and he might hallucinate so he was careful to take frequent naps and not overtax himself.

Each decision was his alone and every day he made dozens of large and small judgments. His self-reliance was complete, but he needed to be a strong and resourceful individual.

The solo yachtsman operates totally without people. He practices his sport far from shore and far from cheering fans. Singlehanded yacht racing doesn't have the excited watchers of the boxing ring or the baseball diamond. We all know that the tennis champion, the football quarterback, the ace cricket batsman, and the Olympic swimmer have enthusiastic, flagwaving spectators who urge their heroes to greater efforts. The solo sailor has none of this. He functions in intense isolation. If he has any "fans" they are generally a few close friends or admirers who see him at the beginning or end of a passage. When the singlehander completes a race he sometimes even has to take his own finishing time ("if anybody cares"). The whole sport has an aura of remoteness and isolation. The participants are a special brand of sportsmen who speak with a strange vocabularly and who get their kicks from competence in maneuvers that keep their vessels using the winds to best advantage. All this is done in utter isolation—far from land and other people. The whole zany business is a bit like stagecoach driving in the rain, hunting with falcons, or hot-air balloon ascensions in South Dakota. Yet solitary sailing—like mountaineering or soaring high in the sky in gliders—takes its practitioners into the great outdoors, gives them wonderful peace and tranquility, and gets them supremely close to nature. Except for the few dabblers—who don't count—the commitment to singlehanded sailing is usually total and complete. The solitary sailors treasure their special life and seek no other.

The contestants in the round-the-world competition were all avowed sailors, but instead of a twenty-day passage between the Azores and Barbados, for example, this race went on and on.

There were times when the nine men got sick of the endless race and craved something different. Anything different. The trip around the world was long, too long, infinitely long. At the slow speed of a yacht you logged 100 miles or so each day. The whole distance was thirty thousand miles, more or less, which meant 300 days or ten months of sailing. That's 300 dawns and dusks, 300 noons and midnights, 900 solitary meals. No wonder most of the nine spoke of quitting at one time or another.

Five of the men—Blyth, Carozzo, Fougeron, King, and Ridgway—stayed in the race from twenty-six to ninety-eight days. Ridgway pulled out because of a structural failure. Blyth panicked when salt water got into his gasoline supply. In truth, these two men knew that their vessels were small and ill-suited for the race. More sailing experience would have helped both, and more resourceful captains might have kept their vessels going. Ridgway and Blyth were hard as nails physically, but they needed seasoning and a bit of the cunning of a Francis Chichester. Alex Carozzo withdrew because of bleeding stomach ulcers. Fougeron and King were wiped out in storms. King would have continued, indeed he was keen to complete the race, but he lost one mast and cracked the second when he was rolled over. Fougeron was shocked by the severity of the storms off South Africa and seemed quite pleased to retire from those awful seas. On November 27th (his 98th day) he wrote: "I am less than 100 miles from St. Helena . . . At 1800 hours I drop anchor. I go to Jamestown, visit the authorities, go to the doctor, where I am invited to dine."

These five men got along with themselves fairly well. The other four entries stayed in the race for much longer periods— seven to ten months. On November 1st, in the Indian Ocean, Moitessier wrote: "I find myself taking a long look at Mauritius, not very far north of here." The next day Knox-Johnston, nearing southeast Australia, echoed the same sentiments: "I think I'll give up at Melbourne. I've had enough. I'm tired, exhausted would be nearer the truth, frustrated because nothing I do seems to make any difference to the course, and scared to think what will break next." Tetley was far behind and nearing South Africa, but on November 27th he wrote: "An almost overpowering me." We know from Crowhurst's own words that he never wanted to leave on the race in the first place and ever afterward schemed how to withdraw without losing face.

Five of the nine were out. The four who were left—grumbling now and then—sailed hard for England. All four wanted to win.

25. *Homeward Bound*

IT TOOK KNOX-JOHNSTON SIX DAYS to sail the 450 miles between Cape Horn and Port Stanley in the Falkland Islands. The English captain kept trying to make radio contact with someone in Punta Arenas (Chile) or Port Stanley. His receiver worked perfectly and he could hear lots of Spanish and English voices on the commercial frequencies. But nobody answered. Evidently *Suhaili*'s transmitter did not work. Knox-Johnston headed for Port Stanley to make himself known, but on January 20th the wind began to blow hard from the north-east—the direction of the port. The choice was either east or northwest. The captain chose east because he feared running into the southern coast of the Falklands, especially if the wind backed to the southeast. Unfortunately this put *Suhaili* within an area of the chart marked: "extreme limit of pack ice" (in red).

The fickle northeast wind began to blow harder and harder and by midafternoon it shrieked at fifty knots. As the wind increased, Knox-Johnston stripped off the sails. The freezing spray and rain blasted the captain's face and hands and both were soon numb. The spray also ripped off the scab on the sensitive burn on his right hand. It had been ten days since he had spilled boiling porridge on his right wrist and hand and now the healing process would have to start all over again.

In spite of the bitter cold, Knox-Johnston felt he had to keep an ice watch because of the danger of icebergs and loose ice. By evening, the wind had eased; so the captain hoisted the mainsail again. He kept falling asleep in the hatchway and dimly realized that since the wind was down and the ketch was not going very fast the danger from ice was slight. He gave up and turned into his sleeping bag, wet clothes and all.

For the next few days the wind continued to blow mostly from the northeast so Knox-Johnston abandoned his call at the Falklands. He did not feel well, was sick to his stomach, and his head hurt so badly that he gulped two codeine tablets to ease the pain. Nevertheless he managed to repair several chafed lines and did his daily sewing on the sails. On January 23rd the wind finally settled in the west; which gave *Suhaili* a free wind on her port quarter. The captain discovered that he had gotten sick because he had pumped his drinking water from a tank with contaminated water. When he changed to rain water from a plastic container he soon got better. During a squall a few days later he managed to catch five gallons of water, which he reckoned would last a month.

One day before sunset *Suhaili*'s captain noticed patches of royal blue on the slate-gray sea. "Ice!" was his first thought. As he looked closer he saw that hundreds of fast-moving tadpole-like creatures about six inches long caused the blue color. The tadpoles were just at the surface and appeared to have long silver tongues. Incredible. Could they be the larval stage of something? Knox-Johnston leafed through his fish book for an identifying clue but he found nothing. What could they have been?

After lunch on January 26th the jib halyard carried away and the headsail fell into the sea. Knox-Johnston pulled the sail on deck and began trying to climb the mast to reeve a new halyard. He made three attempts, all failed, and he was fortunate not to have injured himself. The problem was the yacht swinging into the wind after he had gone partway up the mast. With the yacht heading into the wind she pitched forwards and backwards into the head seas. And the higher up the mast a sailor climbs, the worse the motion. A person hauling himself aloft on a four-part tackle and a bosun's chair is liable to start swinging back and forth like a marble on a thread and to crash into the mast with bone-smashing results. (Oh for a friendly hand at the tiller to run the boat off away from the swells.) After his third failure, Knox-Johnston decided to disconnect the topping lift from the

main boom and to hoist the headsail on the topping lift. He would
have to get along without the main boom lift until he found
smoother waters.

Both Moitessier and Knox-Johnston were heavy smokers.
North of the Falklands Knox-Johnston accidentally dropped his
last cigarette over the side. Now he would have to quit. A good
thing. He stopped smoking for a whole day. The next evening,
while drinking a cup of coffee, he craved a cigarette. Wait a minute! Hadn't he hidden twenty packs at the bottom of his clothing
bag? Maybe yes. Maybe no. "No mole ever dug as furiously as I
did into my large clothing bag," he wrote. "Arms, head and
shoulders disappeared as I scrabbled to the bottom, and emerged
clutching a precious 400 fags. In my diary I promised 'I'll keep
to four a day,' and then added more realistically 'or there-
abouts.' "

On February 3rd *Suhaili* crossed forty degrees south latitude
and left the Southern Ocean behind. She headed into the variables, the zone of uncertain winds between the westerlies of the
high latitudes and the trade wind of the tropics. As the wooden
ketch plowed northward, each day got a little warmer. The sea
was still too cold for swimming so Knox-Johnston continued to
wash in a bucket of sea water he heated on his Primus stove. The
captain spent a lot of time trying to coax his engine into life, but
his only results were two cracked cylinders. As the weather
warmed up he washed and dried all his damp clothing, scrubbed
and aired the settee cushions, and wiped out and cleaned the
interior. On some days *Suhaili* looked like a floating laundry.
Knox-Johnston began to check his stores and he threw out almost
one hundred cans of food that had been corroded and pierced
by salt water. Warm air poured in through the open hatches and
filled the interior of the yacht. The damp woodwork dried out
and the jammed locker doors began to work smoothly. Instead
of sweaters and oilskins the captain now went without a shirt and
wore only trousers. Wonderful!

One day Knox-Johnston shot two seven-foot nurse sharks that
he heard scraping against the hull and knocking off anti-fouling
paint. The next day he took his first cautious swim. The cool
water refreshed him and he discovered three pilot fish keeping

station with *Suhaili*. During various swims Knox-Johnston
checked the hull and the worn rudder fittings. He scraped off
the underwater growth, particularly the gooseneck barnacles,
some of which were bloated and six inches long.

Suhaili passed the latitude of Buenos Aires on February 9th.
The yacht averaged only seventy miles a day in this region. A
special problem in the Atlantic east of the Argentine and southern Brazilian coasts are vicious line squalls that demand instant
sail reduction. Between these squalls the sun burned down on
the Englishman and the cabin temperature rose to the nineties.
He suffered a lot from the heat because his one-month transition from the coldness of the Southern Ocean to the broiling
sun of the tropics was too short. Now instead of sentences about
a frozen face and numb fingers, the log spoke of mild sunstroke,
headaches, and weakness caused by the heat. The captain got
busy and sewed a sun hat from old canvas.

Knox-Johnston did everything he could to get northward,
but his tubby vessel sailed poorly in light airs. What he needed
were moderate seas and brisk, steady winds on the beam. Light
headwinds were hopeless. At night he steered by stars because
the compass light had given out long before and his last flashlight had stopped working. He also had to concern himself with
catching drinking water. The water catching was no joke because
the British sailor had only seven gallons of water, no engine, no
radio, abysmal winds, and the yacht's generally poor condition.
In the scorching heat a sailor had to drink a fair amount of fluids
each day just to stay alive. He still had plenty of food, however,
and reported that he had finally perfected a cheese sauce to pep
up some of his dishes.

On February 19th he logged forty miles; on the 20th he did
thirty-six; on the 21st *Suhaili* made only eighteen miles noon-to-
noon. At 0330 on February 22nd, the captain got up to look
around and he noticed a squall coming. He was ready when it
arrived, but he was unsure of his course as the rain had obscured
the stars and he couldn't see to steer properly. Nevertheless, he
collected four gallons of water from the bucket hanging on the
gooseneck of the mizzen boom. At 0630 he got another two gallons of water from a second squall. At 0825 one more gallon and

at 1005 two more. Now Knox-Johnston had a total of sixteen gallons of water, almost a two-month supply if he rationed himself. On this day he logged eighty-seven miles and slipped into the southeast trade wind; which meant a steady twelve knots or so of wind across *Suhaili*'s starboard beam or quarter for the next 1500 miles—from twenty-four degrees south latitude to roughly the equator.

"Now that we were moving again my spirits shot up," wrote Knox-Johnston. "Like most sailors I immediately began calculating when I would reach my destination using the best day's run achieved so far; a totally unrealistic calculation, of course, but tremendously exciting."

On February 24th *Suhaili* passed 140 miles east of Ilha Trindade, 600 miles east of the Brazilian coast. The captain had begun to think of England and home and tried to smarten up his vessel a little. He worked on some new rope netting beneath the bowsprit and splashed a bit of paint here and there. In truth the ketch looked terrible. The paint on her white topsides and cabin was dull and chalked and in places blistered and peeling. Various iron fastenings and the chainplates bled ugly streaks of rust. Her waterline showed grass, bits of marine growth, and traces of the captain's efforts at scraping off barnacles. The rudder fittings—once tight—had worn until there was one-quarter of an inch of play in them. Knox-Johnston put lashings on the rudder head to take some of the pressure off the fittings. At times the loose rudder made frightful thumping noises. He hoped the worn gudgeons and pintles would last until the end of the voyage.

In spite of his various problems, the captain kept the sails well trimmed. By now he was an expert at getting his small ketch to steer herself by adjusting the sails. *Suhaili* glided along smoothly before the trade wind. The sailing was delightful. Knox-Johnston enjoyed it immensely and his spirits soared. The wind blew steadily, but not too strongly. There were no storms. The sun shone brightly and the trade wind clouds made distinctive patterns in the sky. The wind reduced the temperature to a comfortable degree and the sea sparkled and glittered as the sun bounced off the ocean swells that rolled along in an even rhythm. *Suhaili* averaged almost 120 miles a day in the trade wind and took only twelve days to reach the equator. The captain continued to spruce up his vessel and somehow managed to give himself a haircut and beard trim (he had planned to shave, but somehow his razor blades had been left behind). *Suhaili* neared the major shipping lanes where Knox-Johnston hoped to get a message off to England by means of a merchant vessel.

By March 6th, he had finished all his cigarettes; but, far worse, he developed terrible stomach pains, a medical problem that turned into the most harrowing episode of the entire voyage. The sea can be dealt with in some fashion or another, but illness cannot. Knox-Johnston got out the *Ship Captain's Medical Guide* and began to read about possible problems based on his symptoms. The more he read the more alarmed he became. The possible troubles ranged from appendicitis to ulcers. As recommended, he commenced on a soft diet of spaghetti, cheese, and rice puddings but when the location of his stomach pains moved, he really got upset. It was appendicitis for sure!

The nearest port was Belem at the mouth of the Amazon, one thousand miles or ten days away. He had no antibiotics on board and in ten days he would be dead. A few days later he sighted a ship and tried to get help, but after a flicker of recognition the ship steamed away. Two other ships came close during the next days, but they also failed to answer *Suhaili*'s signals; which included flashing light signals and powerful flares. After a few more days Knox-Johnston's stomach pains eased; he began to think that his problem had been a bad can of corned beef plus chronic indigestion and acute imagination. Never give a layman a medical book!

While Knox-Johnston struggled northward and tried in vain to get word to the outside world, the newspapers back in England speculated at length about his location and whether he was even still alive. He had last been seen leaving New Zealand on November 21st when he reported his radio transmitter out of order. Now it was the middle of March, sixteen weeks later. Had he struck an iceberg? Had the Southern Ocean swallowed up

Suhaili? Had Knox-Johnston's sails and running gear simply worn out? Was he at sea somewhere floating around helplessly? Moitessier had been sighted off Port Stanley in the Falkland Islands on February 9th, but no one had seen Knox-Johnston. Who was ahead? Indeed who was alive?

The *Sunday Mirror* newspaper, always on the alert for headlines, attempted to launch a giant search for Knox-Johnston, who was presumed to be near the Azores if he had kept up his 90- to 100-mile daily average. By chance, a thirty-ship NATO naval fleet was on maneuvers in the area. The newspaper asked the navy captains to keep an eye out for a small weather-beaten ketch. The United States Air Force base at Terceira in the Azores agreed to watch for Knox-Johnston on its daily patrol flights. The *Sunday Mirror* also broadcast a notice to residents and fishermen in the Azores.

Meanwhile *Suhaili* had left the southeast trade wind, slipped through the narrow doldrums, and entered the northeast trade wind. The wooden ketch continued to make good runs—up to 125 miles a day. On March 17th, Knox-Johnston celebrated his thirtieth birthday and one week later, at eighteen degrees north, he sailed out of the northeast trade wind into the northern zone of variable winds. As usual, he was soon fed up with fickle winds and regarded any light winds from bad directions as personal insults. The only way he could let off steam was to swim until he was exhausted and then to lose himself on some bit of maintenance. On March 23rd he did sixty-seven miles with headwinds; two days later he ran before a south-southeast gale until the sea conditions obliged him to reef and slow down. Then more variable winds. Unfortunately the captain often had to steer by hand in the variables because the winds were so fluky.

In the Sargosso sea he saw clumps of gulfweed, pulled some on board, and was fascinated with the tiny brownish-yellow shrimps and crabs that fell on deck when he shook the weed. Once a five-inch eel or snake shot out of a clump of gulfweed and startled the amateur biologist.

On April 2nd, a Norwegian cargo vessel passed *Suhaili* at a distance of 150 yards. Knox-Johnston signalled frantically and even fired five shots from his rifle into the air but got no response.

Other ships also paid no attention. Finally on April 6th, a little west of the Azores near thirty-nine degrees north latitude, he made contact with the British Petroleum tanker *Mobil Acme* and sent the following message by flashing lamp signal.

> **Sent:** British *Suhaili*. Round the world non-stop.
> **Received:** Please repeat name.
> **Sent:** *Suhaili*. Please report me to Lloyd's.
> **Received:** Will do. Good luck.
> **Sent:** E.T.A. Falmouth two weeks.
> **Received:** Roger.

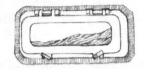

26. *A Separate Peace*

THE FOUR MEN STILL IN THE RACE desperately craved news of their fellow contestants. Where were the others? Was the competition still on? Were the rest of the men ahead or behind? What sort of hair-raising adventures had the others been through? Had there been any mishaps? Record daily runs? How could anyone make plans or decide what risks to take or even feel settled if he had no news of the race in general?

Every sports participant needs a milepost, a stopwatch gauge, a glance at his competitors' scores, or a glimpse of the other people on the race track to reassure himself. He can relax a bit if he is ahead, or redouble his efforts if he is lagging behind. Without some idea of his progress and standing and a thought of the goal ahead, a man's mind is liable to wander. He may think he is far ahead and has won, or he may decide that he has failed miserably. His mind may rejoice in aggrandizement or he may sulk because he is depressed and discouraged.

The solo round-the-world race required a tough nut to survive it physically. It was even more demanding on a mental level. Imagine sailing by yourself for ten months! Twenty-four hours a day, in all seas and in all sorts of weather! Imagine dealing with large and small problems every day for 300 consecutive days and nights! Some of the yachts had been back in port for months, and the news had not been made known to those who were still at sea. Moitessier had rounded Cape Horn in February, but he was quite unaware that Bill King and Loïck Fougeron had been knocked out of the race the previous November.

The comradeship between the nine men who had started the

race was a thin link, but it was palpable and real. Some of the sailors were close friends; others hadn't even met. Yet they were all in this marathon together and they struggled with the common problems of morale, endurance, determination, and resourcefulness. While each man hoped to win or at least to finish honorably, each wished the others good sailing and good fortune. Even Donald Crowhurst had begun with good intentions.

One would think *The Sunday Times*, a giant in the communication business, would have had enough sense to have made twice-monthly briefings available for all contestants. This could have been done by long-range radio broadcasts at certain hours. Or the contestants could have been given low-powered radios to make contact with shore stations in, say, the Azores, Cape Town, Kerguelen, Perth, Hobart, Christchurch, Hao, Juan Fernandez, Port Stanley, and Trindade. Low-powered radios have only a short range, but their size, complications, and power requirements are modest (a kite or balloon aerial put up on a calm day can increase their range enormously). A contestant within range of one of the shore stations could have been read a prepared message or have listened to a taped commentary of the race up to that moment. The range of a low-powered radio might have been extended by patching through a long-distance set on a passing merchant ship. A ham radio link could have been arranged. Or pilot boats at various key ports could have been alerted to deliver an information bulletin when they made sightings of the yachts. If the communication or visual sighting link had been two-way and obligatory, it could have given the newspaper valuable up-to-the-minute information about each contestant that would have enabled the reporters to have written longer and better stories. And with a positive, short-range look at each man, it would have been impossible to cheat.

The Sunday Times relied on long-distance radio communication, which required expensive, delicate, bulky equipment with high electrical demands, which in turn meant large, noisy, smelly generators. Long-distance equipment also needed special antennas, a certain amount of expertise, and radio schedules made out months in advance. No wonder some of the contestants balked at burdening their vessels and themselves with such gear.

The newspaper didn't sponsor the race to encourage long distance yacht racing or because of feelings of good will toward men. The paper put the race on in order to generate exciting, on-going news stories. If the contestants had a bit of trouble now and then, well, all the better. The readers would eat it up and the circulation and profits of the paper would increase. Newspapers have been putting on circulation drives for decades and this was merely another scheme to make money.

Right from the beginning it was a decisive blunder for *The Sunday Times* not to have kept everyone in the race informed about the progress of the race. Certainly the sponsor of such an undertaking had a moral responsibility to the men it sent out. What the effect of twice-a-month briefings would have had on the contestants is hard to judge, but a few paragraphs of authoritative information would have reassured everyone and eased the mental load on the men at sea.

Bernard Moitessier's behavior might have been different; he hadn't heard about anyone for five-and-a-half months even though he listened carefully to the BBC, which occasionally reported yachting news. On February 5th—only nineteen days behind Knox-Johnston now—we last saw the bearded Frenchman speeding past Cape Horn. Four days later Moitessier's red ketch *Joshua* lay hove-to in a stiff north wind at Cape Pembroke at the eastern extremity of the Falkland islands. It was Sunday. No one replied to Moitessier's mirror signals that he flashed at the lighthouse, a black iron tower ringed by a white horizontal stripe. Port Stanley lay out of sight to the west. A sail to the settlement meant a hazardous detour to the far end of a complex fjord. It meant some night sailing in constricted waters littered with rocks and kelp and beset with strong tidal streams and hard squalls. The French captain was extremely tired and he lacked local knowledge. Yet he wanted very much to let his family and friends know that he was well. In the end he refused to tackle the fjord. He had made it safely around the three great capes of the world and he decided that he was not going to be wrecked in an insignificant sound on a mission that might not even prove successful.

Reluctantly, he sailed onward. The first order of business was to get out of the ice zone so he headed northeast. His second requirement was to recover his strength. The rounding of Cape Horn and the Falkland Island episode had drained away every bit of vitality and zip from him. Consequently, he slept a lot and prepared his meals with care. He read a little and climbed to the masthead three or four times a day to look for icebergs. He took long naps and did yoga exercises. Gradually he grew stronger and forgot about the gale south of the Falklands, the difficult landfall, and the disappointment at the Cape Pembroke light.

Sometimes Moitessier dreamed about the other men in the race and sailors he had known from earlier voyages. Bill King and Loïck Fougeron were in his dreams a few times but not Nigel Tetley. Moitessier had heard that you can't dream about a dead person. "Nigel is the one I think of most often, yet I have never seen him in my dreams. Good Lord! I hope nothing has happened to Nigel."

The surface of the Southern Ocean is usually turbulent and upset because of the perpetual westerlies and ground swell that sweep around the world. In the lee of South America, however, the South Atlantic is often quite smooth by comparison. As *Joshua* pushed northeastward and crossed forty degrees south latitude the sea warmed up little by little and the ice danger receded. One day during a calm, Moitessier dropped his headsails, sheeted the mainsail and mizzen flat to ease the rolling, and put on his wetsuit. He checked around for sharks and dropped over the side with a scraper to peel off the barnacles on the hull. In half an hour he was done and *Joshua* was on her way again. During another calm, the French captain did a little restitching on the mainsail and replaced a few luff slides. Soon *Joshua* was halfway between Cape Horn and the Cape of Good Hope. On March 8th, the red ketch crossed her outbound track from England and completed her circumnavigation of the world. But the captain was strangely unexcited. Unlike Tetley he opened no bottles of champagne nor cooked any special dinners.

"She [has] sailed round the world . . . but what does that mean, since the horizon is eternal?" he wrote in a strange philosophical outburst. "Round the world goes further than the ends of the earth, as far as life itself, perhaps further still."

Moitessier decided to withdraw from the race! It was a step that had been percolating in his brain for a long time, an action that jolted his soul and made him stroke his beard in wonderment. He had the best yacht in the race and he was making the fastest runs. If he won the competition he would collect the prize money, receive awards from England and France (perhaps the Légion d'honneur), and make a handsome sum of money from a book, endorsements of equipment, and personal appearances. He would see his wife and children and his mother again.

But after the beauty of the sea and his marvelous run around the world, how could he debase himself by going back to Europe? It was the snakepit. A business hell. A place where men brutalized one another for the sake of a few daily coins. Crass juggling of ledger accounts to make money for pointless purposes: to buy a new car when the old one was perfectly good; to acquire stylish clothes when last year's were still excellent; to pay a ransom to moor his yacht in a fancy marina where people would bother him. And so on and on. Why did he need money? He already had *Joshua* and good sails and plenty of food. *Why seek more when he already had everything?* Why lose his peace and self-respect? He was happy and content and he would keep circling the globe until he passed Good Hope, the Indian Ocean, Australia, and New Zealand. In the Pacific he would head north a little, pick up the gentle southeast trade wind, and sail to Tahiti where he had friends. Or he would travel a little further east to the Galápagos islands where he could see the marvelous seals and penguins that were so friendly and genuine. Yes, he was done with the stupid race. It was over. Finished. Kaput. Terminated.

Moitessier thought of his childhood and youth in Indochina where he was born and where the value structure was more sensible. "All at once I see my Chinese nurse again, teaching me, as a child, to lie face down on the ground when I had worn myself out, or been bad. And when I was bigger, she told me that the earth gives her strength and peace to those who love her." He thought of his native land where people still greeted one another by joining palms in front of their chests, which means: "I greet the God in you" exactly as one addresses a divinity.

By March 18th *Joshua* was at Cape Town where Moitessier tossed a three-gallon plastic jerrycan to a sailor on a ship chandler's launch. In the can were movie films, tape cassettes, and still films, some of which included photographs of *Joshua's* logbook entries. On the same day Moitessier fired a slingshot message on board *British Argosy*, an oil tanker anchored in the bay. The cable that was radioed to *The Sunday Times* read: "The Horn was rounded on February 5th, and today is March 18th. I am continuing nonstop towards the Pacific islands because I am happy at sea, and perhaps also to save my soul."

When Moitessier's wife heard the news from Cape Town she made a quick diagnosis and said that seven months of solo sailing had temporarily unbalanced her husband. "I can't think what has made Bernard do this," she said. "It can only be some sort of *cafard* [fit of the blues] after seven months alone at sea."

Even Sir Francis Chichester, the chairman of the race committee, found Moitessier's decision incredible. Sir Francis searched into his own great experience of solo voyaging for a theory that would account for Moitessier's action. "He is a very unusual man and a yachtsman of exceptional experience," said Sir Francis. "But the trouble is that on these long voyages you develop a sort of rhythm of life with the boat and the sea and you are very loathe to break that rhythm.

"When I was pulling towards Britain on my own round-the-world voyage I had the very strong feeling that instead of heading to Plymouth, I'd prefer to go on sailing for ever," said Sir Francis.

Moitessier realized that the world would think him deranged so he wrote a long letter to his publisher, which said in part:

Why am I playing a trick like this? Imagine yourself in the forest of the Amazon, looking for something new, because you wanted to feel the earth, trees, nature. You suddenly come across a small temple of an ancient, lost civilisation. You are not simply going to come back and say: "Well I found a temple, a civilisation nobody knows." You would stay there, try to understand it, try to decipher it . . . And then you discover that 200 kilometres further on in another temple, only the main temple this time. Would you return?

So on March 18th the favorite in the race withdrew with a spectacular bow. It was an incredible exit and hard to believe. This able French seaman had had no sailing or equipment problems at all; he had had the race within the grasp of his hand. Now for personal reasons that sometimes seemed hard to understand he opened his hand and let the bird of victory fly away. Whether he had won his own personal race we will let the reader judge. . . . In any case now there were only three men left. All were in the Atlantic and charging hard for Plymouth.

(It forms no part of this story, but Moitessier continued around the world a second time as he had planned. The French sailor finally entered the lagoon at Papeete, Tahiti in French Polynesia on June 21st, 1969, after completing a ten-month non-stop voyage of 37,455 miles.)

27. *Meeting with Himself*

IN EARLY APRIL, after he was reported by a ship near the Azores, all odds were on Robin Knox-Johnston to win the race and collect the Golden Globe trophy for the first man to circle the world singlehanded. The £5,000 for the fastest solo circumnavigation, however, was a different matter and it looked as if one of the other two sailors in the race would scoop up the big cash prize.

As we have seen, after nearly three months of radio silence Donald Crowhurst sent his April 9th telegram to England. The next day Crowhurst's press agent, Rodney Hallworth, announced that his man had rounded Cape Horn and was rushing toward Plymouth ("Donald is proving to be one of the greatest sporting sailors of our time," crowed Hallworth). An analysis of Crowhurst's mileages since his departure the previous October showed incredible irregularities. He had started out badly, claimed a record run, mentioned a few place names in his later telegrams, lapsed into silence, and now was again claiming sensational times.

The men at *The Sunday Times* kept correcting their old figures and revising their estimates of *Teignmouth Electron*'s arrival in England. First it had been November and then September 30th (after "the record run"). Later revisions put the date at September 8th (following the telegram from supposedly near Tristan da Cunha); then August 19th (when he was "in the Indian ocean"). After the latest barrage of misinformation the new arrival date was posted at July 8th or before. One set of bizarre calculations put *Teignmouth Electron*'s speed at 188.6 miles a day for 13,000 miles. Evidently the sleek blue and white trimaran had grown wings as she had sped around the world. Some people theorized that as Crowhurst had settled down and learned how to sail his craft and had worked into his stores and provisions, his speeds had naturally increased. Additionally, in the roaring forties of the Southern Ocean a vessel would make better time, his admirers said. Of course these arguments applied to all the yachts. . . .

According to the reporters' calculations, Crowhurst's time was fourteen days ahead of Tetley's time up to Cape Horn. Tetley, who had started the race forty-five days before Crowhurst, had been speeding northward in the Atlantic since March 18th, but it appeared that Crowhurst was sailing faster. None of Crowhurst's figures would have stood up to scrutiny, but no one dreamed of foul play and there was no expert inquiry except in the mind of Sir Francis Chichester who had made no public statement. All the newspapers meekly accepted Hallworth's numbers or calculated their own.

It began to look like a possible racehorse finish between the captains of the two Victress class trimarans. One man was a veteran naval officer; the other was a brash young challenger who was proving to be a formidable threat. *The Sunday Times* was delighted and planned full coverage; the picture department was checking into the hiring of airplanes and fast launches for its best photographers when the multi hulls appeared near England. There would probably be front-page stories plus inside feature articles about each man as he crossed the finish line.

On April 12th, Crowhurst received a message from Hallworth:

YOURE ONLY TWO WEEKS BEHIND TETLEY PHOTO FINISH WILL MAKE
GREAT NEWS STOP ROBIN DUE ONE TO TWO WEEKS-RODNEY

Crowhurst now knew that his plan to win the race by staying in the Atlantic hadn't been detected. Also his stop in Argentina hadn't been exposed. So far so good. All he had to do now was to complete the false logbook and to start back to England. He had been sailing steadily northward from the Falklands and on April 18th he answered a direct radio call from England querying whether he had received Hallworth's recent message. Crowhurst gossiped in morse code with the Portishead operator and found out Tetley's position and that Moitessier was out of the race. Now the captain of *Teignmouth Electron* knew about his competitors; it was time for his move.

Crowhurst's problem was how to coordinate his fake passage with his real position. He needed to advance his fraudulent daily positions closer and closer to his true positions so that he would finally meet himself and could use his actual daily positions henceforth. Further north he would be reported by ships, which would authenticate his latitude and longitude and expose any irregularities.

Instead of sailing northward as fast as he could to implement his master plan, however, Crowhurst hesitated, almost on purpose it seemed. Again and again he was guilty of indecision and delay. Sometimes you felt he almost wanted to lose. He would work out a scheme to do something and then be reluctant to act, as if he hoped someone else would make up his mind for him or push him this way or that. Even in the beginning Crowhurst was not a strong captain; his resolve appeared to be growing weaker and weaker.

By now he was roughly 700 miles east of Buenos Aires and within easy radio range of the Argentine capital. He repeatedly tried to arrange a direct land-link telephone call to his wife, Clare, in England via New York. It was easy to speak to the Argentine radio operators, but the South American overseas telephone facilities were primitive. Crowhurst prepared telegrams to Clare asking her to wait for his call. He tried again and again, but the telephone connections did not succeed. It seemed that Crowhurst wanted to speak to his wife directly without going through the ears of the English radio technicians who by this time had become interested in the race and who might not respect his privacy. By routing his call via local Spanish-speaking operators and New York, where he was not known, he could talk without the radio people in England monitoring his words.

Donald Crowhurst was a lonely and thoroughly confused thirty-seven-year-old man who knew he was not dishonest by nature but who had been caught in a complex spider's trap of his own making. He wanted to quit the race, to somehow back out of the marathon, to get away from this endurance contest that stretched on and on like the hard blue line of the horizon. He wanted to confide in someone and perhaps confess his deception. He wanted help from a human being he could trust, who would advise him, and tell him what to do. The world was certainly an unjust place; it was not fair to him when he had so many important things on his mind.

Was this situation unique for Crowhurst? Had he ever deceived people before? What was his background?

He was born in 1932 in India, where his father was a railroad superintendent. Crowhurst's childhood and youth reveal a sensitive, intelligent, sharp-tongued, gutsy young man who was clever at fixing things. He left school in England at sixteen and spent the next six years in the Royal Air Force where he learned to be a pilot. He purchased an old sports car and liked to rush from place to place. His mind moved quickly and he was usually a brash showoff when he was out with his fellow pilots. "Let's paint a telephone box yellow," he would shout. . . . "Who can drink the most gin backwards from a beer glass?" . . . "I hear that sniffing mothballs increases potency, let's try!" and so on. Eventually his obstreperous behavior caught up with him, however, and his superiors asked him to leave the RAF.

He promptly enlisted in the army, was again commissioned, and took a course in electronic control equipment. Again he led his fellow officers on merry evenings and barroom highjinks. He smashed his car into a bus, was caught several times driving without insurance, lost his license, yet kept driving. One night during a beery escapade he tried stealing a car and was arrested and fined; the local police sent his photograph to the criminal records office of Scotland Yard. Again he was asked to resign his commission. At twenty-four, Crowhurst began work at the Reading University laboratories where he was soon considered both an intellectual and a rather dashing figure. He met Clare in 1957 and after a flamboyant courtship married her the same year. It wasn't long until the first of four children arrived. He impressed everyone by being an excellent, devoted father.

Crowhurst began work as an equipment salesman for a

prominent electronic company, but left after a year because of trouble following a car accident. In his mid-twenties now, he had already blown three budding careers and his record was not good. He dabbled with several other companies but finally decided he must work for himself as an electronics engineer and salesman. He would get rich by inventing new electronic gadgets and marketing them. His first successful product was a clever radio direction-finding device he called a Navicator. Though not brilliant nor especially original it was a useful and saleable device and he set up a small factory with six employees.

Crowhurst lived in a village named Nether Stowey near Bridgwater in Somerset in southwest England. He was a typical small-town intellectual, a bit loud-mouthed, and after a time got elected as a Liberal councillor, not by his record, but by an image he somehow projected of himself as a skillful executive who would solve all of Bridgwater's industrial difficulties. He generally shouted down his opposition with a series of computer-like questions that had only one answer: Donald Crowhurst.

About the time he began his political efforts he bought a new Jaguar sports car. The same dreary pattern repeated itself. He drove too fast and in six months had another mishap. This time the car flipped and Crowhurst got a nasty smash on his head. Clare said that his personality was different after the accident. He became more introspective, often sulked, and sometimes became infuriated and lost his temper and was liable to throw and smash things. In this behavioral change one is reminded of the Argentine small-boat sailor Vito Dumas who also underwent a marked personality change after he struck his head in a swimming pool accident.

When Crowhurst's biographers reconstructed his story they found two Donald Crowhursts. One was an unpleasant bore, a braggadocio whose swaggering manner was so blatant that after an amusing minute or two his cockiness began to disgust people. This was the military Crowhurst who led his young officer friends from one noisy bar to another. This was the fast-driving Crowhurst who roared across the English countryside and wrecked car after car. This was the yachtsman Crowhurst speaking on radio interviews and BBC tapes where he was the hale and hearty, tough, two-fisted, jocular, unforgiving sea captain who liked to mock his opponents and the world.

Oh tis 'orrible to be out matey. Mountainous seas eighteen inches high an' horrible great black clouds, roll upon roll of them matey, stretching away as far as the eye can see. Now I will cast me optic on the wind recorder. Me gawd six knots . . . Oh I have been in some tight spots on this voyage matey, but this is diabolically tight matey.

The second side of Crowhurst's personality revealed a quiet, introspective, moody person. The vaudeville posturing was gone. The serious Donald demanded intellectual challenge. He was a man who searched and probed his mind and past activities like an explorer walking into a range of uncharted mountains. All of mankind over its whole course of history added up to a blank, a meaningless void, he said. Crowhurst's mind and the system of the universe were really rival mathematical computers. His gloomy, morbid writings of this were all mixed up with religion and his childhood. Instead of sailing his yacht and concentrating on his great deception which, after all, was a fiendishly clever scheme, Crowhurst spent more and more time escaping in mental fantasies.

Crowhurst considered himself an engineer and mathematician. No novels or light humor or travel books for him. He needed tough stuff. Books with muscle. One of the volumes he had taken on board with him was *Relativity, the Special and the General Theory* by Albert Einstein, a book the great scientist had written to explain his work to popular audiences. Crowhurst studied the book day after day and gave deep thought to Einstein's theories and explanations. Crowhurst read into Einstein all sorts of mystical meanings and interpretations the renowned physicist certainly never intended. Crowhurst made extensive notes on the margins of the book, wrote a critical commentary, and later prepared a confused and puzzling essay on Einstein's book. What Einstein considered mere mathematical and logical explanations, Crowhurst turned into cosmic meaning and God-like associations. The amateur sailor saw great things in $E = mc^2$, a mathematical statement that according to Crowhurst was the same as the Christian formula: God is Love.

Crowhurst wrote at length about his childhood and how he had learned about God and man. He did his writing with difficulty and his pages were filled with deletions and changes. The content made some sense, but it was a confused, melancholy business and certainly not done by a person in control of himself.

One night while looking at the stars and wondering about God I thought I detected a pattern in the stars resembling the head of Christ with a crown of thorns [he wrote]. I turned to my companion and tried to point it out, but she could not see it. Nor could I. I had been brought up on miracles, and decided that this was a miracle . . .

One day soon afterward I noticed a fruitcake in the pantry and ran to my mother to thank her for obtaining my favourite food. "I bought no fruitcake," said my mother. "Yes you have!" "No I haven't." I was worried. What could the explanation be? You see, it never occurred to me that my mother could be lying. "But I have just seen it in the pantry." "Oh," said my mother, 'I bought it as a surprise.' My mother had lied to me! I reeled under the mental blow.

All these depressing, unhealthy mutterings were drops of corrosive acid on the thin cord that connected him to the social world. Crowhurst's personality was crashing about him in ruins. The pressure of his loneliness, the bad work at the boatyard before he left, the supplies that got left behind, the other sailors who were honest and winning, his refusal to give up, the deception, the months of hiding in the Atlantic, the illegal stop in Argentina, the falsified logbook—all these separate pressures converged on him and gradually drove him toward madness. After five-and-a-half months at sea Crowhurst, was a mental case who should not have been loose.

28. *Valiant to the End*

LIEUTENANT-COMMANDER NIGEL TETLEY rounded Cape Horn on March 18th and immediately shaped a course to the northeast in the South Atlantic. Knox-Johnston had slipped past Cape Horn sixty days earlier, but Tetley was sailing faster and gradually gaining on the leader. At least he thought he was. Who knew what the final outcome would be? Tetley wondered where Crowhurst and the others were, and as the question pulsed through his mind, he turned and looked around the horizon for a sail although he realized there was only a million to one chance of spotting anyone.

Tetley always had plenty to do aboard *Victress*. The day after he had rounded Cape Horn he noticed his yacht was not keeping her course properly. When he went aft to check the self-steering he discovered that both the special stainless steel shaft and the self-steering rudder had fallen off. This was presumably impossible because they were secured to their metal frame with a washer and a stout cotter pin that could not wriggle loose. Yet somehow the cursed cotter pin had sheared off and allowed the vital parts to drop into the sea. Damn! Tetley steered by hand for several hours while he considered alternatives. He tried a combination of small sails which did not work at all; the storm jib got flogging so violently that its sheets whipped back and forth and lashed Tetley's face hard enough to close one of his eyes for several hours. He was too tired to think properly so he hove to and slept.

The next day Tetley managed to get *Victress* to steer herself by flying and adjusting larger sails. Meanwhile he thought about making proper self-steering replacement parts from odds and ends on board. He passed Port Stanley in the Falkland islands on March 23rd. During the afternoon *Victress*'s main steering wires broke again so Tetley fitted new wires. So far he had been reasonably successful in getting the trimaran to steer herself by adjusting the sails. He hesitated to rebuild the mechanical self-steering, which was a lot of work.

Victress was now north of the Falklands, clear of ice danger, and sailing quite fast. On March 26th, Tetley gave himself a haircut; the next morning he spoke to his English newspaper contact in Buenos Aires on the radio and was amazed to learn that Bernard Moitessier had dropped out of the race. Tetley reckoned that only he, Knox-Johnston, and Crowhurst were left. This was certainly a strange race; two-thirds of the starters had withdrawn. Fortunately all were safe. The day had been squally, but the air and sea were gradually warming up. Tetley brought up new food stocks from the bilges including twenty-four cans of beer he had been saving for the tropics. On March 30th it rained heavily and the captain was pleased to see water gurgling into his tanks from the wheelhouse roof scuppers.

As the days passed, Tetley broke and repaired a spinnaker pole, fitted a new compass light, sewed sails, and read in Palgrave's *Golden Treasury*. To his delight he managed to find a corroded fuse on the rectifier of his radio transmitter; a new fuse restored the unit to full power. Tetley was not pleased at all, however, with water that was running into the trimaran's floats and the main hull from beneath the connecting wings. The leaks were bad signs.

By April 7th *Victress* was level with Rio de Janeiro and bumping and slatting through the variables. This meant a lot of sail drill, hand steering, and frustrations. One day Tetley tuned in to an American religious station that played classical music. He thought it wonderful. On April 9th, during a calm, he checked the structural damage under the wings of the trimaran and considered going for a swim when a nasty-looking shark suddenly reared up out of the water.

For the next week *Victress* ghosted slowly before light winds from the south. On April 16th Tetley sat on deck eating his supper, a large bowl of stew. His vessel had gradually come to a stop as the wind died. The radio played native Brazilian music, which alternated with commercials in Portuguese. One commercial was repeated over and over by a hard-driving announcer who seemed to delight in his job. Tetley got curious about the commercial so he looked up a few key words in his dictionary and discovered that the advertisement was extolling a patent medicine for tapeworms.

On April 17th Tetley received a new radio message from Buenos Aires. Robin Knox-Johnston had been seen near the Azores; Donald Crowhurst was reported in the eastern Pacific. "What a relief to hear that both were still afloat," said Tetley who figured that Robin's arrival in England would siphon off most of the race publicity. "Crowhurst's challenge to me from the rear was a different matter. . . . I still wanted to win; or put another way, I didn't want anyone to beat me, least of all in a similar type of boat."

Sometimes Tetley thought about the long trip he had made.

While going through the Pacific I had the absurd notion that I was under judgement by the "spirit" of the Southern ocean. It would, I knew, be touch and go whether he allowed me through. In so many ways, I was wanting. That I would have to undergo a period of trial and some ultimate pennance I realized only too well. But because of my love for the seabirds I believed the "spirit" might spare my life.

Bernard, the only competitor who knew exactly what to expect, refused to regard the voyage as a race. "It will be a question of survival," he had said. "Everyone who gets round will have won." How right he was! I now understand why there was a complete absence of rivalry in his make-up.

On April 18th Tetley inspected his trimaran again. It was a grim survey. The starboard float had four cracked frames. The fastenings on most of the inner beams were in bad condition. In addition there was all the cabin damage from the Pacific storm. "The old girl will see me home, but . . . she is a write-off," he concluded. Almost as if to counter this bad news, a steady eight-knot wind began to blow, and with one thousand square feet of sail, *Victress* pressed onward, her three hulls furrowing the smooth sea.

At noon the next day the trimaran was only 100 miles from crossing the track of her outbound voyage. Tetley was anxious to hang up his shark's tail at the bow, the sign of a successful circumnavigation. At 0300 on April 20th the wind freshened. Keen to outpace Crowhurst, Tetley kept his big sails flying and *Victress* raced ahead at high speed. An hour later the genoa tack fitting—held with only wood screws—pulled out, something else to fix. The tack fitting was small stuff, however, compared with what happened next. As dawn rose over the tropical sea Tetley heard the sound of water spashing forward. When he rushed into the bow section of the main hull he was horrified to see daylight coming through the access section to the port wing. The whole forward part of the port wing back to the crossarm—which would correspond to the left shoulder of a bird—had come away, beams, plywood, braces, doublers, fiberglass sheathing and all.

Tetley hurried out to the bow of the port float where he found split and holed plywood, the deck sprung, and five ruined frames. "Squatting in the narrow hull, knee deep in water, I could feel the sides moving in and out like a concertina," he wrote. "It looked as if the voyage were over . . . and with the gods' true gift for irony, sixty tantalizing miles short of circling the world."

He quickly pulled down all the sails and scanned his charts for the nearest port. It was Recife, on the easternmost bulge of Brazil, where John Ridgway had gone the previous July when he had withdrawn from the race. "The yacht is too badly damaged to make the West Indies," Tetley scribbled in his log. "I will patch up the worst of the holes and steer for Recife."

Tetley sawed away the wing decking over the damaged area and put a piece of plywood over the hole in the main hull. He began to fit strengthening crossbeams to the broken frames in the port float but he was unsure how to fasten the new bracing. He started to saw wooden battens which he planned to bolt to the float sides. Once the battens were in place he would fasten the new crossbeams to the battens. Partway through sawing the battens, however, he remembered that he had some stainless steel straps with predrilled holes. He decided to bend the metal straps into brackets that he would fasten between the beams and the hull of the float. Tetley worked throughout the day and the following night, pausing only to pump and eat. The repairs seemed stronger than mere patches and Tetley began to think about continuing toward England. After a long sleep on Sunday night he went on with his carpentry and metal bending; by late Monday afternoon he had fastened the last beam and metal bracket in place.

It was impossible to make the forepeak of the port float watertight because of all the cracks and the delaminated plywood. When Tetley put up the sails, got underway, and looked in, the forepeak was like a shower bath. Since the forward compartment was sealed off from the rest of the float, however, Tetley drilled several holes below the waterline to let the water out as fast as it came in from above.

The work was makeshift and no doubt a shipwright would have fainted away. Yet *Victress* was sailing again. By the evening of April 22nd the battered trimaran had crossed her outbound track. In 179 days she had logged 20,500 miles and averaged 114.5 miles a day. Tetley raised his glass: "To Miss *Vicky*. Much abused yet great-hearted to the end."

The next day the wind increased to twenty-five knots. The captain watched gravely as the port bow crashed into wave after wave. Everything seemed to be holding so on he went. At 1300 on April 26th, *Victress* crossed the equator and neared the doldrums between the two trade wind zones. Tetley sat on deck and toasted Father Neptune with his last two cans of beer. In the evening the fickle winds of the doldrums blew first one way then another. Sheet lightning crackled from towering banks of purplish clouds. The moon seemed to float beneath a halo. The following day the temperature soared into the nineties and Tetley had to steer by hand to keep going at all. "I was beginning to feel the strain when, towards evening, squall clouds brought a spanking wind," wrote the captain. By this time I no longer cared if the port bow should drop off. I decided to keep her going at full tilt as long as the wind lasted." Three days later *Victress* picked up the northeast trade wind and logged 150 miles.

"I screwed back the hatch over the port bow—an unnecessary precaution in view of the space's self-draining qualities," he wrote. "What I might have found going on down there, as *Victress* bashed to windward on the starboard tack, must have been secretly worrying me. I could not afford to waste any more time in repairs. Even if the whole section came away it shouldn't matter too much—the space retained little buoyancy anyway. I was quite prepared to bring *Victress* home minus one bow."

On Friday, May 2nd, the captain discovered that most of the fiberglass sheathing had peeled off the port float. Now bare plywood showed. During the night the wind freshened and the vessel assumed an alarming angle of heel to port. Tetley, dreading to look, figured that the center section of the port float had filled with seawater. The next morning, sure enough, when he peered into the float he found the compartment full. He got busy and improved the pumping arrangement from the float to the main hull. The center compartment of the port float had always been watertight before, but now was taking water beneath the wings in the same way as the starboard float. None of the frames of the port center compartment were damaged, but the plywood sides bellied in and out as waves passed. To ease the strain Tetley emptied the compartment of all stores and supplies, some of which he tossed over the side.

While he worked on the float compartment, *Victress* charged northward. On May 8th she was at twenty-three degrees north latitude and thirty-four degrees west longitude, almost out of the northeast trade wind. Two days later Tetley spoke to *The Sunday Times* on his radio. The yacht continued to sail well. By now the hard-driving, resourceful Tetley had the knack of adjusting the sails to keep his vessel sailing herself at good speed. One evening at dusk a small merchant ship steamed close by and asked if the yacht needed any supplies or assistance: which cheered the captain a good deal. Another night Tetley's radio picked up some splendid Spanish music from the Canary islands.

By May 16th *Victress* was about 800 miles west of Portugal and close to the Azores. These islands had six radio beacons that helped Tetley determine his position. During the day he saw two westbound cargo ships. The wind blew at eighteen knots on the beam of *Victress* and she raced along in great form and covered 100 miles during daylight hours. At dusk the wind increased so Tetley took down some sails before he turned in.

Tuesday morning, May 20th, marked *Victress*'s 245th day at sea. The wind whistled at thirty knots. Tetley reefed the mainsail, but the yacht continued at speed. The seas kept increasing and Tetley knew he was in for a gale. He substituted the mizzen for the mainsail and later lowered the mizzen as well. That evening the wind shrieked at forty-five knots; large seas with dense streaks of foam rumbled past the trimaran. Tetley dropped all sails and drifted in front of the storm. Before he went to sleep he drew a line on his chart to Plymouth. The distance to go was exactly 1,100 miles. Only a few days more.

At midnight Tetley suddenly awoke. He heard a strange scraping sound. He knew at once the noise meant the port bow had come adrift. He hurried on deck and looked. The damage was far worse than he had imagined. Not only had the bow of the port float come off, but it had slammed into the main hull and holed it. *Victress* was filling with water. By the time the captain had returned to the cabin the water was six inches deep. Her roll and light motion had become drugged and ponderous from the weight of water pouring into the yacht; even if she did not sink she would be prey for every sea now. Tetley picked up his radio-telephone microphone and transmitted a Mayday call. He received an immediate response from a Dutch ship.

Tetley collected his life raft, survival gear, and items of value. Water continued to flood in so the captain heaved the life raft into the sea, inflated it, tossed in his gear, and climbed aboard. "Give over, *Vicky*, I have to leave you," he cried as he pushed off into the wild Atlantic. "I could easily get sentimental over the moment of parting now. The yacht had become a person to me during the long voyage. I would often talk to her, call her all the names under the sun sometimes, though always in jest." From a downwind position he looked back and saw the lights of *Victress* blink out. She was gone.

Tetley's life raft equipment included an emergency hand-cranked transmitter. By the afternoon he had contacted a big four-engined Hercules aircraft from the United States Air Force

57th Rescue squadron in the Azores which directed a commercial ship to the tiny life raft. A little after 1700 hours Tetley was aboard the Motor Transport *Pampero,* Italian manned and owned, on charter to British Petroleum, and bound for Trinidad.

Tetley went to the mate's cabin for a change into dry clothes and then to see Captain Diego de Portada who gave the castaway a big whisky. It was all over. Finished. The bitter end. Everything had happened so fast. *Victress* was gone. Part of Tetley's life was gone too. Maybe it was all a dream, a hazy, smokefilled dream that would stop when he woke up. Certainly *Victress* was still beneath him. He could almost sense the familiar handholds, his bunk, the galley, the chart table, the compass, and the cleat for the long mainsheet. Of course everything was still there; England was not far now. Soon the powerful lighthouse beacons and the pretty green hills would appear. He was still ahead of Crowhurst. But as Tetley saw the big ship around him, sensed the throbbing engine, and felt the comradeship of the kind Italian officers he knew the rescue had been real. The sailing and the three-hulled yacht were all through. The seventh man to start was no longer in the race.

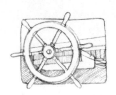

29. *The Winner*

WHEN THE BRITISH PETROLEUM TANKER *Mobil Acme*
acknowledged Knox-Johnston's signal on April 6th he
was overjoyed. Finally! He had spoken to no one for four-and-
a-half months. What had his family and friends and sponsors
been thinking? The worst no doubt. Now everyone would know
that he was safe and where *Suhaili* was. That night Knox-Johnston tuned to the BBC hoping that he might be mentioned on
the evening news. Nothing was reported, however. He thought
that Moitessier might have already crossed the finish line and
that the excitement of the race was over.

The *Mobil Acme* had in fact radioed London at once. Shortly
afterwards Lloyds telephoned Knox-Johnston's family. The officer on *Mobil Acme* who had received the flashing lamp signal
from *Suhaili* had added to the message: "Standard of signaling
excellent." This told everyone that the captain was still in good
form and in control of things.

When *Suhaili* had met the *Mobil Acme* the yacht was in the
zone of westerlies: which meant fair winds across the ketch's port
quarter. Knox-Johnston had calculated his arrival date on the
basis of these winds. But the wind veered perversely to the north,
a turn that reduced the next two days' runs to eighty-nine and
seventy-nine miles. Knox-Johnston did not feel well and had a
severe headache. "Probably due to food poisoning," he conjec-
tured. The following day *Suhaili* ran before brisk southwest winds
that gradually fell away to nothing. "We are completely becalmed
and there are ships all around so I dare not sleep—not that I

could with the booms banging as they are," he wrote. "I feel completely licked. I don't think, even in the variables, I have felt so low the whole voyage."

On April 12th, Knox-Johnston signaled to a French ship, *Mungo* of Le Havre, and found that he was able to use his radio to talk to the captain. The astonishing news was that Moitessier was continuing around the world and that *Suhaili* was "Le Premier." The following day Knox-Johnston logged ninety-eight miles. In the evening he heard a high frequency commercial sta-

KNOX-JOHNSTON and MIZZEN

tion in England and idly tried a call. To his surprise the Baldock operator answered at once and even patched through a connection to Knox-Johnston's family. After months of no news *Suhaili*'s master now seemed to be getting daily reports. Knox-Johnston's brother confirmed that Moitessier was in the Indian

Ocean for the second time and that only three British contestants remained in the race. The two trimarans were in the South Atlantic, with Crowhurst just around Cape Horn and Tetley somewhere off Brazil. Knox-Johnston's family and friends planned to meet *Suhaili* when she appeared off the English coast.

On April 16th, Knox-Johnston spoke to the *Sunday Mirror* newspaper, which by now had run dozens of stories about him and was flogging one headline after another ("ROBIN IS SAFE"; "THEY THOUGHT HE WAS DEAD"). The paper's latest request was for exclusive material. Knox-Johnston and the paper had worked out a code before the race; henceforth the captain was to radio his positions and arrival times in cipher. He almost felt part of a cloak-and-dagger scheme and it all seemed good fun.

The wind dropped again and *Suhaili*'s battery charger stopped working and there was no way to charge the batteries for the radio. Knox-Johnston started to overhaul the charger, but he had all his big sails up and he had to spend a lot of time in the cockpit steering. At noon on April 18th, *Suhaili* had 280 miles to go to Falmouth, the port in England from which the yacht had started. The *Sunday Mirror* radioed that it was sending a Beechcraft G–ASDO plane for photographs and that the other newspapers were shadowing the power yacht that belonged to Knox-Johnston's friends. More cloak-and-dagger stuff.

In the evening a small gray bird with a slender beak suddenly appeared next to the captain who was sitting in the cabin reading *Timon of Athens*. A bit later, ships' lights began to appear around the horizon and the captain got ready for a sleepless night. Two vessels, one small and one large, worked up close to *Suhaili*. At first the captain was wary until he realized that people were shouting his name. One vessel had Knox-Johnston's parents on board; the other sported a contingent of his friends. There was a lot of shouting back and forth. The wind and sea increased, however, and Knox-Johnston had to reduce sail and get some sleep. The next morning when he looked out on the ocean he was alone. At noon he worked out his latitude and radioed it to the escort but the wind was contrary and up to gale force. He stopped *Suhaili* and napped for a bit in the afternoon until the escorts found him.

Unfortunately the wind continued from the southeast: which tended to blow *Suhaili* northward toward the Bristol channel. Knox-Johnston wanted to sail eastward up the English channel; so he tacked to the south until the following morning, when he tacked again and headed for Land's End, 150 miles away. In the evening, with a cup of cocoa in one hand, he began to work through a fleet of French fishing boats. A little before noon the next day the Bishop lighthouse hove into view.

"I suppose that seeing the slim silhouette of the Bishop on the horizon should have been an emotional moment," he wrote. "Over the centuries it has been the last and first sight of Britain for generations of seamen, but my recollection is that I noted the sighting in the log simply as a navigational mark. My emotions, more prosaically, were concerned with a pint of beer, a steak, a hot bath, and clean white sheets."

During the afternoon the two escort vessels continued with *Suhaili*. Now helicopters, a military patrol plane, and a naval minesweeper joined the little flotilla. Knox-Johnston snatched sleep and food when he could and the various escorts darted back and forth to land to refuel. By Tuesday morning, April 22nd, *Suhaili's* accompanying fleet had been joined by the Falmouth lifeboat, the tug *St. Mawes,* and various private yachts. Light aircraft buzzed overhead. Helicopters, with photographers leaning out, fluttered here and there.

The wind swung to the north-northwest which obliged *Suhaili* to tack back and forth. Slowly, ever so slowly, she gained on her goal. By now there were large and small vessels everywhere on the sea. As he neared Falmouth, Knox-Johnston saw lines of parked cars; people and flags waved from all sides. This tiny, wooden, rust-streaked tubby white ketch and her modest captain had sailed all the way around the world without stopping. They had made it back to the port from which they had started. Some 30,123 miles in 313 days. At 1525 hours *Suhaili* crossed the finish line. A cannon echoed across the waterfront and thousands of people cheered a new popular hero. The first contestant to complete the race had returned.*

* Knox-Johnston was the first sailor to go around the world under *The Sunday Times'* rules, which were essentially from England to England south of the three great headlands of Good Hope, Leeuwin, and Cape Horn. During the race two other entrants also circumnavigated. Bernard Moitessier crossed his outbound track on March 8th, more than a month before Knox-Johnston. Strictly speaking, therefore, Moitessier should get credit for the first solo circumnavigation. Nigel Tetley touched his earlier wake on April 22nd, the third man around. Depending on your definition of solo sailing you can take your choice. Maybe the best answer was from Moitessier when he said (page 270) "Everyone who gets around will have won."

30. *The Loser*

ON APRIL 22ND, the day that Knox-Johnston crossed the finish line in England, Donald Crowhurst was slowly sailing northward about 700 miles east of northern Argentina. Nigel Tetley, whose *Victress* was not to sink until May 21st, was approximately two thousand miles to the north-northeast, off the easternmost bulge of northern Brazil.

In his usual deceptive message to Rodney Hallworth, Crowhurst claimed that he was near the Falkland islands and sailing well. In a separate cable to the BBC, he congratulated Knox-Johnston, but pointed out that although the Golden Globe had now been won, the overall prize was far from decided, and that he, Donald Crowhurst, was certainly going to try to win the £5,000. When these two messages had been transmitted, Crowhurst was back in the race. He had decided to join his false and true positions on May 4th and it seemed as if everything was set for the final dash up the Atlantic to England.

Although Tetley was some two thousand miles ahead of Crowhurst we must remember that Crowhurst had started the race forty-five days after Tetley. Crowhurst's *alleged* position on April 30th was at the Falkland Islands, another one thousand miles to the south, or roughly three thousand miles behind Tetley.

By May 4th Crowhurst had begun to sail northward with determination. He advanced rapidly before strong following winds and made some first-class runs. Two days later he logged only a little less than the 243-mile record he had falsely claimed months earlier. This fast run clearly demonstrated that Crowhurst and his trimaran had plenty of potential. The captain scarcely mentioned this remarkable mileage, however, because he had too many other things on his mind. A few days later the strong southerly winds died out as *Teignmouth Electron* entered the variables. Soon fickle headwinds slowed the progress of the white and blue multihull to a crawl. Crowhurst tacked to the east, seeking the southeast trade wind.

Whenever he could, Crowhurst worked on his grand scheme of deception. He sent a cable to England explaining that his direct connection to Portishead radio had been an isolated stroke of luck. He recorded long excuses on his BBC tape recorder concerning his lapses in radio communication. He invented complicated lies and all sorts of fanciful stories.

Hallworth and Crowhurst exchanged cable after cable. Hallworth realized that elapsed time victories mean little to the general public and urged Crowhurst to cross the finish line in a neck and neck duel with Tetley. Crowhurst's wife and friends began to send adulatory messages ("very proud").

Hallworth cabled:

TEIGNMOUTH AGOG AT YOUR WONDERS WHOLE TOWN PLANNING HUGE WELCOME—RODNEY

Although Crowhurst made efforts to perfect his fraudulent log and to account for the lapses in his radio messages, his efforts weren't wholly sincere. Again and again he procrastinated and failed to follow up his scheme to win. The other men in the race had used every bit of their skill and energy to keep their yachts going as fast as possible. Knox-Johnston, Tetley, Moitessier, and Bill King were hard drivers. Crowhurst, by contrast, was a weak sister. He failed to press on regardless as the others had. He treated the actual sailing as if it was a peripheral task, not his main business, which by now had become the saving of Donald Crowhurst.

On some level or other Crowhurst wanted to lose to Tetley. If that happened, no one would care a fig about the fake logbooks. Maybe the best thing would be to lose to Tetley at the last minute. This approach would still get a lot of publicity for *Teignmouth Electron,* his sponsor Mr. Best, and for Crowhurst himself.

After May 15th, *Teignmouth Electron*'s daily average slumped to seventy miles. *The Sunday Times* again calculated his estimated arrival date and added one week. Admittedly he was in the zone of variable winds, but he simply wasn't paying attention to his sailing.

Now came the most ironic twist of the entire race. On May 21st, as we have seen, *Victress* fell apart and was abandoned. The plucky captain took to his life raft and was rescued. Tetley's three-hulled yacht had disintegrated because he had driven the old trimaran too hard and had subjected her to trials that her California designer, Arthur Piver, had never dreamed of when he had drawn the plans.

Tetley was desperately keen to win. He got message after message that Crowhurst was gaining so he drove *Victress* harder and harder when she was getting weaker and weaker and beginning to splinter to pieces. If Tetley had nursed and coddled *Victress* and continued to patch her he might have limped into Plymouth and won the £5,000. Fame, fortune, and perhaps a title would have been his. Crowhurst could have come home just behind Tetley and would have nailed down a respectable place in sailing history. Crowhurst could then have retired to Nether Stowey and his electronic business with his logbooks unexamined.

When Tetley's *Victress* disintegrated, and Tetley was suddenly out of the race, it meant a whole new cave of horrors for Crowhurst. Now he would win the race for the fastest time and the £5,000 for sure. He would become famous and respected. He would get money and prestige. Or would he? What about the cursed fiddled logbooks? What about the interviews with the damned reporters and their endless, probing questions? A magnifying glass would be focused on his every action. Could he keep up such a folly, and lie with certainty? Or would he trip himself up? And what about the race committee? Would that ace navigator, that damned old fox Sir Francis Chichester, be there with a devastating inquiry into Crowhurst's uneven daily runs and his peculiar radio silences? One slip and Crowhurst's whole world of Let's Pretend would come crashing down. He would be humiliated and scorned. His family and friends would be horrified. It was a grim prospect, and Crowhurst must have felt remorse and have regretted that he had ever started in the race. The only escape was to let Knox-Johnston win the £5,000 and that would require Crowhurst to stall around for months, something not possible because now everyone knew where he was.

What could he do? Exactly what he had done during the long months when he had hidden on the fringes of the South Atlantic while the others had sailed around the world. He would abandon the sailing of *Teignmouth Electron* and start a solo voyage into the depths of his mind.

How do we know all this? From a mass of radio transmissions, tape recordings, and motion pictures that Crowhurst made while he doddered in the Atlantic. Crowhurst's biographers sifted through all this material and patiently unwound the captain's mental foibles. Taken piece by piece, up to the time of his final collapse, each bit seemed normal. Perhaps a little strange but within the bounds of credulity. Taken altogether, however, as the sum of a thousand morbid fragments, the evidence pointed a hard finger toward explaining the eventual shattering of Crowhurst's personality.

On May 23rd Crowhurst radioed his condolences to Tetley regarding the abandonment of *Victress*. A week later *Teignmouth Electron* was well north into the tropics. But instead of speedy daily runs in the trade winds, the captain often didn't even bother to set his mainsail and poked along at three or four knots. He still had to bail out the floats with a bucket, and his mechanical self-steering hadn't worked for a long time. He began to run low on certain supplies and his food had become dull and monotonous. Not only was he short of gasoline for the electric generator, but suddenly there was a new crisis. His radio transmitter, his all-important connection with the outside world and a vital tool in his efforts at deception, failed. When this happened, Crowhurst abandoned everything and started working sixteen hours a day soldering wires and parts together in a frenzied attempt to get back on the air. Meanwhile he kept talking into the BBC tape recorder:

Teignmouth Electron

The tea's gone off. Something's happened to it. . . . I think it's gone mouldy or something, but it makes me ill.

By now the trimaran was north of the equator and jogging along under jib and mizzen in the northeast trade wind. Crowhurst, the expert electronics engineer, was determined to repair his radio transmitter. He soon found that he was unable to fix his big Marconi Kestrel set; so he undertook to modify a small Shannon radio-telephone. The Shannon was designed for short-range work on medium wavelengths. Crowhurst decided to try to modify the Shannon for long range transmission on the short waveband. This was a major project, which meant redesigning and rebuilding various circuits and adding parts from other radios. The captain needed books on design, and test equipment to check his work as he went along. Undaunted, he started work at once while the trimaran bounced along on the trade wind waves and the equatorial sun burned down from overhead. While he soldered and tinkered he listened to his receiver. On June 18th the BBC sent a long telegram, the first of a series:

> CONGRATULATIONS ON PROGRESS HAVE NETWORK TELEVISION PRO-
> GRAMME FOR DAY OF RETURN YOUR FILM URGENTLY WANTED CAN
> YOU PREPARE FILM AND TAPES INFORMATION ANY SUGGESTION
> PLEASE ON GETTING IT BACK AT LEAST FOUR DAYS BEFORE TEIGN-
> MOUTH ARRIVAL CAN ARRANGE BOAT OR HELICOPTER HOW CLOSE
> AZORES BRITTANY OR SCILLIES REPLY URGENTLY-DONALD KERR

In response to the telegram, Crowhurst shot new 16mm film of himself doing various jobs: shaving, baking bread, using the sextant, working at the chart table, and so forth. All these scenes were done by clamping the camera and using a self-timer on the shutter, a tedious and time-consuming job for a singlehander who was involved in radio design and reconstruction.

Finally on June 22nd, Crowhurst got his rebuilt transmitter working. He fired off messages in morse code to the BBC, Hallworth, and his wife. He still hoped to speak directly to his wife, Clare, however, so he took the transmitter to pieces again and tried to modify it for long range voice transmission. In spite of all his skill and determination, he didn't succeed.

On June 24th, Crowhurst's mind made an abrupt spiral turn. He started on something entirely new, a long, complex, hard-to-follow religious-philosophic essay. During the next week he scribbled twenty-five-thousand words while *Teignmouth Electron* drifted slowly along in the calms of the Sargasso Sea north of the northeast trade wind. Each word that Crowhurst wrote was of supreme significance, he said. He had a great message, and his contribution to mankind had to be committed to paper in seven days. By now he had given up the race, sailing, and the radio modifications. He had retreated into a private, arcane world whose dimensions only he could fathom and appreciate. He had given up housekeeping on his yacht—still less than one year old—and the cabin was filthy and smelly. His bedding lay unwashed, radio parts were scattered everywhere, and the sink was stacked high with dirty dishes.

Again he turned to Einstein who would help Crowhurst deal with the nightmare that he faced. "Man is a lever whose ultimate length and strength he must determine . . . The shattering revelation that $E = mc^2$ is one supreme example of this activity . . . I introduce this idea because [it] leads directly to the dark tunnel of the space-time continuum, and once technology emerges from this tunnel the 'world' will 'end.' "

Crowhurst spoke of mathematics as the language of God. He talked of an Antichrist. He rambled on and on, working to one conclusion that the next great change in human society would be the liberation of the mind from the body so the mind could soar to an abstract existence. The moment for this move was at hand, and Crowhurst, Crowhurst himself, was to present this message to the world. Those who made this leap, this total jump, became like a God. *"If* creative abstraction is to act as a vehicle for the new entity . . . it lies within the power of creative abstraction to produce the abstraction!!!!!!!!!!!!!!!!!!!!" He got so excited as he wrote that he almost pressed his pencil through the paper.

Crowhurst claimed that he had reached a state so elevated that he could free his mind from his body and float away—leave *Teignmouth Electron*—whenever he desired. Now he could escape from his predicament. Forget the cheating and lying. Forget the radios and the schemes for money. Forget the fools in England.

Forget all the earthly impedimentia. Not only could Crowhurst obtain salvation, he could become God.

All these words were a jumble of prophesy, scientific doubletalk, mathematics, religion, and nonsense. This self-taught engineer-cum-sailor suffered from a psychiatric complaint called *paranoid grandiosity*. Crowhurst showed all the symptoms, and his delusions revolved around complex, highly organized beliefs that he was a great prophet and scientist.

He was insane.

Meanwhile back in England great preparations were going on for a colossal reception for Crowhurst. In Teignmouth the Crowhurst Welcome Home Sub-Committee met and outlined every minute of the hero's grand entry. *Teignmouth Electron* would be escorted by a naval minesweeper, the yacht club would fire its cannon at a suitable moment, and the trimaran would be towed along the seafront of the resort town so that the thousands of cheering visitors and townspeople could catch a glimpse of the world hero. While helicopters with the press buzzed overhead, Crowhurst would be formally presented to the town council. There would be a press conference at the theatre and receptions at the hotels. Enormous TEIGNMOUTH WELCOMES CROWHURST banners would be draped all over town, particularly along the seafront.

Rodney Hallworth had become respected and important in Teignmouth. The early civic doubters had come round and the pubs and inns rang with praise for Hallworth's astute handling of Crowhurst. The companies that had donated equipment and supplies for the trimaran relished the publicity prospects; a sculptor proposed a special trophy to commemorate the arrival. Crowhurst was scheduled to present awards for Prince Phillip, and the post office readied a special franking mark. Hallworth had ten thousand postcards printed with Crowhurst's picture, and the press agent wrote fawning copy for a welcoming edition of the local newspaper and even got Crowhurst's wife to write about "My Life as an Ocean Widow."

It was enough to make an ostrich sick.

Meanwhile on board *Teignmouth Electron,* Crowhurst continued to write. By now his pencil had worked back to the actions of cavemen who in the past had shocked society into change. As he wrote he got so excited that he could scarcely put down the words. He had had a great revelation but it needed to be handled with care. "When we decide to act we must be careful not to rush things. Like nuclear chain reactions in the matter system, our whole system of creative abstraction can be brought to the point of 'take off.' "

On June 26th, Crowhurst worked hard on the linked ideas of escape from his body. Words poured onto the paper. "Mathematicians and engineers used to the techniques of system analysis will skim through my complete work in less than an hour. At the end of that time, problems that have beset humanity for thousands of years will have been solved for them," he wrote.

Later he said: "Do we go on clinging to the idea that 'God made us', or realize that it lies within our power to make GOD? The system IS SHRIEKING OUT THIS MESSAGE AT THE TOP OF ITS VOICE why does no one listen I am listening anyway"

Crowhurst had become so deeply involved in his theories that he was unable to treat them as abstract ideas. Now whatever he wrote about he *became*. At one time he thought of abstract intelligence as a conceptual idea. Now his mind went through the actual change. Once it had been a game; now it was the actual, palpable truth.

As his dream world blurred into his real world, time had begun to be important to Crowhurst. A defective chronometer was not simply a clock that had gone wrong. It was not a symbol of his own condition. It *was* his own condition. *Crowhurst was the clock.* "God's clock is not the same as our clock. He has an infinite amount of 'our' time. Ours has nearly run out."

Crowhurst's verbal outbursts grew increasingly morbid. He wrote of his dead father, his mother's religious ties, about secrets of his past, and the idea of himself as a new God. It was all a demented, pathetic, jumble. He hinted increasingly of death. "[Christ] had arrived at the truth. . . . People witnessed the manner of his death. I must consider whether to . . ." he wrote. The flow of sentences went on and on. Thousands of tortured words. He talked of apes, revolutionaries, Julius Caesar, and problems of the world. Crowhurst's only real problem, of course, was how to get out of his faked sailing trip. His answer was a tortured, roundabout view of his own death. He was so far gone, however, that one wondered whether the demented captain understood what he was writing.

He began a discussion with himself about the false voyage. Should he confess? Or should he destroy all the evidence? If he pitched everything into the sea it would be contrary to the principle of always telling the truth and would keep mankind from Crowhurst's great revelation. He wrote about three levels of pain. Again he spoke of time. He raged against the devil who had tricked him unfairly. He wrote slogans: "IT IS THE MYSTERY OF FREEWILL."

Crowhurst was now so far gone that he had decided he would be a better God than God himself. He spoke directly to cosmic beings. The faults with the voyage were really the 'Gods' ' faults. He was beyond human morality. "The truth was that there was no good or evil, only truth." Finally he spoke of death, a quick death. Afterward he would be in the universe with the Gods.

In the motion pictures that Donald Crowhurst took of himself the man we see is not the smooth-faced Englishman who had joked and laughed with his friends before the voyage. We see a man who had aged incredibly. His eyes had become furtive; lines of strain puckered his mouth and nose and eyes. The smooth, boyish look was gone, replaced by haggard middle age.

By June 30th, Crowhurst had lost all track of time. His watches and chronometer had run down. He used the Nautical Almanac and the moon to establish the date and time. It was really 1000 hours, July 1st, but he no longer cared about anything. His writing had become even more confused and rambling. Death had become paramount in his sentences. He decided to leave evidence of his wrongdoings so that anyone who found *Teignmouth Electron* would be able to understand what he had done. "There can only be one perfect beauty that is the great beauty of truth." he wrote. A little later on that morning the weary captain penciled these words:

I will only resign this game if you will agree that [on] the next occasion that this game is played it will be played according to the rules that are devised by my great god who has revealed at last to his son not only the exact nature of the reason for games but has also revealed the truth of the way of the ending of the next game that

It is finished

It is finished

IT IS THE MERCY

A little later he added the words "I will resign the game [at] 11 20 40." Crowhurst climbed to the stern of *Teignmouth Electron* clutching his chronometer. When the time reached 11 20 40 he jumped into the sea.

His long race was over.

31. *The Last Word*

ON JULY 10TH the Royal Mail Vessel *Picardy,* outbound from London for the Caribbean, came upon *Teignmouth Electron* gliding slowly along on a smooth North Atlantic 525 miles southwest of Ilha Flores in the Azores. The trimaran only had her mizzen sail set. Captain Richard Box blew his foghorn three times and maneuvered to pass close astern of the multi-hulled craft. There was no sign of life so the captain stopped his ship, lowered a boat, and sent an officer and three men to have a look. The inspecting crew found no one on board. There was no trace of anyone in the water and no small boat or life raft to be seen. The last entry in the vessel's three logbooks was a notation in the radio log for June 29th, eleven days earlier. Captain Box had a derrick rigged on the *Picardy* and hoisted *Teignmouth Electron* on board. In the meantime he alerted his London owners who immediately called the Royal Navy, which flashed the United States Air Force unit in the Azores and requested an aerial search. Both the United States Air Force and the *Picardy* criss-crossed the area but found nothing. It appeared that Donald Crowhurst, the singlehanded captain, had fallen overboard. A regrettable accident.

Back in England, sympathy poured into the Crowhurst home. On July 12th *The Sunday Times* started a fund drive for the Crowhurst family with £5,000. Because of Crowhurst's death, Knox-Johnston was to receive the £5,000 race prize, but in a gesture of supreme magnanimity he donated the entire amount to the fund. No one dreamed of duplicity or foul play.

Meanwhile on board the *Picardy,* which was steaming toward

the Caribbean, Captain Box studied the logbooks. Most of the entries seemed routine enough, but in the last log there was a good deal of disorganized and peculiar writing that suggested psychological unrest and mental disorder. Captain Box continued reading.

The story of Crowhurst's disappearance could not be investigated without the logbooks. All the newspapers coveted Crowhurst's records and asked for a look. Rodney Hallworth, who worked at the speed of light whenever he detected the glimmer of money, naturally arranged an auction among the various newspapers. *The Sunday Times* finally won with a bid of £4,000.

Hallworth, along with a reporter and a photographer from *The Sunday Times,* now flew to Santo Domingo to get the logbooks and to inspect the trimaran. On July 16th, when the *Picardy* came into port, the three journalists met Captain Box who took Hallworth aside and showed him the log entries that contemplated suicide. At Box's suggestion, Hallworth ripped out these pages to spare the Crowhurst family. Hallworth held the pages aside and planned to show them to the editor of *The Sunday Times* privately. Meanwhile the reporter started going through the logbooks and soon discovered that Crowhurst had never sailed further than the Atlantic Ocean! Incredible! Even these hardboiled British journalists must have wondered how to handle the story. It seemed obvious that the abbreviated voyage and the death of Crowhurst were somehow connected. Hallworth soon realized that he could not keep back the secret of Crowhurst's death so he handed back the log pages he had ripped out.

The three journalists hurried back to London and huddled with the paper's senior editors. What to do? The Crowhurst story was sensational copy but its unfolding might cause a lot of bruises. There was the negative effect on the Crowhurst family, still reeling from the shock of Crowhurst's death. *The Sunday Times* itself, the sponsor of the race, would not look too good when the truth of its incredibly sloppy race administration spilled out. But feelings and egos aside, the story had to be printed. A confidential warning was passed to the BBC, which was busy working up a triumphant version of the Crowhurst circumnavigation based on the films and tape recordings. *The Sunday Times'* editors did a lot of teeth-gnashing, and decided to publish the full account after a review by Mrs. Crowhurst and Hallworth.

On the weekend of July 27th, 1969, the story came out. It was an immediate national sensation as front-page news. Every newspaper in the land picked up the story and amplified the bizarre tale of Donald Crowhurst's faked trip around the world, his mental failure, and his final suicide. The story spread to the foreign press, and newspaper wire services telegraphed details to the corners of the world. The cunning twists of the story intrigued radio and television news editors everywhere, and enormous pressure poured into London from abroad for more details. French and American news magazines prepared special coverage, and Italian and Polish readers looked at photographs of Crowhurst. A herd of reporters from all over the globe stalked Mrs. Crowhurst for a month. Her telephone rang day and night. What did she think of it all? What did his vessel look like? What was a trimaran anyway? Captain Box was asked to repeat the details of finding *Teignmouth Electron* over and over. A dozen fanciful rumors of Crowhurst's reappearance were published, speculated upon, and finally quashed as the story ran its course. The mighty *Sunday Times* itself came in for plenty of criticism for sponsoring circus stunts without adequate control. The overall feeling, however, was that the fault was the mental collapse of a weak man rather than an overzealous and careless sponsor.*

The great victory dinner of the Golden Globe race was postponed. The Teignmouth town council hastily cancelled its huge

---

*In future races of this type, the yachts would be inspected for design suitability and seaworthiness. The contestants would need to demonstrate their sailing proficiency in qualifying trials in the actual vessels to be used. This would be obligatory well in advance of the starting date to prevent a rush of last-minute building and qualifying. The entries would depart from one place at the same time. Simple radio communication—improved since 1968—would assist safety, help with compliance of the route and rules, and would foster general race information. If these rules had been announced in 1968 before *The Sunday Times* race, however, there would probably have been no competition at all because the two Frenchmen would have objected to the radio rule, Carozzo and Crowhurst wouldn't have been ready, and Blyth and Ridgway might not have qualified. With only Tetley, King, and Knox-Johnston—all ship officers—there wouldn't have been enough entrants.

civic homecoming for Donald Crowhurst. The town elders sum-
moned Hallworth to task, but the loquacious press agent pointed
out that although Crowhurst was regretfully dead, the resort had
received millions of pounds' worth of publicity. Hadn't Hallworth done a good job?

What of the others in the race? John Ridgway and Chay Blyth,
who both had tried to make up in guts what they lacked in experience and whose small yachts seemed inadequate for the task,
liked their taste of deep sea adventuring. Quite separately and
in different areas, they continued ocean racing in various spon-
sored yachts. In 1970–71, Blyth soloed westabout around the
world in a fifty-eight-foot steel ketch. Ridgway started a school
for physical fitness and adventure training in Ardmore, Scotland.

Bill King, the retired submarine commander, who was among
the first to suggest a solo round-the-world voyage, shipped his
sleek *Galway Blazer II* back to England from Cape Town after
the yacht was dismasted. Following several setbacks he eventually sailed south and east again. West of Australia, in the Southern Ocean, his vessel was struck and seriously damaged by a whale.
King managed emergency repairs and struggled into Fremantle
to a shipyard. He continued eastward, rounded Cape Horn, and
returned to England in May, 1973, to fulfill his dream.

The spirited Italian, Alex Carozzo, disappeared from the
yacht racing scene after Lisbon and has left no further wake.
Loïck Fougeron, who sailed into St. Helena after getting rolled
in the great storm, has also slipped into anonymity.

Bernard Moitessier sailed to French Polynesia where he lived
for eleven years, sailing among the islands and doing a little
farming when he could. He wrote a splendid book *The Long Way*
about his 37,455-mile nonstop voyage. He has remarried and
has a young son. Still aboard his beloved *Joshua,* he lives in San
Francisco.

Robin Knox-Johnston immediately became well-known after
his return to England where he was lionized and feted as he
deserved. The British empire and her military heroes were mostly
gone; now the sporting heroes of soccer, football, and sailing

took the place of the intrepid admirals and gallant generals of the past. The round-the-world race had been a tough sporting event. Not everyone had understood the race or why it had been held, but Knox-Johnston was quite a fellow and the English rewarded their heroes well. Both Francis Chichester and Alex Rose had been knighted for their sailing trips around the world. Knox-Johnston received a C.B.E. (commander of the British empire), a great honor for a thirty-year-old man. He wrote a best-selling book and was soon involved in various marine enterprises. Less than a week after he docked, a newspaper reporter wrote: "Accompanied by four friends and 20 dozen cans of beer, Robin Knox-Johnston sailed for London on the *Suhaili* yesterday, after four days of skilful tacking through business negotiations which could bring him £100,000 in the next year."

During his long solo trip Knox-Johnston had had plenty of time to reflect on his life up to that time. He decided to have a new look at his earlier marriage, which had broken up in India. Shortly after he returned to England, Knox-Johnston remarried his former wife Sue. It was a nice step.

We have now accounted for eight of the nine contestants, all except Nigel Tetley, the tall, handsome, retired naval commander whose voyage in an experimental yacht had been so exemplary, but who had been victimized by the machinations of Crowhurst and maybe by fate itself. Tetley, perhaps more than any other, deserved to win the £5,000 and some share of the accolade that had cascaded on Knox-Johnston's shoulders. *The Sunday Times* had awarded Tetley £1,000 as a consolation prize, but this seemed trifling. Knox-Johnston had become a national hero. Tetley remained an obscure mariner.

Tetley had put so much into the race and had gotten only gall and bitter lemons for his trouble. Even his vessel, the only one of the nine, had been lost. He wrote a book about his part in the race, but its sales were poor. He discussed multihull construction and safety aspects with other sailors and he commenced construction of a new yacht for upcoming voyages. But he had trouble dedicating himself to future enterprises. When *Victress* had broken up during that stormy night in the North Atlantic, part of Tetley had gone down with his ship. He tried hard to recoup and to start again, but his heart wasn't in it. On February 5th, 1972, thirty-three months after *Victress* sank, Tetley committed suicide by hanging himself. Like Crowhurst, Tetley's long race had ended.

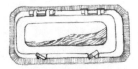

Bibliography

PRIMARY SOURCES

Blyth, Chay and Maureen. *Innocent Abroad*. Lymington, Hampshire, England: Nautical Publishing Company, 1970.

King, Commander William. *Adventure in Depth*. New York: G. P. Putnam's Sons, 1975.

King, Commander W. D. AE. *Capsize*. Lymington, Hampshire, England: Nautical Publishing Company, 1969.

Knox-Johnston, Robin. *A World of My Own*. London: Cassell & Co., 1969.

Moitessier, Bernard. *The Long Way*. London: Adlard Coles Limited, 1974. (First published in 1971 in France by Editions Arthaud, 6 rue de Mézières Paris 6 as *La longue route*.)

Ridgway, John. *Journey to Ardmore*. London: Hodder and Stoughton, 1971.

Ridgway, John and Marie Christine. *Round the World with Ridgway*. New York: Holt, Rinehart and Winston, 1978.

Tetley, Nigel. *Trimaran Solo*. Lymington, Hampshire, England: Nautical Publishing Company, 1970.

Tomalin, Nicolas and Ron Hall, *The Strange Last Voyage of Donald Crowhurst*. London: Times Newspapers Ltd., 1970. New York: Stein & Day, 1970.

Issues of *The Sunday Times, Daily Express,* and *Sunday Mirror* between 11 January 1968 and 24 February 1972.

SECONDARY SOURCES

Gliksman, Alain. *La Voile en Solitaire*. France: Éditions Maritimes et d'Outre-Mer/Denoel, 1976.

Heaton, Peter. *The Singlehanders*. London: Michael Joseph, 1976.